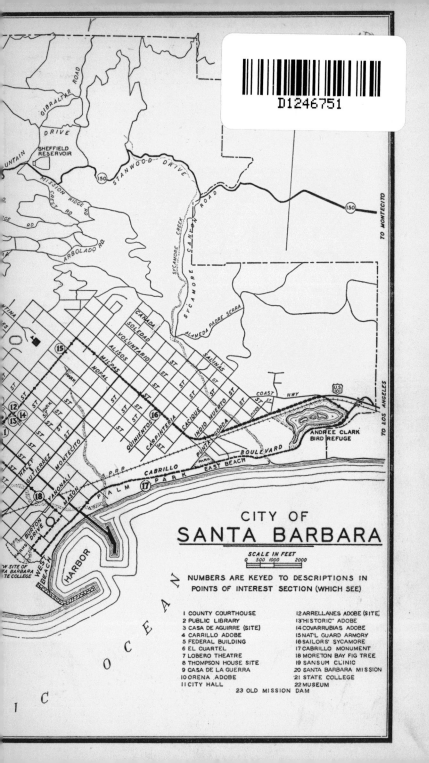

CITY OF
SANTA BARBARA

SCALE IN FEET

0   500 1000   2000

NUMBERS ARE KEYED TO DESCRIPTIONS IN
POINTS OF INTEREST SECTION (WHICH SEE)

1 COUNTY COURTHOUSE
2 PUBLIC LIBRARY
3 CASA DE AGUIRRE (SITE)
4 CARRILLO ADOBE
5 FEDERAL BUILDING
6 EL CUARTEL
7 LOBERO THEATRE
8 THOMPSON HOUSE SITE
9 CASA DE LA GUERRA
10 ORENA ADOBE
11 CITY HALL

12 ARRELLANES ADOBE (SITE)
13 "HISTORIC" ADOBE
14 COVARRUBIAS ADOBE
15 NAT'L GUARD ARMORY
16 SAILORS' SYCAMORE
17 CABRILLO MONUMENT
18 MORETON BAY FIG TREE
19 SANSUM CLINIC
20 SANTA BARBARA MISSION
21 STATE COLLEGE
22 MUSEUM

23 OLD MISSION DAM

SANTA BARBARA

A Guide to the Channel City and Its Environs

SANTA BARBARA

A GUIDE TO THE CHANNEL CITY AND ITS ENVIRONS

Compiled and Written by the Southern California
Writers' Project of the Work Projects
Administration

AMERICAN GUIDE SERIES

ILLUSTRATED

Sponsored by Santa Barbara State College

HASTINGS HOUSE · Publishers · NEW YORK

MCMXLI

CALIFORNIA STATE DEPARTMENT OF EDUCATION

Official Sponsor of the
Southern California Writers' Projects

FEDERAL WORKS AGENCY

JOHN M. CARMODY, *Administrator*

WORK PROJECTS ADMINISTRATION

HOWARD O. HUNTER, *Commissioner*
FLORENCE KERR, *Assistant Commissioner*
HENRY RUSSELL AMORY, *Administrator for Southern California*

 199

Foreword

The Santa Barbara Guide, made possible as a Southern California Writers' Project through the facilities of the Work Projects Administration, gives evidence of careful planning and great diligence on the part of those who have carried the project through to completion. Fortunately, the task of preparing this volume has been carried on by those who have had the feeling that a piece of work must be done, but who also have had a purpose to make it reveal beauty and exude the historical atmosphere of the region with which it is concerned.

The present completed project is the most comprehensive descriptive guide that has been prepared of this city and its surroundings. It gives much general information. There is adequate detail about travel, accommodations, recreation and recreational areas, places of interest, and cultural opportunities. The wealth of information contained on natural features makes even old residents aware of riches they had failed to comprehend fully. The Guide thus becomes a gift of unmeasured value even to those to whom beautiful, healthful Santa Barbara is an old story. It can serve, therefore, not only to guide visitors, but also as a source of information and pleasure to others, even to many Santa Barbarans.

Very clearly the compilers and writers of the book were not concerned solely or even chiefly with making a local Baedeker or another orthodox visitors' guide, but rather were interested in compiling information, presenting a picture, and telling a story colored perchance with spirit tints of Santa Barbara's past. In doing this, they intended to reveal Santa Barbara as unique because of its location and a history that was different—a purpose amply fulfilled.

To be sure, a work such as the *Santa Barbara Guide* must be fitted into a pattern. This requires that liberties must be taken with form and content, but under the limitations necessary in the nature of the case a picture is presented that on the whole is true. All of us owe a debt of gratitude to the Work Projects Administration for making the *Guide* possible, and to those who toiled with devotion to

v

give an artistic, and, in the broad sense, an accurate presentation of historic and present Santa Barbara.

WILLIAM H. ELLISON
Head of Social Science Department
Santa Barbara State College

Preface

Questing galleons and swift pirate craft once plied the waters of the Santa Barbara Channel; priests, explorers, soldiers, and adventurers tarried on both the mainland and the four islands—lived and died there.

Tierra Adorada (Sp., beloved land) of that day it was, and not less so today.

Through four centuries of hope, turmoil, and progress Santa Barbara has remained what a beneficent nature made her, a gracious place in which to live. In her venerable adobes was made not only the history of California, but also the history of Spain, Mexico, America. Here was the flowering of the great mission system, and here alone the mission endured.

Waters of the friendly channel long since have washed over the grave of Cabrillo, dissolving his bones in the sea he loved. Governors, bishops, priests, and soldiers lie undisturbed in this haven where land and sky and sea unite to bring a serenity seldom found elsewhere.

Four centuries through which troop the great and small of many nations have seen the birth and the passing of many legends, most of which, in spite of all that has been written, may never be recorded.

Those who have shared in producing this book have tried to present a well-rounded picture of Santa Barbara, have tried to fill its pages with the atmosphere of the channel mainland and islands, the great National Forests, the rich valleys to the north—they have tried to produce a volume which will be authentic in the minds of the pioneers and their descendants, from the pages of which school children may learn, and which visitors may use as a guide in passing through.

Practically every member of the staff of the Southern California Writers' Project has contributed to this book and their work hereby is acknowledged gratefully. Scores of Santa Barbarans gave freely of their time and knowledge. Without help of the county supervisors this book could not have been written.

Particular thanks are extended to Clarence L. Phelps, president of Santa Barbara State College, co-sponsor of this volume; Sam J. Stanwood, county supervisor; Owen H. O'Neill, county surveyor and historian; Fr. Maynard Geiger, historian of Santa Barbara Mission; Dr. David Banks Rogers, formerly curator of the Santa Barbara Museum of Natural History; Dr. William H. Ellison of Santa Barbara State College; Mrs. Frances B. Linn, librarian and staff; Dr. Philip Orr, paleontologist of the Santa Barbara Museum of Natural History; S. A. Nash-Boulden and C. S. Robinson of the United States Forestry Department; Thomas M. Stork, editor and publisher of the Santa Barbara *News-Press;* Leo Preisker, county supervisor.

Much valuable assistance was given by Earl Plescia, C. C. Christiansen, Pressley Lancaster, Jr., Hobart O. Skofield, Alec Bullock, Bertha Zachrison, Herbert Orriss, Wallace Penfield, Frank F. Flournoy, Winsor Soule, R. H. Pitman, E. E. Ericson, Dr. William Sansum, Maunsell Van Rensselaer, Arthur Sterry Coggeshall, Fr. Augustine Hobrecht, Francis Noel, Jane Kimberly, Capt. George Kimberly, Capt. Edwin J. Gourley, F. A. MacKenzie, Dr. C. T. Roome, Dr. R. C. Main, Chester Moore, Faye Canfield, Curtis E. Warren, Muriel Edwards, Hubert Voight, Pearl Chase, H. G. Chase and staff, P. Stanley Belford, vice-president, County National Bank & Trust Co.; Walter L. Hanson, editor and publisher of the Santa Ynez Valley *News;* R. T. Ambrose, postmaster; Edward F. McCaffrey, assistant postmaster; L. Dexter Barnard, Security Title & Guarantee Co.; and Phil Weidman.

JOHN DENNIS KEYES, *State Supervisor*
Southern California Writers' Project

Contents

Page

FOREWORD By William H. Ellison v

PREFACE vii

MOSAIC xiii

Part 1: General Information

WHAT, WHERE, WHEN, HOW 3

PLACES TO PLAY 8

PUBLIC INVITED 14

Part 2: Past and Present

PRESIDIO TO CHANNEL CITY 25

TIERRA ADORADA 56

BACKDROP 60

SIERRAS IN THE SEA 65

SANCTUARY IN THE CHAPARRAL 79

HUMAN SIDE OF A CITY 86

FIESTA LAND 99

Part 3: Points of Interest and Tours

POINTS OF INTEREST 111

TOUR 1   Montecito and the South Coast Region 132

TOUR 2   The Back Country 144

TOUR 3   Coast and Mountains 165

Part 4: Appendices

	Page
CHRONOLOGY	187
BIBLIOGRAPHY	194
INDEX	199

Maps

	Page
CITY OF SANTA BARBARA	front end paper
SANTA BARBARA CHANNEL ISLANDS	67
SANTA BARBARA COUNTY	rear end paper

Illustrations

Page
Between 6 and 7

ANDREE CLARK BIRD REFUGE

SNUG HARBOR FOR SMALL CRAFT, SANTA BARBARA

RESIDENTIAL AND BUSINESS AREAS, SANTA BARBARA, SHOWING STATE
    STREET (*Center, Left to Right*)

RESIDENTIAL DISTRICT, EASTERN OUTSKIRTS OF SANTA BARBARA

SANTA BARBARA HARBOR AND STEARNS WHARF

OIL DERRICKS ON THE SHORE NORTH OF SANTA BARBARA, WITH SANTA
    CRUZ ISLAND SHOWING IN THE DISTANCE

TWILIGHT ON THE MESA

Between 38 and 39

ANACAPA ARCH AND LOOKOUT TOWER, THE COURTHOUSE, SANTA BARBARA

INDUSTRIAL EDUCATIONAL BUILDING, SANTA BARBARA STATE COLLEGE
    (*Center R.*), AND MCKINLEY ELEMENTARY SCHOOL (*Center L.*)

THE ADMINISTRATION BUILDING, SANTA BARBARA STATE COLLEGE

SUNGLOW AND SHADOWS IN THE SUNKEN GARDENS, SANTA BARBARA
    COURTHOUSE

ARCADES AND SYLVAN COURT, SANTA BARBARA STATE COLLEGE

VISTA THROUGH COURTHOUSE ARCH

Between 70 and 71

SANTA BARBARA MISSION, THE CATHEDRAL OF EARLY CALIFORNIA

MISSION SANTA INÉS

A PATH OF THE PADRES, SACRED GARDEN OF SANTA BARBARA MISSION

RUINS OF ANCIENT MISSION AQUEDUCT, SANTA BARBARA

FRAGMENT OF REREDOS (c. 1820), MISSION SANTA BARBARA
    Courtesy WPA Art Program

FOUNTAIN, MISSION SANTA BARBARA
    Courtesy WPA Art Program

xi

Page

Between 102 and 103

RIBBON OF CONCRETE THROUGH ROCKY GAVIOTA PASS

ANACAPA ISLAND (*Left*) AND SANTA CRUZ (*Right*), AS SEEN FROM THE MAINLAND AT VENTURA

ARCH ROCK, SANTA CRUZ ISLAND

PELICAN BAY, FAIR ANCHORAGE AT SANTA CRUZ ISLAND

FORNEY'S COVE, BLEAK HABITAT OF SEA LIONS, WEST END OF SANTA CRUZ ISLAND

A BROKEN SHIP MAST MARKS THE GRAVE OF BENJAMIN FOXEN, SANTA BARBARA COUNTY

MORTON BAY FIG TREE, GROWN FROM A SAPLING OF THE 1870'S

Between 134 and 135

THE RUIN OF A CLOISTERED CORRIDOR (1900)

THE CORRIDOR RESTORED TO ITS ORIGINAL CONDITION (1941)

RUINS OF LA PURISIMA MISSION (PRIOR TO 1935), LOMPOC VALLEY

LA PURISIMA MISSION UNDER RECONSTRUCTION

THE RESTORED CHAPEL, LA PURISIMA MISSION

A CCC WORKER IN LA PURISIMA MISSION WEAVES TULE STALKS WITH RAWHIDE THONGS, EXACTLY AS DID THE NEOPHYTES WHEN THE MISSION WAS BUILT

Between 166 and 167

FLOWER SEED HARVEST IN LOMPOC FIELDS

"EL REY DE LOS REYES", DWIGHT MURPHY'S GOLDEN BROWN PALOMINO

NATIONAL GUARD ARMORY, SANTA BARBARA

"RANCHEROS VISITADORES"—SANTA BARBARANS RE-LIVING THE PAST

THE HOUSES THAT JACK AND JILL BUILT, BLOCHMAN CITY

A CREAKING CARRETA IN THE FIESTA PARADE, SANTA BARBARA

HOME, SWEET HOME, IN THE SANTA YNEZ MOUNTAINS

A HOME IN MONTECITO, WEALTHY SUBURB OF SANTA BARBARA

Mosaic

IT IS a small room—in which Don Sebastián dreams and works. The ceiling is beamed—adz-hewn with accurate strokes by an accustomed hand. The walls are rough adobe, stained with age and use. A lion-figured *serape* curtains a doorway in a bare wall relieved only by an oaken crucifix—nothing more. Wooden pegs driven into another wall hold a varied assortment of leather trappings and riding gear. Strips of leather hang from a cord, others soak in a tub of water. A low bench stands beneath two windows, and upon it are strewn the tools for the tasks at hand—punches, knives, awls, small spindles of silver and gold wire, pieces of metal worked in design, others awaiting the touch of the silversmith—rosettes of leather for stirrups, *tapaderas,* and saddle skirts—mounts for cantle, saddlebags, and horn—inlays for cinch and *látigo* rings.

The windows shed a revealing light upon the head of the lone occupant of the room and the things of beauty upon which he has been working—a pair of engraved spurs with solid silver rowels, a woven quirt with silver butt, saddlebags, a pair of carved leather arm cuffs studded with jewels, elaborately decorated riding boots, and a saddle fit for the greatest king.

Here is one who has "kept the even tenor of his way" in a "sequestered vale of life." The clean, musky odor of tanbark, and the cool clayey smell of adobe and earth emphasize the atmosphere of age-old

peace. Yet beyond the walls are the raucous blasts of traffic, the babble
of many tongues, the quarrel of a modern city's conflicting sounds.
Yesterday and Today—worlds apart.

> *"Cuando me veras en la desierta playa,*
> *Con el vaivén incesante de las olas,*
> *Acuerdate—acuerdate de mi . . ."*

> ("If thou should see me on ocean shore deserted,
> While all the waves incessantly are stirring,
> Remember me—ah, then remember me . . .")

So sings Don Sebastián de la Peréz y Aguilár.   Don Sebastián "the
very greatest *talabartero*—artist supreme in leather and silver."   Don
Sebastián, great troubadour, who sings as he works—though, according
to the good padre, "for some of his songs he will surely lose his soul."
Don Sebastián, gracious man, old and stooped and grizzled.   What
matter if the padre cluck disapproval at some of his songs?   What
matter if each prick of an awl or sweep of a knife bring words meant
only for the walls, the work, his dreams?   So Sebastián sings in a
low and plaintive voice while he tools his dream of nearly four centuries gone.

The sweeping scroll in your saddle leather is, perhaps, the red-and-
yellow banner of Spain fluttering above a tiny caravel and intrepid
Cabrillo—bold explorer, first to look upon *Tierra Adorada* (Beloved
Land)—safe in quiet azure waters and a last haven for his bones
upon a Channel Isle beyond the Bay of Santa Barbara?   *Si!*

My friend, there is no forgetting in Arcadia Land, named for
"the fairest saint in all the calendar."   Now in song and story, fiesta
and pageant, Cabrillo and *conquistadores* and the long line of those who
followed, are well remembered.   And you will tell it well, Sebastián,
in the intricate designs in silver embroidery, inlay, and tooled leather
of your saddle—the trappings of your trade.

Today is Fiesta Day, and beyond your door are all those you dream
of so fondly—as real as yesterday.   Out of the past and in physical
being, your beloved mingle upon the streets of Santa Barbara—in the
byways.   They are descendants of the kingly, courteous, hospitable
dons.   Their dashing sons, austere but gracious *señoras,* spirited but
demure *señoritas,* bold *caballeros, vaqueros*—worshipful, loyal retinue,
cast their approving spirit over tourist, Midwest tycoon, field-worker,
movie star, yachtsman, office girl, laborer, and sweep them into the days
long gone.   Hearts are joyous for today and full for yesterday, Sebastián.

Banners of the explorers still wave from mainland shores to island
crags.   Those sails and spars dotting the sea and channel and cove
today leave their wake in the selfsame waters all those others sailed so

bravely—only a part of what the yesterdays have sent down to this "Spanish Riviera."

Your patterns are of this very day, Sebastián, though you know it not.

Don Sebastián cocks his hoary head and contemplates the articles about him—they are like friendly children watching from the shadows.

He has worked the leather cuffs in a simple inlay and a few jewels which offer no interference with the work of the wrists and forearms of the man they are to adorn, a lowly vineyardist, one who works among berry vines, harsh tangles and thorn pricking.

His deep, black eyes twinkle as he lifts the riding boots. They are for a woman—they are small and shapely. With those upon dainty feet, and only blue denims and a silk shirt, the wearer will cut a pretty figure during the carnival, even for one of humble birth.

But what of your saddle, Sebastián?

A sharp knife parts the smooth surface of the leather. Beneath the flashing blade a picture unfolds. Music, Song—gay *caballeros* and not so demure *señoritas*—flutes and guitars, violins and cellos—dancing and horsemanship—passion and love.

> "Light of my dawn and of twilight my star,
> I come to thy presence with rapture."

Think of your soul, Sebastián!

> "And let's woo, let's coo
> To the Jota, the Jota, the dance of little care."

Sebastián, Sebastián—but continue—penance can be made—*mañana*

> *"Si te admiro, las gracias que tu tienes."*
> ("I do love thee dearly, thy graces I adore.")

This knot behind the cantle—so. It shall be a religious symbol of the Orient. Circular conchas—serrated edges—thus—like a Buddhist wheel—sign of a happy journey. It shall represent the Ancient Ones, the Oak Grove Men, and the Hunting People of mongol cast who once roamed these shores, valleys, and mountain slopes. Hunters, fishers, fighters—forebears of the gentle Canaliños.

> *"Cuando los indios vinieron . . .*
> *Bajaron por el estero . . .*
> *Ay! Ay! Ay! Ay! Ay! Ay!"*

> ("When the Indians came
> They came down through the inlet . . .
> Aye! Aye! Aye! Aye! Aye! Aye!")

Those lines upon the saddle skirt? Trails to ancient forest camps —hunting and fishing grounds, and paths above the sloping beach?

They have them still. True, modern roads now skirt the selfsame shore and climb to forests primeval—to hunting grounds—the home of deer and mountain cat. Grouse and quail still call and mate through the selfsame woods—pheasants and doves await a later hunter. Trails still wind to scenic heights, the public camps and mountain ranches, lodges—streams that flash with trout and bass—a hunter's Paradise it yet remains. The deep seas and fighting denizens of the ocean's roll are close at hand.

Happy journey, indeed! *Ay! Ay! Ay!*

He has finished his Oriental design behind the cantle, and now Sebastián begins to embroider in gold a chaste cross before the saddle horn—that the rider, descendant of the *dons,* might ever have that symbol before him—that the steed beneath would ever know a guide beyond the pressure on the rein, and ever carry his master to an honorable destination, sturdily and swiftly, truly and safely.

Worked upon an unadorned background of brown leather, the cross is pure in design and expression. Simple lines above it and to each side are arched as cathedral windows—three—the Blessed Trinity. Where the leather overlay meets the saddle skirt, a border of lightning flashes and one sword completes the legend of Saint Bárbara's virginity and martyrdom. Upon the skirt, itself, Sebastián carves a bundle of reeds that the *Canaliños* plucked along the *estero* and brought down as a roof for Father Serra's altar and received, in return, his blessing at the first Mass of *San Joaquín de la Laguna.*

Don Sebastián lays aside his tools under the spell of the seraphic Serra—he seems to drowse—arms outstretched, fingers entwined, his head bent low upon his breast. No sound intrudes from the street. The air is very still. Only the sunlight and the glittering saddle picture upon which it shines seem to live. Pictured there an imposing mission rises from the humble *enramada* of boughs. Granaries, weaveries, tanneries—an adobe village clusters about its sacred walls. The orchards thrive, the herds increase, and fields of grain wave golden in the sun. Through the years the settlement grows and populous *rancherías* know the benign spirit of holy fathers and the spell of mission bells.

That has not passed, Sebastián. A noble structure surmounts *El Pedregosa* (The Rocky), like a crowned spirit casting its benediction over the jeweled city at its feet. Here, beneath the willows in the shadow of its towers, sleep the dead of ages past—the bones of a bishop—the ruler of a State—Franciscan friars who tended to their flock—neophytes who toiled and sang and danced before its porticos. Within her walls Indian carvings grace the ceiling and beneath are carved statues brought from Spain—sacred relics of ancient days—cloisters and chapels as they were. High above the altar is the statue of Saint Bárbara and before her the lighted candle which never has been dimmed.

But Don Sebastián does not sleep. He rouses and crosses himself. The quiet smile that wrinkles Sebastián's mouth might have been akin to that of Father Serra's as the good Padre contemplated the bough-covered altar on the shores of the small lagoon—leather-jacketed soldiers with eyes to a rising presidio—the tireless Padre visioning his Mission Santa Bárbara in a day to come. The pious Padre may well have smiled deeply in his heart and exultant soul that his "May God bless it," is for Church before Crown, though the military know it not.

"*En el nombre del Padre Dios, el espíritu Santo y la Virgen Purísima—Amén.*" The murmured words are Sebastián's but the prayer is from all the room.

"Fah! Think of your work, Sebastián. The saddlebags, they must be finished—and dreams do not fill an empty belly! Ha! Fit for a real *caballero,* these bags. One day they would have carried food and tobacco—or messages to a lady—a long, hard ride, and at the end a guitar 'beneath a Gothic window.' But it is not so. These bags are for the modern world, for the one who will own you directs the pictures that move. You will carry script and—nonessentials—bah!"

That plaited quirt hanging from its peg? The silver-embossed leaves on the butt are exquisite things. A woman tourist will take it home this winter to show and treasure. She comes sometimes with the spring, the autumn, fall, or winter. Santa Barbara is her all-year playground, and she visits often—a lovely lady.

And the so-beautiful spurs! Any gay *vaquero* would welcome you, my friends. He would interpret properly these notes of music engraved on bright silver. He would understand how the musical ring of the rowels would attract the ear of the *señoritas.*

> "*Vámonos por Santa Bárbara*
> *Vámonos y lo verás;*
> *Las carretas por delante*
> *Y los bueyes por detrás.*"

> ("Come, let's go to Santa Barbara
> Come, let's go for there you'll find;
> In the lead the wagons harnessed
> And the oxen on behind.")

These are not for the *vaquero,* no. But for a fine fellow, yes. A grand figure is this man O'Shea. During fiesta he discards his spattered brogans, overalls, and begrimed shirt and leaves the oil fields behind. He steps into Santa Barbara, resplendent in his black-tasseled sombrero, slit-laced pants and toe-crowded, handsome boots. His roweled spurs clink on the pavement as did the cutlass of his bucko forebears who made the town a port of call—for more reasons than one.

Is this yesterday or today, Sebastián—you are confusing? What difference? Maids and men dressed as from southern Spain—Seville—Malaga—Cartagena. A gay blade sings beneath a window, fresh from the rodeo and the scars of bold horsemanship upon him—meekly, just a little slyly—a rascal.

"I am your little turtle dove, my darling."

A maiden smiles down disdainfully. Passions run as hot as in days long gone, do they not? But alas! Wooing, as of yore, does not always prove successful.

"¡O blanca virgen a tu ventana,
Asoma el rostro para escuchar!"

("Oh, fairest maiden approach thy window,
Come to the railing and turn thy ear.")

The lady is quite unmoved!

"La noche hablaré
Se van las silfides a costipar."

("Señor, I go to bed,
Sing to the rain instead—
Sing not to me.")

Finalidad! She has closed the window!—Bang!

"y lo pobre bardo suspirou, morreu."

("And the poor bard dropped dead.")

Sebastián laughs uproariously—"Ha! Ha! Ha! Ho! Ho! Ho!" The present is not much changed from the past.

His work is done and he lays aside the tool that made the final stroke. The old man brushes his lips with the tips of his fingers as a salute and gesture to that rider who will proudly sit this saddle someday hence and ride away.

"Un pajarito yo tenía, se me volo."

("I held a little bird, and lo, it fled one day.")

Buenos noches, my friend—and always may you have as pleasant dreams.

Part 1
General Information

What, Where, When, How

Railroad Stations: Southern Pacific Lines (SP), 205 State St.

Bus Station: Pacific Greyhound Lines, NE. corner Chapala and Carrillo Sts.

Bus Tours: Tanner Motor Livery, operating the Grey Line, 20 E. Victoria St.

Bus Service: Local and interurban terminal, 622 Anacapa St. *Local* fares: 5¢ on State St. between Sola St. and West Beach; 10¢ to other parts of city, free transfers, reduced rates for commutation tickets. *Interurban* fares from terminal: Carpinteria, 25¢ one way, 45¢ round trip, 15-trip book $3.00; *Summerland,* 20¢ one way, 35¢ round trip, book $2.25; *Montecito*—two routes, (1) *Miramar Route* via Coast Highway (US 101) to Sheffield Dr. (at Coast Highway), 15¢ one way, 25¢ round trip, book $1.70; (2) *East Valley Road Route* (State 150) to Sheffield Dr. (at East Valley Road), 20¢ one way, 35¢ round trip, book $2.30; *County Hospital,* San Antonio Rd., 15¢ one way, 25¢ round trip, book $2.95; *La Patera,* 25¢ one way, 45¢ round trip, book $3.00; *Hoff Hospital* (new Army Hospital) 10¢, 10-trip books, 75¢. Take Oak Park bus.

Airport: Santa Barbara Airways (United Air Lines) is situated at Goleta, 6 miles west of Santa Barbara on US 101. Special taxi service from downtown Santa Barbara hotels only, 15 minutes to airport not including 10 minutes to be allowed for checking manifests, special rate $1.00 per person each way. Bus service, 20¢ one way, 35¢ round trip, 30 minutes on 1½-hour schedule.

Taxi Services: Rates vary; 20¢ for first 8/10 m., 10¢ each additional ½ m.; five persons may ride at this rate; 6-passenger limousines, $3.00 hour; taxi shopping service, $2.50 hour; cabs also available at 20¢ for first mile, 10¢ for each additional ½ m. Privately owned limousines are available at rates ranging from $2.00 hour.

Piers: Stearns Wharf, foot of State St., dock for shore boats of United States Navy and navies of foreign countries, intercoastal freighters and yachts.

Information Bureaus: Southern Pacific Lines (ticket office), 906 State St., Atchison, Topeka & Santa Fe Ry. (ticket office), 915 State

St.; Spreitz Transportation Service, 622 Anacapa St.; Pacific Greyhound Lines, NE. corner Chapala and Carrillo Sts.; Recreation Center,
100 E. Carrillo St.; Heath International Travel Bureau, 20 La Arcada
Bldg.; World Travel Service, 1018 State St.; Chamber of Commerce,
715 Santa Barbara St.; Public Library, corner Anapamu and Anacapa
Sts.; Automobile Club of Southern California, 1301 Santa Barbara St.

Streets and Street Numbering: There are no streets or avenues designated by letters or numbers in Santa Barbara, and the majority of the
city's streets carry Spanish names. The city's blocks are in general
laid out in equal-sided squares with the streets running at 45-degree
diagonals to the north-south and east-west directions of the compass.
Streets are known as being north or south of Quinientos Street, the
southwest-northeast base line, and east or west of State Street, the
northwest-southeast base line. One hundred numbers are allowed to
the square block.

Business District: Santa Barbara's business district is rectangular in
shape and extends from Cabrillo Blvd., on the water front, northwestward to Sola St., and from De la Vina St., northeastward to Santa
Barbara St. Most of the better-class stores and shops are situated
along State Street and on the intersecting streets between State and
Anacapa extending from Canon Perdido to Victoria. Small shops, spe-
cializing in antiques and a variety of imported merchandise, may be
found in the interior El Paseo group of stores and studios facing De la
Guerra Plaza and adjacent areas. Mexican, Japanese, and Chinese
shops are situated along Canon Perdido to the northeast of Anacapa St.
Shopping areas also may be found in the outlying residential districts.
The principal wholesale district is situated along Chapala St.

Accommodations: Within the limits of Santa Barbara, its suburbs and
adjacent communities, are approximately 40 hotels with a total capacity
in excess of 2,000 rooms, with rates ranging from 75¢ to $12 per day;
many apartments and bungalow courts with rates at $18 to $100 per
month; and a number of automobile and tourist camps with and without facilities for trailers. Rates at these camps range from 50¢ to $3.00
per day.

Restaurants: Numerous restaurants, coffee shops, cafeterias, cafes, and
drugstore fountains offer varied menus; many specialize in sea foods
and foreign cuisine.

Auto Club: Automobile Club of Southern California (AAA), 1301
Santa Barbara St.; National Automobile Club, Emergency Service,
Woods Garage, 400 State St., Telephone 5528.

Public Buildings: Federal Building, corner Anacapa and Canon Perdido Sts.; County Courthouse, block bounded by Santa Barbara, Figueroa, Anacapa, and Anapamu Sts.; City Hall, De la Guerra Plaza; Public Library, corner Anacapa and Anapamu Sts.; Faulkner Memorial Art Gallery, 40 E. Anapamu St.; Department of Motor Vehicles, 938 Rancheria St.; National Guard Armory, 700 East De la Guerra St.

Museums: Museum of Natural History, 2559 Puesta del Sol Road (*open weekdays 9 a.m.-5 p.m., Sun. 10 a.m.-5 p.m., free; closed Christmas*).

Newspapers: Santa Barbara *News-Press,* De la Guerra Plaza, morning, evening and Sunday editions; *Union Labor News,* 32 E. Victoria St., weekly; Santa Maria *Times,* 207 West Main St., Santa Maria, daily except Sunday; Lompoc *Record,* 112 East Ocean Ave., Lompoc, weekly; *The Chronicle,* 115 East Coast Highway, Carpinteria, weekly; Carpinteria *Herald,* 813 Linden Ave., Carpinteria, weekly; Santa Ynez Valley *News,* Solvang, weekly; Goleta Valley *Leader,* Goleta, weekly.

Radio Stations: KTMS (1220 kc.), National Broadcasting Co., Inc., Blue Network affiliate, Santa Barbara News-Press Bldg., De la Guerra Plaza; KDB (1500 kc.), Mutual Broadcasting System affiliate, 15 E. Haley St.

Theaters: (legitimate) Lobero, 33 E. Canon Perdido St., road shows, concerts, lectures, and community plays; Alhecama, 914 Santa Barbara St., nonprofessional plays, lectures, and concerts; Playbox, 1408 State St., amateur plays. Motion-Picture Houses: Fox-Arlington, 1317 State St.; California, 20 W. Canon Perdido St.; Mission, 618 State St.; Granada, 1212 State St.

Amphitheater: Santa Barbara Bowl, county owned, at Milpas and Anapamu Sts., summer concerts, ballets, and operas; nightly productions in connection with annual fiesta, "Old Spanish Days," held during the full of the moon each August.

Climate: Rainy season from November to March; average seasonal rainfall for 68 years, 18.2 inches annually; no snow in coastal region; average yearly wind velocity, 4.0 m.p.h.; average daily temperature over period of 60 years, 60°. Light clothing and sportswear suitable for daytime most of year; wraps desirable for general evening wear.

Traffic Regulations: Speed limit, 15 m.p.h. when passing schools; 20 m.p.h. in business districts; 25 m.p.h. in residential districts. Parking limit, 15 minutes in congested areas; restricted zones designated by signs and painted curbs. State Vehicle Code available at office of California Highway Patrol, 929 Rancheria St.

Liquor Regulations: No alcoholic beverages sold between 2 a.m. and 6 a.m. It is unlawful to drive while under influence of alcohol. It is unlawful for a dealer to sell to a minor, or for a minor to purchase alcoholic beverages.

Forest Regulations: Visitors to the national forests of California are required to observe the following rules:

1. A campfire permit must be secured before building any fire, including fire in stoves burning wood, kerosene, gasoline, etc., on national forest land. The nearest forestry officer will issue permit without charge.

2. Every camping party in the national forests must be equipped with one shovel and ax per vehicle or pack train—shovel, with blade at least 8 inches wide and with over-all length of 36 inches; ax not less than 26 inches long overall, with head weighing 2 pounds or more. Both tools to be in serviceable condition.

3. During the fire season smoking is prohibited in the national forests. In camps, at places of habitation, and in special posted areas smoking is allowed, but smokers must be careful to extinguish their lighted matches, cigars, cigarettes, and pipe heels. Watch carefully for "No Smoking" and "Smoke Here" signs.

4. In periods of high fire hazard, camping and camp picnic fires are restricted to posted campgrounds, and part or all of the forests may be closed to public use and travel. Watch for the "Closed Area" signs.

5. Build small fires. Clear an area not less than 10 feet in diameter before starting fire.

6. Never leave a fire without totally extinguishing it with water.

7. Keep camp clean. Where garbage pits and incinerators are not provided, burn or bury all garbage refuse.

8. Do not pollute the springs, streams, or lakes.

9. Observe the State fish-and-game laws.

10. Drive carefully on mountain roads.

Fish-and-Game Laws: License required for hunting and fishing except for nongame marine fish. Special permit required to fish in Gibraltar Reservoir. It is unlawful to fish inland between one hour after sunset and one hour before sunrise. Licenses and latest information may be obtained at leading sports-goods stores.

Wild-Flower Protection: Destructive picking of wild flowers, shrubs and plants is prohibited by State law. Permits for picking wild flowers

ANDREE CLARK BIRD REFUGE

SNUG HARBOR FOR SMALL CRAFT, SANTA BARBARA

RESIDENTIAL AND BUSINESS AREAS, SANTA BARBARA,
SHOWING STATE STREET (*CENTER, LEFT TO RIGHT*)

RESIDENTIAL DISTRICT, EASTERN
OUTSKIRTS OF SANTA BARBARA

SANTA BARBARA HARBOR AND STEARNS WHARF

OIL DERRICKS ON THE SHORE NORTH OF SANTA BARBARA,
WITH SANTA CRUZ ISLAND SHOWING IN THE DISTANCE

TWILIGHT ON THE MESA

for scientific purposes may be obtained without charge from the U. S.
Forest Service office in the Federal Building, Anacapa and Canon Perdido Sts.

Garden Tours: Arranged by the Plans and Planting Branch, Community Arts Association.   Through this service visitors and residents
may study and enjoy the numerous private gardens on estates in Montecito, Santa Barbara, and the Hope Ranch area.   During certain seasons of the year, tours supervised by a landscape gardener are conducted
on Friday (*starting 10 a.m. and 2 p.m. from Recreation Center, 110
E. Carrillo St.   A charge is made; higher for guests without own cars.*)
Programs may be secured at Chamber of Commerce, hotels, banks, or
Public Library.

Places to Play

Recreation: The following alphabetical list gives the outstanding recreational facilities of the Santa Barbara area:

Aquaplaning: Aquaplaning is a popular sport off the Santa Barbara beaches, with motorboats available through private parties or commercial establishments. General information regarding rentals may be obtained at the office of the harbor master on the Breakwater, or at Stearns Wharf at the foot of State St. The waters off both East and West Beach frontage as well as the inner harbor, protected by the Breakwater, are used for this popular sport.

Archery: Manning Park, 419 San Ysidro Rd., Montecito, no equipment; Walton Sports Field, El Sueno and Foothill Blvd. (just off US 101), no equipment; La Cumbre Junior High School, Modoc Rd., equipped with 8 butts and all ranges, used every Sunday by the Santa Barbara Archers Club; Dwight Murphy Field, situated just off E. Cabrillo Blvd. at Mar Monte Hotel, equipped with 2 butts and 100-yard range, no equipment furnished; Oak Park, W. Junipero St. and Alamar Ave., two 50-yard ranges.

Badminton: Santa Barbara Badminton Club, at "Flying A" Studio, corner State and Mission Sts.; Montecito Home Club, 460 E. Valley Rd., Montecito (*Summer: 1 p.m.; winter: 9 a.m.-10 p.m. except Sundays*); Community Center Gymnasium, 1230 De la Vina St., (*supervised play mornings, afternoons and evenings, players must furnish rubber-soled shoes, birds and racquets*).

Baseball: California Baseball League, (Santa Barbara "Saints" play scheduled games during season, Apr. 19 to Sept. 1, at Laguna Field, entrance on East Cota St., near Laguna St.) Santa Barbara County League, composed of Lompoc, Santa Maria, Carpinteria, and Santa Barbara teams, (*games at Pershing Park each Sunday during season May 15 to Aug. 15 at 2 p.m.; admission is charged*). Santa Barbara Young Men's League, composed of Santa Barbara and Carpinteria amateur teams, Cabrillo Field, E. Cabrillo Blvd. near Mar Monte Hotel (*Sundays, 2 p.m. during season, May 15 to Aug. 15, no admis-*

sion charge). These games under guidance of City Recreation Commission. Night softball is played by both men's and women's teams at Pershing Park during the summer (*Monday through Friday evenings, no admission charge*).

Basketball: Played in season (*Dec. 1 to Mar. 15*) at Santa Barbara High School Gymnasium, interscholastic and intramural games; Community Center Gymnasium, 1230 De la Vina St., and National Guard Armory, 700 E. De la Guerra St., City League games with 25 teams sponsored by local merchants and organizations participating under guidance of City Recreation Commission, (*games from 5:15-10:15 p.m. during season, no admission charge*).

Beaches: Four beaches provide playgrounds for Santa Barbarans the year round. East Beach, along E. Cabrillo Blvd., and West Beach, along W. Cabrillo Blvd., are reached by bus from any section of the city; Leadbetter Beach lies west of the Breakwater. Playground facilities and barbecue pits are provided and lifeguards are on duty. Arroyo Burro Beach (also known as Hendry's Beach) is situated at the mouth of Arroyo Burro at the west city line. No lifeguard.

Boating and Yachting: Stearns Wharf, foot of State St., small boats, $2 per hour; powerboats may be chartered with operators, fees vary; for Channel and Island trips a charge of $25 and more per day is made. No fixed schedules; speedboats operate from water-ski headquarters, Stearns Wharf, fee 50¢ up.

Bowling: Figueroa Bowling and Billiard Bowl, 14 E. Figueroa St., private ownership, 10 alleys, free instruction, (*open daily 11:30 a.m. to 1:30 a.m.*). Montecito Home Club, 460 E. Valley Rd., (State Highway 150) 1 alley, free.

Bowling: (Lawn): Community Center Outside Recreation Area, 1230 De la Vina St. (*open daily except Monday from 1-5 p.m., free*). The Santa Barbara Lawn Bowling Club has the use of greens and lockers and welcomes players and beginners; players furnish own bowls.

Boxing and Wrestling: Mission Athletic Club, 635 E. Montecito St., professional wrestling matches (*each Thursday 8:30 p.m.*); amateur boxing bouts (*second and fourth Mondays each month, 8:30 p.m.*).

Cards, Checkers, Chess: Community Center Outside Recreation Area, 1230 De la Vina St.; Oak Park, corner Alamar and W. Junipero Sts.;

Plaza del Mar, end of W. Cabrillo Blvd. and Castillo St. (*9 a.m.-6 p.m., no admission*). Cabrillo Community Center, 1100 E. Cabrillo Blvd., (*10 a.m.-10 p.m., weekdays, 1-6 p.m., 7-10 p.m., Sun.*).   The Santa Barbara Chess Club is situated in separate quarters at 1230 De la Vina St. (*members only, nominal fee, telephone 27368*).

Cricket: Dwight Murphy Field, Por la Mar Dr. off E. Cabrillo Blvd., (*Sunday afternoon, April through September, for information and schedules telephone 7171 City Hall, Montecito or Santa Barbara Cricket Clubs*).

Croquet: Community Center Outside Recreation Area, 1230 De la Vina St., (*2 courts, equipment furnished, free*); Plaza Del Mar, end of W. Cabrillo Blvd. and Castillo St., (*2 courts, equipment furnished, free*); Manning Park, 419 San Ysidro Rd., Montecito, and Oak Park, Alamar Ave. and W. Junipero St.   (*1 grass court each, no equipment, free*); Ortega Park, Salsipuedes and Ortega Sts., (*1 grass court, free*).

Fishing (fresh water):   Many trout streams flow through Santa Ynez Mountains; fishing in Gibraltar reservoir by special permit during open season (*May 1 to Oct. 1*).   Consult authorities in local sports-goods stores for information on current fishing areas.

Fishing (ocean):   Surf fishing year round; from Stearns Wharf, except on causeway, (*tackle rented for fishing from wharf, pole and line 25¢ all afternoon; bait 5¢ and up*).

Football: Santa Barbara State College conference games at La Playa Field on Leadbetter Beach (*by automobile, end of W. Montecito St. over Cliff Dr. to Leadbetter Dr., turn L. to foot of Leadbetter Dr.*); Santa Barbara High School games at Peabody Stadium, situated between Olive, Anapamu, Nopal, and Canon Perdido Sts.

Golf: Montecito Country Club, Coast Highway (US 101) near east entrance to Santa Barbara, private membership, (*privileges granted with restrictions and fees*):   La Cumbre Country Club, Modoc Rd. at intersection of La Cumbre Rd., (*open to public, reasonable green fee*); Valley Club of Montecito, restricted to membership.

Golf (miniature):   Two privately operated courses, one of which is situated at corner of W. Cabrillo Blvd., and Bath St., and one at corner of Chapala and Micheltorena Sts. (*fee*).

Hiking: Canyon roadways, mountain trails and beaches offer challenges to the hiker.   Information concerning mountain trails obtainable from U.S. Forest Service office, 204 Federal Bldg.

Horseback Riding: Gudgeon's Riding School, 1899 Coast Highway (US 101); Montecito Riding Academy, 1640 Coast Highway (US 101); Santa Barbara Riding and Hunt Club, Las Palmas Dr., Hope Ranch; San Marcos Trading Post and Riding School, Modoc and Las Positas Rds.; San Ysidro Ranch Stables, 900 San Ysidro Rd., Montecito; Vandever's Riding School, Nogales Dr., Hope Ranch; (*rates vary according to stable, 75¢ to $1.50 first hour, 50¢ ensuing hours*).

Horseshoes: Oak Park, corner Alamar and W. Junípero Sts., 9 courts, (*open day and evening, equipped, no charge*): Santa Barbara Horseshoe Club plays Tuesday and Thursday evenings; Plaza Del Mar, foot of W. Cabrillo Blvd. and Castillo St., 6 courts; Manning Park, 419 San Ysidro Rd., Montecito, 2 courts, no equipment; Community Center Outside Recreation Area, 1230 De la Vina St., 4 courts, (*open daily 9 a.m.-6 p.m., Sundays 10 a.m.-6 p.m., equipment furnished*).

Hunting: Excellent hunting available in back country of Santa Barbara Mountains, State license required; large deer herds in Los Padres National Forest, season varies, limit 2 bucks; dove, Sept. 1 to Oct. 15, limit 15 twice weekly; quail, Nov. 15 to Nov. 28, limit 10 twice weekly; wild band-tailed pigeons, Dec. 1 to Dec. 15, limit 10 twice weekly. Licenses and information available at sports-goods stores.

Kayaks and Beach Umbrellas: Kayaks and beach umbrellas may be rented from W. H. Austin, 310 W. Cabrillo Blvd.

Parks and Playgrounds: Andrée Clark Bird Refuge, end of E. Cabrillo Blvd.; Plaza Del Mar, end of W. Cabrillo Blvd. (*picnicking, wading pool, tennis, horseshoes, etc., no charge*); Oak Park, Alamar Ave. and W. Junípero St. (*picnicking, barbecue pits, tennis, horseshoes, wading pool, no charge*); Rocky Nook Park, Mission Canyon Rd. near Old Mission (*picnicking, barbecue pits, etc., no charge*); Foster Glen, San Marcos Rd. (State Highway 150), (*picnicking*); Tucker's Grove, Foothill Blvd., 3 miles west of Santa Barbara (*picnicking, barbecue pits, dance floor, no charge*); Alameda Plaza Park, 1400 Blk., Santa Barbara St., (*family*); West Beach (*picnicking, barbecue pits in sheltered area between municipal pool and Breakwater*); Franceschi Park, (*floral, family*); Ortega Park, Blk. bounded by Salsipuedes, Ortega, Cota, and Quarantina Sts., (*picnicking, tennis, playground, no charge*); Palm Park, E. Cabrillo Blvd., (*picnicking, no charge*). There are 14 playgrounds, 9 of which are attached to local schools and are supervised during the school year. The remaining 6 are supervised the year round.

Polo: Fleischmann Field, 6 miles south of Santa Barbara on US 101, national and international matches (*nominal admission charge*), practice games Tuesday and Thursday during seasons, July 4 until mid-September, mid-November until April 1, (*no charge*).

Putting Green: Community Center Outside Recreation Area, 1230 De la Vina St.

Roque: Community Center Outside Recreation Area, 1230 De la Vina St. (*daily 9 a.m.-6 p.m., Sundays 10 a.m.-6 p.m., no charge*).

Rugby: Santa Barbara's rugby team, associated with the Southern California Rugby Union, plays during the season (*Nov. 1 to May 1*) at Dwight Murphy Field, Por la Mar Dr., off E. Cabrillo Blvd., (*admission free at some games, nominal fee charged at others*).

Shooting: Izaak Walton Sports Field, off Foothill Blvd., 2 miles west of Santa Barbara, ranges for skeet, rifle and pistol shooting, Naval Reserve practice range (*open to public at all times*).

Shuffleboard: Community Center, 1230 De la Vina St., 3 courts (*open daily, 1-6 p.m., no charge*): Plaza Del Mar, end of W. Cabrillo Blvd. and Castillo St., 3 courts, (*open daily 9 a.m.-6 p.m., no charge*).

Skating: Santa Barbara Roller Skating Rink, privately owned, 322 State St. (*open daily, 7:30-10:30 p.m., no instruction*).

Swimming: Samarkand Plunge, club privileges at pool (*admission charged, season tickets for June, July, and August may be bought*). Municipal pool, on beach at Plaza Del Mar, end of W. Cabrillo Blvd. and Castillo St., (*open daily during summer, nominal admission fee includes dressing room, towel, and locker*). City-supervised summer classes for children (*weekdays 10 a.m.-2 p.m.*). Lifeguards on duty all year at East and West Beaches and during summer, west of Breakwater.

Tennis: Municipal Tennis Stadium, US 101 near Bird Refuge, 9 courts, 4 lighted for night play (*minimum service charge*), players furnish own equipment; Plaza Del Mar, end of W. Cabrillo Blvd. and Castillo St., 2 courts, day or night play; Oak Park, corner Alamar Ave. and W. Junípero St., 2 courts, day or night play.

Tennis (table) : Cabrillo Community Center, 1100 E. Cabrillo Blvd., 6 tables (*open daily, 10 a.m.-10 p.m., Sun. 1-6 p.m., 7-10 p.m.*).

Water Skiing: Santa Barbara Water Skiing Club, operating under guidance of City Recreation Commission. Facilities and instruction at Stearns Wharf, adjoining yacht club building, foot of State St. (*Launches available from private parties and skis may be rented for 50¢ per hour.*)

Public Invited

January 1st	National observance of New Year's Day (special programs).
Jan. through March Sundays	Continuation of Winter-Spring Polo Season, Fleischmann Field, Santa Barbara. Admission nominal (practice games free). Special tournaments, special rates.
February through month	Annual Santa Barbara Artists' Winter Exhibition, Faulkner Art Gallery, East Anapamu Street, Santa Barbara (free).
nfd	World Day of Prayer.
12th	National observance of Abraham Lincoln's birthday (special programs).
22nd	National observance of George Washington's birthday (special programs).
March first week	Japanese Festival of the Dolls, Buddhist Temple, 131 East Canon Perdido Street, Santa Barbara, Traditional Flower Arrangements and Formal Tea Ceremony included.
all of 2nd week	California Conservation Week (7th year).
all of 3rd week	Wild Life Restoration Week (4th year).
mid-March to mid-May Fridays 10 a.m. and 2 p.m. (Tuesdays when announced)	Spring Garden Tours, from Recreation Center, Carrillo and Anacapa Streets, Santa Barbara. Sponsored by Plans and Planting Committee of the Community Arts Association. Landscape gardeners as guides. Each estate tour is dif-

		ferent. Admission identification tags must be purchased.
	late March or early April—three days	*La Primavera* Flower Show of Santa Barbara, National Guard Armory (parades are a feature). Admission nominal.
April	through April	California Open Road Month.
	nfd	Wild Flower Season.
	6th	National Army Day.
	nfd	Public Schools Week.
	23rd	Annual Exhibition of Shakespeare's Flowers. Public Library, Santa Barbara. Local gardeners vie in producing flora mentioned in the works of Shakespeare, for this exhibit; first presented in 1916.
	two days	Santa Maria Spring Flower Show, Santa Maria (76 miles north of Santa Barbara on US Highway 101). Veterans' Memorial Building. Admission nominal.
	late April	Observance of National Youth Week.
	two days	Carpinteria Spring Flower Show, Carpinteria (12 miles south of Santa Barbara).
	week	Better Homes and Gardens Week, Santa Barbara.
	nfd	Dance Festival in Sunken Gardens of Courthouse.
May	1st	National May Day.
	1st week	Opening of California Fresh Water Fishing Season.
	5th	*Cinco de Mayo,* celebrated in the Mexican sections; commemorates victory over French usurpers.
	5th	Japanese Boys' Festival, celebrated in Japanese section of Santa Barbara. (The carp balloons flown from the housetops indicate number of sons in family and their comparative ages. Carp are symbols of courage and daring.)
	2nd Sunday	National Mother's Day.

nfd	Annual Tri-County Open Tennis Tournament for men and women. Also Junior Tri-County Open Tennis Tournament.
mid-May	Annual Romería de Charros (rodeo), Fleischmann Field, Santa Barbara.
19th	National Citizenship Day.
nfd one week	Annual ride of *Los Rancheros Visitadores* (members and their guests).
24th	American Legion Poppy Day.
25th	Harbor Day.
last week usually	Tour of Flower Farms at Lompoc, Guadalupe, and Santa Maria (fields of the commercial growers).
latter part	Annual Barbecue at Nojoqui Park. Sponsored by Santa Barbara County Fish and Game Protective Association. Held since 1924— several thousand participate.
30th	National Memorial Day.
latter part or **early** June	Annual Festival at Guadalupe. This is a Portuguese celebration of thanksgiving and, on Sunday, is of a religious nature.

June

early June through October	First Annual $10,000 Open Southern California Salt Water Fishing Tournament (sponsored by Los Angeles Junior Chamber of Commerce). An official weighing-in station in Santa Barbara. Tournament boundaries are: San Diego to Santa Barbara—many trophies.
5th	Danish Constitution Day.
14th	National Flag Day.
all of 2nd **week**	National Flag Week.
three days nfd	Rose Show, Flower Room, Santa Barbara Museum of Natural History, sponsored by the Garden Club of Santa Barbara and Montecito (free).
nfd	Santa Ynez Valley Rodeo, Buell Ranch, Buellton (north on State 150 or US 101).

	latter part	Danish celebration at Solvang (north on State 150). Folk dancing in costume; dramatization of Hans Christian Andersen's fairy tales; religious and historic pageants.
	latter part	Lompoc Flower Show at Lompoc, Veterans' Memorial Building.
July	4th	National Independence Day (special programs).
	4th, week of	*Semana Náutica,* Santa Barbara. Marine events predominate: water sports and pageant, boat races and athletic meets. Annual Anacapa Yacht Race is the opening event of *Semana Náutica.*
	4th three days	Annual Lipton and Santa Barbara Perpetual Trophy Races.
	4th	Lompoc Western Street Parade and Rodeo at Lompoc (60 miles north of Santa Barbara).
	4th	Annual Scots' celebration at Tucker's Grove, Santa Barbara.
	4th	Fourth of July celebration at Carpinteria (12 miles south of Santa Barbara).
	nfd	Santa Barbara State College Summer Session (annual outdoor Shakespearean or other classic performance).
	nfd location varies	Biennial Yacht Race to Hawaii.
	nfd	Biennial Southern California Championship Regatta. (This event is substituted for Hawaiian race biennally.)
	through July and August	Band Concerts in Santa Barbara Parks.
	through July and August	Santa Barbara Drama and Music Festival, usually held in Santa Barbara County Bowl, East Anapamu Street.
	nfd one day only	Santa Barbara Dog Show (all breeds); auspices of Santa Barbara Kennel Club.
	early July to mid-	Summer Polo Season, Fleischmann

September, Sundays · Field, Santa Barbara (practice games free). Admission nominal. Special events, special prices.

late July to early September
Fridays 10 a.m. and 2 p.m.
Tuesdays when announced · Summer Garden Tours, from Recreation Center, Carrillo and Anacapa Streets, Santa Barbara. Sponsored by Plans and Planting Committee of the Community Arts Association. Landscape gardeners as guides. Each estate tour is different. Admission identification tags must be purchased.

latter part · Santa Barbara County Fair, Santa Maria (76 miles north of Santa Barbara on US 101).

latter part · Santa Barbara Annual Open Tennis Tournament for Men and Women; also Santa Barbara Junior Open Tennis Tournament.

last week usually · Santa Barbara National Horse Show and Fair, Pershing Park, Santa Barbara. Many prizes. Cattle, Flower, and Lemon Exhibits are included.

August
through August
week days 10 a.m. to 5 p.m.
Thurs. eve. 7-9 p.m.
Sundays 2-5 p.m. · Annual Summer Exhibition of Santa Barbara Artists, Faulkner Art Gallery. East Anapamu Street. Other art exhibits, national and international, throughout the year.

full of August moon · Old Spanish Days Fiesta, Santa Barbara.

1st day 8 p.m. · Official opening of fiesta, also a pageant, at the Santa Barbara Mission.

2nd day 3 p.m. · Famous historic pageant and parade.

2nd day 8 p.m.
3rd day 8 p.m.
4th day 8 p.m. · Historic presentation at Santa Barbara County Bowl, East Anapamu Street (incidents of Spanish history and tradition).

3rd day 2:30 p.m. · Dance Pageant in Sunken Gardens of County Courthouse.

2nd eve. 9 p.m.
3rd eve. 9 p.m. · Old Spanish dancing and entertainment by descendants of Spanish

4th eve. 9 p.m.	and pioneer families in Courthouse gardens.
3rd day 2 p.m.	Stock Horse Competition, Pershing Park, Santa Barbara; rodeo events also.
4th day 2:30 p.m.	Children's **Parade**, followed by "Santa Barbara Fifty Years Ago." (State Street reserved for carriages and horses.) Old costumes a feature.
every eve. 8:30 p.m.	Fiesta Play at Lobero Theater, also Early American or Spanish Drama by Community Players at Alhecama Theater.
continuous	Programs are arranged throughout the Fiesta.
mid-August	Santa Barbara School of Natural Science.
September first Monday	National Labor Day.
nfd	National Rice Bowl Charity Day. La Purísima Mission State Park Fiesta, near Lompoc (special programs).
9th	State Admission Day (special programs).
15th and 16th	Mexican *Fiesta Patria*.
28th	State Indian Day.
October early October 3 days nfd	Autumn Flower Show at National Guard Armory (sponsored by Santa Barbara Horticultural Society; outstanding flower exhibits).
Saturday and Sunday nearest the 9th	Leif Ericson Festival, Santa Barbara; sponsored by Norroenn Federation of America (awards for characteristic national costumes, also for folk dances).
12th	Columbus Day (special programs).
mid-October	Opening of Football Season.
nfd	National Navy Day.
31st	Halloween.
November November through March usually 1st Sundays 8 p.m.	Series of six Concerts by Mozart Society (in costume). Old masterpieces revived. Clerbois Studio. Admission nominal.

11th	National Armistice Day.
2nd week	National Book Week.
mid-November through March	Opening of Winter Polo Season at Fleischmann Field, Santa Barbara.
Sundays	Special events, special prices (practice games free).
2nd and 3rd weeks	National Red Cross Roll Call.
by Proclamation	National Thanksgiving Day.
December 4th	Saint Barbara's Day (Patroness of Santa Barbara). Special services at the Santa Barbara Mission.
24th evening	Christmas Carols and Tableaux. (Locations vary — see current press.)
25th	Christmas Day (special programs).
25th	Community Hearthstone — Open House at Public Library. Librarians as Hostesses (blazing log fires).
nfd	Annual Southern California Intercollegiate Symphony Concert (usually conducted by Leopold Stokowski or Henry Eichheim).
nfd	Annual Concerts generally by Los Angeles Philharmonic Orchestra; at Santa Barbara.

THROUGHOUT THE YEAR

daily 9 a.m. to 5 p.m.	Santa Barbara, Queen of the Missions, Santa Barbara. Tours conducted and lectures by Franciscan guides.
daily 3-5 p.m.	St. Anthony's Seminary, adjoining Santa Barbara Mission. Chapel open to visitors.
daily	Mission La Purísima Concepción. The Civilian Conservation Corps and the State government have restored this mission recently; it is now included in La Purisima State Park, Lompoc Valley.
daily 9 a.m. to 5 p.m.	Santa Barbara Courthouse, Santa Barbara, a famous structure—open to visitors.

daily	Santa Inés Mission, Solvang. Art collection of special interest—open to visitors.
weekly	Sunday Horseback Rides, arranged by the Recreation Commission, also frequent rides by Santa Barbara Riding and Trails Associations; visitors included.
periodically	Federal Music Project Concerts; Oak Park and other recreation centers.
visitors' cards will admit to	The Rancheros Club (*Los Rancheros Visitadores*). Inquire at headquarters, 715 Santa Barbara Street.
daily	Special Parks and Botanic Gardens; no admission card required.
daily except Sunday	*El Fureidis,* Parra Grande Lane, Montecito (estate of J. Waldron Gillespie).
daily	Manning Park, San Ysidro Road, Montecito; also Hillside Park, Moreno Road and Alameda Padre Serra, Santa Barbara (labeled specimens).
daily 8 a.m. to 6 p.m.	Franceschi Park, Riviera, Experimental Gardens; Santa Barbara Botanic Garden, Mission Canyon. Native California plants growing under garden conditions.
daily	Faulkner Art Gallery, national and international art exhibits.
daily 9 a.m. to 5 p.m. Sundays 10 a.m. to 5 p.m.	Santa Barbara Museum of Natural History, Puesta del Sol Road, Santa Barbara. Prehistoric fossils from local asphalt pits. Canaliño Indian and prehistoric dwellers' artifacts. Local gems and minerals, flora and fauna; also spring and winter series of lectures for members.
periodically	Lectures at Santa Barbara Women's Club, Rocky Nook, Mission Canyon Road, Santa Barbara. Many

events are open to visitors by
ticket. Club will supply information.

Call Chamber of Commerce for additional information, also (see
What, Where, When, How). All dates subject to change.

Part 2

Past and Present

Presidio to Channel City

"THE ANCIENT ONES"

IN OCTOBER, 1542, two tiny, vest-pocket caravels, *La Victoria* and the flagship *San Salvador,* sailed up the California coast from Mexico and passed through what is now the Santa Barbara Channel.

It was fifty years to the month since Columbus had discovered the New World. Under the leadership of Juan Rodríguez Cabrillo,* a Portuguese navigator sailing for the Spanish Crown, the vigorous threads of empire were spinning a fateful web along the California coast. Unfurled before the stiff, coastal breeze, the proud banner of imperial Spain, flashing crimson and gold in the sunlight, cast its shadow over the swarthy mariners who dropped anchor in Santa Barbara Bay.

A fleet of large Indian canoes swarmed out to greet the first white men to visit the sunny, crescent harbor. The canoes, made of boards ingeniously lashed together and caulked with asphaltum, were paddled

---

* Juan Rodríguez Cabrillo—Cabrillo was his mother's name; according to Portuguese and Spanish custom this follows his surname, and as is often the case, he became known as Cabrillo rather than Rodríguez.

by *Canaliño* Indians, who lived in large villages near the present site of Santa Barbara. In some two score villages along the channel coast line nearly 15,000 Indians were still living when Spanish soldiers and padres came into the region more than two centuries later.

Of their own history, the Indians spoke with awe and vagueness, referring to ancestors whom they called "The Ancient Ones." In recent years scientists have unearthed skeletons and artifacts far antedating the "Ancient Ones." These discoveries imply a culture dissimilar to those of later times, a culture which may have been the earliest to exist within the confines of the present United States.

The first people believed to have inhabited the channel region, at a time preceding the Bronze Age in Europe, lived in deep-set circular huts in the humid climate of oak-forested crests in the foothills. This fact has led archeologist David B. Rogers, formerly Curator of Anthropology of the Santa Barbara Museum of Natural History, to name them "Oak Grove Men." Mongoloid in type, they were heavy-set, slant-eyed, with flattened noses. Their stonecraft was of the crudest; for grinding the acorns composing their diet, they used a primitive forerunner of the present Mexican *mano* (Sp., handstone) and *metate* (Sp., concave grinding slab) ; the latter of these was broken and overturned on the grave of its owner, presumably to insure household goods for the hereafter. Recent archeological discoveries lead to the belief that the Oak Grove people occupied their crested slopes for several centuries and that they may have disappeared before a new race, bringing a new culture, came to the channel area, probably almost two thousand years ago.

Weapons found in a higher stratification indicate a culture much more advanced than that of the Oak Grove Men; from these weapons is derived a name descriptive of the newcomers, the "Hunting People." They appear also to have been of the mongoloid type. With the passing centuries, they improved their weapons. They discovered, for instance, that asphaltum seeping up from the sand and outcroppings in the cliffs could be applied to strips of sinew in order to fasten spearheads to shafts with rocklike rigidity. Food refuse found in kitchen middens shows that giant Pismo clams and other shellfish were part of their diet. While traces of sea lion and seal indicate that they may have hunted from the shore, scarcity of fishbones indicates that these people had no boats and knew little of sea fishing.

But of hunting and fighting, their weapons, arrows, and clubs indicate they knew a great deal. They were nomads, yet from the remains of their household goods it appears probable that they formed villages of from 10 to 100 structures. Stone bowls found in fire beds suggest that in their later years they had adopted a more settled mode of life, since these heavy objects would not have been easy to carry from camp to camp.

Their dead were buried in the embryonic position, knees under chin, the head usually pointed toward the west.   Unlike many other tribes, they put few personal belongings in the graves.   Anthropologists believe that the Hunting People came to the channel region about the beginning of the Christian Era and remained fully a thousand years. Apparently, about the eighth to the tenth century, A.D., another race arrived and eventually intermarried with them, merging the two cultures.

It was the descendants of these merged peoples who were named by the Spanish explorers *Canaliño* * (Sp., channel) Indians, and who became the neophytes of the Santa Bárbara Mission.   Among North American tribes, only the *Canaliños* and the *Shoshones* possessed the unique canoes of lashed boards which formed the native entourage for Cabrillo.

Father Juan Crespi, in his diary of the Portolá expedition, dated August 14, 1769, wrote of the *Canaliños* and their canoes: "They have surprising skill and ability in the construction of their canoes which are made of good pine planks, well joined and of a graceful shape, with two prows.   They handle them with equal skill; three or four men go out into the open sea, and they hold as many as ten men.   They use long oars with two blades and row with indescribable lightness and speed."   Again, in a letter to José de Gálvez, visitor-general in New Spain, February 9, 1770, Father Crespi refers to the canoes: "All of these towns have many canoes with keels. . . . At one town we counted as many as fifteen canoes, some of them not so small, as they measured seven or eight *varas* [20 to 24 feet]; but all were equally light so that two men could launch them in the water."   Fire beds with ashes of tremendous depth on cliff tops in the Channel Islands have resulted from huge beacon fires lighted to guide the seagoing *Canaliños*.

In common with other North American tribes, however, the *Canaliños* possessed no written language, but they did use symbols to communicate with one another.

Progressive centuries show improvements in the fashioning of the *Canaliños'* weapons and utensils, from which can be discerned an expanding culture.

The Oak Grove Men had inhabited the forested hilltops, and the Hunting People the open ground and headlands, but the *Canaliños,* for the most part, clustered together on ledges of land adjacent to the marshes.   Here huts, often as many as one hundred, were thatched

---

* *Canaliño*—variable, *Canaleño*. Both spellings are used by historians. A majority of contemporary anthropologists employ *"Canaliño."*

with coarse grass or tules, the hearth in the center. Of these, Father Crespi, in 1769, again recorded in his diary: "This channel has eight or ten regular towns containing a number of heathen, with very round houses in the form of half oranges, roofed with grass. . . . These people have their own form of government, all the towns have three or four captains, one of whom is head chief and is obeyed by all the rest. Each chief has two wives, while the rest of the men have only one. They have two cemeteries, one for the men and the other for the women, all surrounded by high, sharpened palings, painted many colors."

Of the Indians on the Channel Islands, Bartholomew Ferrelo, who kept log for the Cabrillo expedition, laconically recorded that they were very poor. "They are fishermen; they eat nothing but fish; they sleep on the ground. In each house they say there are fifty souls. They live very swinishly. They go naked."

The natives on the mainland worked communally; the women pounded meal, often seasoned with grasshoppers, in groups at pot holes; the men built canoes. The village *temescal* (sweat house) was a customary gathering place for the men. Round and earth-covered, almost air tight, it offered a surprisingly modern "steam bath" which was followed by a plunge into cold water as a preventive against disease.

Canaliño women apparently were treated with higher regard by the men than was usual in most North American tribes. Vanity took form in elaborate coiffures, the women entwining their hair through mother-of-pearl rings and embellishing it further with shell daggers. A profusion of bead ornaments, claws of birds and animals, and animal teeth bedecked both men and women, and on ceremonial occasions a dancer wore the beak of the swordfish, in honor of the "Provider of meat." Abalone shells were used for plates. Needles were of polished bone.

Monogamy prevailed, although chiefs were allowed more than one wife. Women were required to give undivided loyalty to their husbands. To be seen walking with another man meant chastisement, and a second offense often brought death.

Occasionally women ruled a tribe. Cabrillo's record states: "Most of the Indian chiefs were men, but the ruler of one of the villages was a very wrinkled old woman, which seemed very queer to us."

For their services to the tribesmen the chiefs apparently received food and shell money. The tribal medicine man was called the *shaman;* a creature of mystery and of meditation, he was deeply venerated as the intermediary between the tribe and the forces of good and evil. The chief god was *Chupu,* whose blessing was invoked upon the bounty of the sea, the acorn harvest, and young married women by rites which included sprinkling with sacred flower pollen.

THE QUEST FOR EMPIRE

During the sixteenth century, questing galleons spun a tenuous thread between the Old World and the New. In 1513, Balboa discovered the Pacific; in 1519, Cortez began to drive the wedge of empire into Mexico; in 1579, Drake explored the Pacific coast for England. Then, in the summer of 1602, sixty years after Cabrillo had been welcomed by the *Canaliños,* Sebastián Vizcaino set sail from Acapulco with three vessels and a supply transport to explore the California coast for possible ports.

Among the company was a Carmelite friar, Father Antonio de la Ascención, whose custom it was to name each new place for the saint upon whose festival day the discovery chanced. When, therefore, on December 4, 1602, they entered the channel first charted by Cabrillo, the name of Saint Bárbara, Virgin and Martyr, the "fairest saint in all the calendar," was given to the channel and to the shore where the city of Santa Barbara now stands.

Although Vizcaino records that a *Canaliño* chief offered him ten wives for each man if he would come ashore, he was not to be tempted, and for more than a century and a half after the bay was named, the Indians of the channel remained in undisputed possession of their ancestral villages. Not until the encroachment of Russia and England threatened the loss of the Californias, did Spain decide that the time had come to establish her unequivocal dominion in Alta California.

Doughty Captain J. Gaspar de Portolá was chosen by José de Gálvez, Spanish inspector general for Mexico, to command two expeditionary units, one by land and one by sea, which were to extend the Spanish frontiers in manifest form to Monterey. Frail and crippled Father Junípero Serra accompanied Portolá by land, representing the Franciscan order of friars who planned to establish missions in Alta California.

In July, 1769, Portolá's overland expedition reached San Diego Bay from Mexico City. Here they reunited with the expeditionary force which already had arrived by sea. Both land and sea groups had suffered hardships; the crews of the ships were greatly weakened from starvation, thirst, and scurvy.

One of the vessels bound from Mexico, the *San Antonio,* had lost its course, and had landed first on an island in the Santa Barbara Channel. Here, a padre lost a small iron cross which was found and later returned by the friendly natives. In commemoration of the circumstance, the island was named Santa Cruz (Sp., Holy Cross) before the *San Antonio* turned back on its course to San Diego Harbor where it anchored, April 11, 1769, to be joined shortly thereafter by the *San Carlos* from Mexico.

FORGING THE MISSION CHAIN

On July 16, 1769, Father Serra dedicated the site for the Mission San Diego de Alcalá, first link in the series of twenty-one Franciscan missions which were to dot the California coast "a day's journey apart" from San Diego to Sonoma, Alta California.

Meanwhile, Captain Portolá, with Father Crespi and a small band of men whom scurvy, thirst, and hunger had spared, proceeded northward to Monterey, where the Crown had ordered a garrison established. Among the company breaking the trail for El Camino Real (Sp., the Royal Highway) was Captain José Francisco de Ortega, whose descendants still live in Santa Barbara (*see Human Side of a City*).

As Portolá and Ortega proceeded northward through the channel villages, the natives impeded their progress and the indefatigable Father Crespi again reported in his diary: "Our only object in traveling today was to get rid of so many people. . . . They were not satisfied with spreading food before us, but also desired to amuse us. We dismissed them . . . but in vain. As soon as darkness had set in, they returned, blowing horns, the infernal noise of which was sufficient to tear our ears to pieces."

Following the founding of the mission presidio at Monterey, other missions were established along the coast, but Santa Bárbara, Virgin and Martyr, patiently waited her turn. Father Serra long had wanted to establish a mission amidst the Indian population, but his spiritual plans met a temporal checkmate in the hard-headed, realistic Governor Felipe de Neve, who insisted, first, on a fortified presidio.

On April 21, 1782, therefore, the governor, the *Padre-Presidente,* and Captain de Ortega who had accompanied Portolá thirteen years earlier to the same spot, jointly conducted the ceremony founding the Presidio Real of Santa Bárbara. The site chosen was on or near the western edge of a lagoon, approximately at the intersection of Santa Barbara and Canon Perdido Streets, and which supported a large Indian village ruled over by the friendly chief, Yanonalit. Father Serra, clad in alb and stole, stood in a hastily constructed chapel of brush before a roughly hewn table used as an altar. Around him were a group of *Canaliños* and thirty-six *soldados de cuera* (Sp., leather-jacket soldiers), their faces bronzed from wind and sun almost as dark as those of their dusky companions.

In a letter to Father Lasuén of San Carlos Mission, Father Serra gave the following account: "On the Feast of the Patronage of Saint Joseph occurred the blessing and erection of the large cross, the blessing of the site, the first Holy Mass with a sermon and the founding of this Mission Presidio of Santa Bárbara, Virgin and Martyr, in the country of Yanonalit. I was and am alone. Hence, there was only a Low Mass, and in place of the Te Deum the Abalado was chanted, which is equivalent to the Laudamus. May God bless it. Amen." Soon after the ceremony the ailing Father Serra, nearly seventy, and bitterly disappointed at the postponement of the building of his mission, left on foot for Carmel where he died two years later.

Following the presidio's founding, four years elapsed before the Comandante Ortega felt he could safely spare part of his men to begin work on the mission. Its location deviated somewhat from precedent. Previous experience had proved the wisdom of choosing a site close to a protecting presidio, but the south bank of *Pedregosa* (Sp., place of stones) Creek was an inviting location and served, the padres felt, to remove the childlike neophytes from the questionable influence of the soldiers.

MISSION SANTA BÁRBARA

In 1786, Father Fermín Francisco Lasuén, third *Padre-Presidente*
of the Alta California missions, presided over the ceremonies dedicating Santa Bárbara, the tenth mission to be established in California.
The formal dedication awaited the arrival of Governor Pedro Fages,
but when the feast day of the Patroness saint had come, the governor
had not. Despite the absence of his superior, Father Lasuén, a successor to the zealous Father Serra, proceeded to consecrate the ground
and raise the cross. Although the first Mass was sung ten days later
in a formal ceremony before the governor, it is the saint's day, December 4, in that year, that is regarded as the day of founding.

Winter storms delayed construction until the following spring,
when a house, 14 by 44 feet in size, was built for the padres. After
the completion of a small chapel 14 by 39 feet, a servant's room, and
one house each for unmarried women and unmarried men were erected.
The plan followed that of the presidio's structure: a group of adobe
buildings about an open square. Since permanency was a consideration, their walls, often three feet thick, were plastered with mortar
and rested on a stone-and-mortar foundation.

The Indians capitulated slowly, but by the end of 1787 one hundred
and eighty-five neophytes had adopted the Christian faith. At this
time, the mission boasted 80 head of cattle, 27 sheep, 87 goats, 32 horses,
and 9 mules. The original chapel, enlarged in 1788, again proved too
small for the increasing number of converts among the Indians, and in
1789 a new church, roofed with red tiles, was built to accommodate
the 428 members of the mission flock.

Nestling close to the buildings of the mission lay the rude adobe
houses where the neophytes lived. Morning and evening they attended
church, where an Indian choir and orchestra of thirty musicians played
violins, flutes, drums, and trumpets in praise to the strange white man's
God they had accepted. Within the courtyard they plied the trades
of mason, blacksmith, carpenter, tailor, and shoemaker, taught them by
the patient padres. The girls and women learned how to spin, to
weave and to sew, and in addition, mastered the art of European cooking. Although most of the neophytes lived at the mission, others remained in *rancherías* (villages) near the cattle and fields where, under
the direction of the padres, they cultivated grain fields and fruit trees.
An important occupation was the tanning of hides, and the remains of
two great vats built for this purpose in 1802 still stand near the church
buildings.

The Indians, who made up 90 per cent of the population, maintained the mission by their labor, in return for which they were fed,
housed, and clothed. At the end of each year they received a blanket

apiece, and at stated times were allowed to visit their relatives outside the mission.

From 1769 until Spanish rule was overthrown by Mexico in 1822, the predominant authority was that of the padres, who nominally held the land in trust until the Indians might be civilized properly. The Franciscan fathers exercised a virtual autonomy over the continuous strip formed by their chain of missions from San Diego to Sonoma. Annually, from 1786 to 1810, the missions received various supplies from Mexico, although much needed consignments of money were seldom forthcoming from their easy-going patrons to the south.

UNDER MEXICAN RULE

The revolution in Mexico against Spanish domination, which began in 1810, soon cut off California from the motherland. Philosophically, the provincial Santa Bárbara folk merely hauled down the Spanish flag and hoisted that of Mexico, but they could not ignore the economic reprisals taken by the disgruntled Spanish Crown during the war. After 1811, Spanish supply ships stopped coming; California became more and more isolated and hard times fell upon the people, who became ragged and hungry. By 1813, manufactured articles were scarce. The native soldiers served without pay for three years; finally, Comandante Don José de la Guerra informed the governor that there was little food for these loyal men, and insufficient clothing.

The destitute residents were almost hysterically eager to welcome traders to their shores. It was impossible for the new government to enforce the old Spanish law prohibiting trade with foreigners. Under the pressure of circumstances and with the canny eye to import duties and licenses, the Mexican government repealed the law. The inhabitants became increasingly aware of Yankee ships nosing along their coast line, bringing sorely needed cloth, implements, and a few welcome luxuries in return for hides and tallow. Americans, and particularly Yankee traders, put in freely at the California ports, many returning to dwell in the towns along the coast, where the tower of a mission church brooded above a friendly cluster of adobe houses, workshops, storehouses, and Indian dwellings.

Mexican independence, which resulted at the end of the war with Spain, sounded the death knell of Spanish Franciscan authority. In 1824, the Indians of several missions, including those of Santa Bárbara, revolted against the Mexican soldiers. The disturbance was quelled after the loss of several lives on both sides.

The California missions had played their role admirably in the development of the wild country. They had accomplished marvels undreamed of even by the visionary Father Serra. The padres had toiled for more than fifty years to bring the white man's creed and culture to a virgin land.

Now their day was done. The large and fertile areas they controlled were coveted by a vigorous society of newcomers who, banding together with discontented native *Californianos,* called themselves *Californios.*

SECULARIZATION OF THE MISSIONS

The Mexican Congress was persuaded by the *Californios* in 1833 to break up the virtual autonomy enjoyed by the padres for more than two generations. In theory, secularization, among other legal changes, was intended to grant the rights of citizenship to the Indians and to restore them one-half the mission land, livestock and farm tools. As drawn up by the newly appointed Mexican governor, José Figueroa, the plan was just and largely painless, except, perhaps, to the padres. The governor's untimely death, on September 29, 1835, left matters in the hands of the *Californios,* who executed the plan to their own advantage.

The approval of the Mexican Congress in 1834 of a measure ordering the mission to be converted into a parish church and the padres to be supplanted by secular curates, had sad effect. The land of the mission of Santa Bárbara was sold, its cattle and orchards ruined through neglect or theft by administrators, its Indians thrown out into an alien world. The padres, abandoned by the Mexican government and plundered by the *Californios,* realized that ruin was inevitable and began to "liquidate" their property. Cattle by the thousands were slaughtered for their hides and tallow. The carcasses, having little immediate value, were left to rot where they fell.

The Indians also suffered under the new order of affairs. Santa Bárbara Mission had led the others in the conversion of the natives. From 864 in 1789, the neophyte population had increased to 1,792 in

1803. Five years after the Decree of Secularization, a scant 246 remained.

Sudden freedom found the Indians totally unprepared to shift for themselves. Many took to the mountains, and the few who attempted to cultivate their ground were so harassed by the *Californios* that their lot became unendurable. For years afterwards, bands of Indians from as far as Mojave and the San Joaquín plains periodically raided the ranches to drive off cattle and horses which they had been taught to consider their own property. When the government made several abortive attempts to regain their confidence, it was too late. Ten years after secularization, the native converts had disappeared almost entirely.

Santa Bárbara Mission suffered less than did the others. This may have been due to the influence of California's first bishop, Father Francisco Garcia Diego y Moreno, who had made his residence at the mission after January, 1842. He was appointed in 1840.

In 1845, the lands belonging to nine of the missions were sold, the rest leased for a term of years. Santa Bárbara Mission, with the exception of the church and cloister, was leased to Don Nicolás A. Den and Don Daniel Hill.

Bishop Diego, his death in 1846 hastened by the ruin growing around him, was buried in the mission church. Though the mortal flame of his life was snuffed, the sacred fire which had been lighted on the mission's altars on the day of its founding in 1786 burned on, nourished and protected by the padres, never to be extinguished. During all the years while the other twenty missions crumbled in ruin and were abandoned, the flickering altar flame at Santa Bárbara, Queen of the Missions, was constant witness that here alone the robed Franciscans remained—remained through rebellion, destitution, and earthquake. Even now, the light persists, immutable, a testament to the devotion of the padres.

YANKEE "DONS"

Although the change to Mexican rule did not at first alter the political fabric of Santa Bárbara life, the era of California-Boston trade it ushered in began a new chapter in the history of the province. Not only did the traffic in hides and tallow make cattle barons out of humble ranchers but it brought the blue-eyed *Yanquis* in increasing numbers and sealed the destiny of Alta California.

In Santa Bárbara, the rapid growth of empire went hand in hand with hasty romance. The terse, laconic wooing of the Yankees won the daughters (and their dowries) of many wealthy *dons:* the suitors adopting Mexican citizenship, the Catholic faith, and the bright *serapes* and bell-bottomed trousers of their Castilian fathers-in-law. The keen-minded eastern newcomers quickly established a place for themselves in the lives of the soft-spoken, passive *Californianos.*

Joseph Chapman, who arrived most inauspiciously in 1818 as an unwilling member of a pirate crew, became one of the city's leading citizens. He talked himself out of a summary execution organized by an irate California posse bent on punishing him for the depredations of

the pirates. Later, he married Guadalupe Ortega, an heiress to the very *rancho* his marauding colleagues had sacked.

A second type of American immigrant, the fur trapper, crossed the Rocky Mountains to participate in a remunerative trade in sea otter skins, which were numerous on the shores of the Channel Islands. A few French, Irish, and a leavening of Old World Spaniards, completed the population of the tiny cosmopolitan city of some nine hundred people in 1840.

Despite the influx of foreigners the atmosphere of the town was little changed. "There was not a timekeeper in the place," said a traveler of that day. "For downright *dolce far niènte,* or double-distilled sweet idleness, Santa Bárbara in 1843 was far ahead of any spot on earth that I have ever visited. . . ." The influence of the brown-robed padres on the community was very marked. Food and shelter and means of conveyance were unhesitatingly extended, and doors never were locked. Everyone was an excellent horseman, since carriages were almost unknown. A guitar was part of every household, and at twilight from all parts of the pueblo were heard the sounds of strumming, and rich, unabashed voices. In the homes of the best people were dignity, elegance, refinement, and charm. Both men and women dressed elaborately; laces, silks, mantillas, and resplendent uniforms bedecked many an occasion of vivid Latin elegance. But their love of finery was no greater than their simplicity of spirit and their inherent dignity of manner.

STOCKTON AND FRÉMONT

There long had been agitation for conquest and annexation of California as the "manifest destiny" of the United States. Matters came to a head in 1846 with the outbreak of the Mexican War. Economic growth had been slow and government lax under Mexican rule. Many of the Californians welcomed the idea of a stable administration of their affairs under the American flag.

In August, 1846, Commodore Robert Field Stockton, in command of American forces in California, sailed from Monterey and anchored at the harbor of Santa Bárbara. Up the long slope into the town, drowsy with the utter somnolence of old-time California, he marched a small force. The American flag went up while a salute was fired. Then, leaving Lieutenant Talbot and a garrison of ten soldiers in command, Stockton proceeded to San Diego.

But the ease with which Santa Bárbara had been captured was deceptive. Two months after Stockton left, Talbot and his ten soldiers found themselves surrounded by two hundred California horsemen. By night the eleven dismayed "gringos" made an escape and struck for the mountains, pursued by their captors and later menaced by burning chaparral fired by the Californians in an effort to drive them out of cover. Fleeing into the San Joaquín Valley, they tramped, half-starved, the 500 miles to Monterey.

News of the rout caused reinforcements to be rushed to Santa Bárbara. Major John C. Frémont, "The Pathfinder," marching from the north with a battalion, 450 strong, to retake the town, was warned before he reached Gaviota Pass (*see Tour 3*) of an ambush set there for him by a group of Santa Barbara *caballeros* who had learned of his coming. Frémont avoided the ambush by taking the little-known Indian Trail through San Marcos Pass (*see Tour 2*). He was guided by Benjamin Foxen, the Sisquoc rancher who had warned him of the trap. On the morning of December 27, 1846, hungry, exhausted from their difficult crossing of the pass, they raised the Stars and Stripes again in Santa Bárbara, without firing a single shot. The Santa Barbarans, emerging from morning Mass, were surprised to find their town recaptured, but offered no resistance.

AMERICAN RULE

As an American city, Santa Barbara began its legal existence on April 9, 1850, when it was incorporated by an act of the first California Legislature, although five months were to elapse before a wrangling Congress voted, on September 9, to admit the infant State to the Union. Word of its new status traveled slowly to the dozing channel town, where everyone felt that *mañana* (tomorrow) was the time to begin the necessary but dull work of instituting the new regime.

Santa Bárbara's earliest civil government had been established under Spanish rule in 1782, with authority vested in the comandante of the presidio. In December, 1826, Mexican rule had established the *Ylustre Ayuntamiento* (Illustrious City Council), which consisted of an *Alcalde* (mayor) and two *Regidores* (councilmen). This governing body had full powers, with the *Alcalde* acting as judge, jury, and executioner. The defendant and plaintiff appeared before him, stated their cases, produced witnesses, if any, and the culprit, if doomed, was executed without delay. Unspurred by "civic consciousness," office-seeking was unknown, and the city fathers, beyond sustaining the dignity of their rank, had little to do.

In the newly minted city of 1850 there was much to do. When, on August 26, 1850, the first Common Council of Santa Barbara finally convened under the presidency of Don Luis T. Burton, it had not only to formulate laws to govern the city, but even rules to govern itself. Eleven days after incorporating the town of Santa Barbara, the State legislature had repealed every Spanish law but one, throwing California towns on the bleak threshold of a new era, without a straw of governmental custom to which to cling. Before the city clerk, Luis Carrillo, lay a book of foolscap stitched together without a mark on it, with "Acts of the Common Council of the City of Santa Barbara" written on the cover.

There was slightly less than $400 in the treasury. It was imperative that the first "Act" provide funds for carrying on the municipal government. The records of the old *Ayuntamiento* were consulted, and "An ordinance concerning licenses" went down on the foolscap as the first official act.

Frugality was the keynote and taxes were light. The mayor, Don Francisco de la Guerra, acted as recorder. He drew no salary; although as police judge he received $2.00 for each conviction, he was required to pay it into the city treasury. The city clerk received $35 a month; the city marshal, $20, plus $1.00 for each arrest, and the city attorney, $10; the city treasurer, 3 per cent of all monies paid in, and the city tax collector, 6 per cent of whatever he could collect.

Since there was no printing press or newspaper, the clerk was required to draw up two copies of all measures, one to be posted on "the eastern corner of Luis T. Burton's house," the other "on the front of Gaspar Oreña's billiard parlor."

On one thing only were the city fathers prodigal. Land, which then seemed inexhaustible, sold in Carpinteria for about 25 cents an acre. Montecito values were higher at 50 to 75 cents an acre. In 1856, three city lots were sold for $1.00 each.

ANACAPA ARCH AND LOOKOUT TOWER,
THE COURTHOUSE, SANTA BARBARA

INDUSTRIAL EDUCATIONAL BUILDING, SANTA BARBARA STATE COL-
LEGE (*CENTER R.*), AND McKINLEY ELEMENTARY SCHOOL (*CENTER L.*)

THE ADMINISTRATION BUILDING,
SANTA BARBARA STATE COLLEGE

SUNGLOW AND SHADOWS IN THE SUNKEN
GARDENS, SANTA BARBARA COURTHOUSE

ARCADES AND SYLVAN COURT,
SANTA BARBARA STATE COLLEGE

VISTA THROUGH COURTHOUSE ARCH

Years were to pass before Santa Barbara possessed the dignity of a city hall; meanwhile the ambulant municipal government rented rooms in various adobe houses. Spanish alternated with English as the language of official records, appointed bodies being designated, for instance, as the "committees on *gastos* (expenses), *propios* (public property), elections, and *arbitrios* (excise taxes)."

THE PLACID FIFTIES

Through its entire first decade the young American town grew slowly. The Santa Barbarans were traditionally indifferent to civic betterment. Only the *Gazette,* Santa Barbara's first newspaper (*see Human Side of a City*), raised a cry against the wilderness of cowpaths that served as city streets in 1855: "There are many deep, uncovered wells, pitfalls, and mantraps in various parts of the city, rendering it extremely hazardous not only for horses and teams, but for foot passengers, to traverse them at night." In a later issue, the civic-minded editor implored the citizens to "tear themselves away from the blandishments of keno, billiards, and cards long enough to examine the route for a post road."

To ameliorate the hazards of night travel, a city ordinance was passed, requiring "every head of a family . . . to cause a lantern containing a lighted lamp or candle to be suspended every dark or cloudy evening in front of his house from dark to ten o'clock; neglecting to do so he will be fined not less than fifty cents, nor more than $1.00 for each offense."

While life in the main was calm during the fifties, Santa Barbara was not entirely without incident and violence, newspaper headlines of 1856 attest:

Severe earthquakes, two persons killed.
Big storm at Santa Barbara.
John H. Kelley drowned while bathing at Santa Cruz Island.
Twenty-three horses stolen from the rancho of the Ruiz Brothers.
José Francisco Sorio killed by José Romero at Montecito.
Patrick Dunne sentenced to two years in the State Prison.
J. H. Moore murdered at Montecito by persons unknown.
Carlos Grimeño fell into an unprotected well and was drowned.

Trade and travel came and went by sea as in the old days. Twice a month a steamship landed a little budget of mail, often water-soaked. Often water-soaked, also, were the passengers, carried ashore on the backs of sailors, for there was no wharf. A generous tip was usually necessary to obviate a "ducking," as the sailors' luck in getting their burden safely through breakers and kelp was often in direct ratio to the amount paid them.

As in the old days, too, hides and tallow were exchanged for flour, boots, sugar, and wine, as well as for silk shawls from China or orna-

mental chests from Spain. Russian otter hunters from Alaska put in at the Channel Islands to repair their ships, take on food and fresh water, and occasionally to carry off the Indian women of the tribes.

Few roads cut the unbroken plains and mountains, and overland travel was practically impossible. Cattle supported everyone. The years between 1850 and 1860 were the golden years of the feudal lords of Santa Barbara; they had cattle on a thousand hills and a king's army of retainers. Cattle drovers pre-empted the place of the hide-and-tallow ships, driving cattle on hoof to San Francisco. Payment was made by six-sided slugs of gold worth fifty dollars each, and guaranteed by the issuing firms of San Francisco merchants.

But the decade of the sixties saw the gradual decline of the cattle empire, thus ending the second era of California's economic history. During the heyday when cattle were the sole medium of exchange, the ranchers settled their bills at the end of each year's rodeo, bringing the whole family to town on a spending orgy which saw the last dollar disappear. Then, confident of many golden *mañanas,* credit would mount again until the next rodeo. When drought seared the land, in 1863 and 1864, most of the cattle died and the few gaunt-ribbed beasts remaining were devalued by the sudden competition of Midwestern cattle raisers. Mortgages doubled, tripled, until the California ranchers, bewildered, unversed in the devious ways of finance, found themselves dispossessed.

Destruction of the district's dominant industry seriously demoralized Santa Barbara. Destitute and discouraged, during the early sixties, it sank deeper into somnolence. Not until immigration brought a transfusion of new vigor, about 1869, did Santa Barbara advance with confidence in its future.

SETTLERS, TOURISTS, AND A LAND BOOM

Reports of the climate and of the agricultural possibilities carried east by visitors, as well as improved steamer communications and the prospect of a coast-line railroad, combined to lure settlers. After the fall of the cattle barons, several great ranches were subdivided in small tracts bought by eastern immigrants. The consequent transition from large-scale stock raising to grain growing, olive and fruit culture on small estates changed not only the face of the country but the character of its inhabitants as well.

Commerce, too, swung from a minor to a major key with the increased tempo of steamship, stagecoach, and railroad operations. Between 1868 and 1872, two piers were constructed, the first, a primitive wharf at the foot of Chapala Street, and the second, of more ambitious proportions, at the foot of State Street (*see Points of Interest*).

In early times the only road between Santa Bárbara and San Buenaventura (now Ventura) skirted the sea around Ortega Hill, Punta Gorda and Rincón Point, and often was impassable during high tide. A new road was built, avoiding the Point, and became the route for a stage line which gave increased mail facilities and regular overland transportation between Los Angeles and San Francisco.

Improved communication with the outside world was a recognized major need, and in 1870, $2,245 of capital stock was subscribed to bring the first telegraph line to Santa Barbara. Lamps were lit with gas for the first time on Wednesday evening, February 21, 1872. The gas was a patent product made from gasoline and shipped in huge drums from the north. With gaslights, "heads of families" took in their lighted lanterns that had served since 1850, and sat back to wait for an increase in property value.

The increase was rapid. Blocks that in 1870 had sold for $100, four years later changed hands at $5,000. Under the Spanish and

Mexican regimes no survey had been made of the pueblo lands. The measurements of so many *varas* (about 33 inches) from some already established grant furnished the boundaries for any new lot. The first city survey, in 1851, had been made with a rawhide riata as a survey chain which, according to legend, stretched in the dampness and contracted in the sun. Although the streets then laid out are today's accepted arteries of travel, dismayed real-estate speculators of the seventies found a progressive difference in the size of several city blocks, and consequent litigations over property lines still stud the court calendars.

In 1872, Charles Nordhoff, grandfather of the Charles Nordhoff who collaborated with James Hall on the best seller, *Mutiny on the Bounty,* visited Santa Barbara. The elder Nordhoff, charmed with the beauty, climate, and agricultural possibilities of the crescent-framed Pacific coast city, wrote about his trip in a book which became a best seller. His propagandizing of the "world's most ideal health resort" brought hundreds of immigrants who disembarked by steamerloads and filled Santa Barbara's few bewildered hostelries to the saturation point.

These enterprising newcomers tuned the economic pulse of the city to that of the nation's own swift arterial flow. Under their leadership, buildings, pavements, street lights, schools, and churches were built. The period between 1870 and 1888 marked the transformation of Santa Barbara from an adobe town to one of brick and wood. The cornerstone of a new courthouse was laid in 1872, and the building completed the following year at a cost of $60,000. In 1874, the long-homeless city council found sanctuary in a red-brick city hall.

The First National Bank of Santa Barbara began in 1876 to serve the financial needs of the community along with the Santa Barbara County Bank, organized in 1875. Santa Barbara College, a coeducational institution founded in 1869 by a joint stock company with more optimism than foresight, struggled for several years to justify its founders' faith in the desire of Santa Barbarans for higher learning, and succumbed in 1878 for want of support. Five years later its 1,200 volumes of government publications swelled the meager assets of the Natural History Society, which had been organized in 1876 with a small collection of exhibits and twenty-one members. In 1882, the city council took advantage of the new State law to establish a free library and reading room, and the first sizable donation was the contribution by the Odd Fellows of their collection of 2,921 volumes.

Contrasted with the surface flow of progress, however, lazed a humorous subcurrent of provincial suburban life. As late as 1873, a man, wife, and child were treed for three hours by a bear at the mouth of Matilija Canyon. In 1876, a horse at the city pound sold for twenty cents and a postage stamp. In 1881, it was recorded that "the household of the Lompoc Hotel were scattered in consternation by the explosion of a stove full of wood, loaded with gunpowder," while on April 18 of that year a fact which seemed worthy of record read, "County jail empty."

The city's mushroom growth, however, assumed orthodox form. Anyone looking north of State Street (anglicized from the liquid *Calle del Estado* of early days) would have imagined himself in a typical Midwestern village. Under the rubber stamp of standardization, Santa Barbara, the quaint, the unhurried, had become unquestionably *"gringo."*

The *Morning Press* of January 3, 1874, "viewed with alarm" in an editorial:

"The old landmarks and most charming characteristics of Santa Barbara are disappearing before the march of 'improvement,' and though our practical people cannot move the mountains, nor change the scenes, nor spoil the climate, they are doing all they can to despoil the quaint beauty of the place and make it just a commonplace American town. . . .

"The very idea of an 'A' Street or a 'First' Street in Santa Barbara seems as inconsistent as a mathematical computation done in verse, and we think that when that change is effected Santa Barbara may be changed to 'Jonesville' and people of extremely sensitive organizations desert the village."

Thus began a conflict between the aggressive protagonists of metropolitan expansion and the idealistic defenders of civic beauty, a conflict that was destined to flare up with intermittent frequency for half a century before it was finally resolved in favor of culture over commerce.

A BOOM AND A RAILROAD

Meanwhile, the Santa Barbara of the eighties congealed in the mold of another "Main Street" village, while the population climbed from 3,460 in 1880 to 5,864 in 1890. The tidal wave of real-estate enthusiasm that swept over southern California caught the placid village in an upward surge. For nearly twenty years, agitation for a line of communication to link their city with San Francisco and Los Angeles had occupied the attention of ambitious citizens. The aggressive newcomers who had been attracted to Santa Barbara in the seventies joined the older residents in enthusiastic demand for the railroad. Anticipating this development, boom times descended on Santa Barbara during the early eighties. When, finally, the Southern Pacific ran a branch from its Los Angeles-Bakersfield line at Saugus, the entire population of Santa Barbara and some 5,000 visitors staged a jubilant celebration in Mid-August, 1887, on the arrival of the first passenger trains.

"Ring the Bell!" cried the *Weekly Independent*. "After years of waiting Santa Barbara's millenium has arrived. Come all ye who are weary of stagecoach and saddle and ride at the rate of thirty miles an hour—so saith the Southern Pacific."

Practical certainty of a speedy completion of the coast line catapulted real-estate sales, and although within a few weeks the railroad stopped laying tracks at Elwood, leaving a "railhead" a scant ten miles beyond Santa Barbara, a frenzied turnover of property shot recorded sales alone to $5,000,000 with an estimated $2,000,000 in unrecorded transactions.

Encouraged by the windfall of capital, the city spent $180,000 to improve State Street for two miles, and to pave it with bituminous rock. Sidewalks were laid and several deep-rutted cowpaths were graded at the same time.   Nevertheless, fourteen years were to elapse before the first train on the Southern Pacific Coast Line from San Francisco to Los Angeles passed through Santa Barbara in 1901.

In 1886, the county assessment roll totaled $8,585,485; in 1887, it went up to $15,035,082, an increase of 75 per cent in one year.   But, when railroad building eased, the reaction came.   Land values dropped. The influx of newcomers dwindled.   After 1888, Santa Barbara attracted few permanent residents.   In 1900, her population was 6,587, a gain of but 723 persons in ten years.

A NEW CENTURY

The long-awaited completion of the railroad to link Santa Barbara with San Francisco and Los Angeles took place March 31, 1901.   The event stimulated the growth of the town.   During the first decade of the twentieth century, the city increased her population more than five thousand, entertained two United States Presidents, and began to replace the old skyline with a new.   A short visit by President William McKinley in May, 1901, set Santa Barbarans agog, and two years later, President Theodore Roosevelt paused for an energetic three-hour visit during a western tour.

Civic improvements were many and substantial.   A modern powerhouse was constructed at a cost of $50,000, and electric lights flooded the city as additional power sites were brought within the territory embraced by municipal holdings.   The Southern Pacific Railroad erected a $20,000 depot and expanded with a double track through the town. Two new schools costing $40,000 were built, and in 1901 the Santa Barbara Mission dedicated St. Anthony's College as a Franciscan seminary to prepare young men for priesthood.   A boulevard was constructed to extend 8,000 feet in a sweeping arc along the beach and paved with asphaltum; and the sewer system received belated attention.

While commercial interests underwent material expansion, improvement of civic attractiveness was not entirely neglected—and landscaping of both public and private property kept pace with building construction. Land was set aside for development into park areas, among them a wild tract of sixteen acres in what is now the Oak Park district. The Potter Hotel, built in 1901 and officially opened January 19, 1902, on a 30-acre area, cost Milo Potter $150,000. At the same time, he sealed the famed medicinal springs of Burton Mound which the hotel tract embraced, thereby sparing Santa Barbara the dubious destiny prophesied by an early enthusiast of becoming the "sanitorium of the United States."

Montecito (Sp., little mountain, or little forest) embarked on an ambitious landscaping project, to emerge from its chrysalis a gay and exclusive suburb with luxurious estates.

Despite the World War, the years from 1910 to 1920 saw Santa Barbara's population mount to 19,441. International attention was directed to the city in 1919 when the King and Queen of the Belgians lingered there for three days. The King and Queen each planted a tree in the mission's Sacred Garden. Otherwise, the decade was unmarked by events other than the inevitable "attack" rumors common to coastal towns during the war.

In September 1923, however, there occurred one of the greatest peacetime tragedies in the history of the United States Navy. An unfortunate accident during Navy maneuvers in thick weather caused seven destroyers to pile up on the rocks at Honda, twenty-three officers and men losing their lives.

THE EARTHQUAKE OF 1925

The pulse-quickening "roaring twenties" produced remarkable economic effects upon Santa Barbara, although the chief cause lay not in hectic boom and subsequent market collapse experienced by the country as a whole, but in the devastating earthquake of 1925.

For fifty years, Santa Barbara had looked with growing apprehension and resentment upon the "gringo" or "Main Street" trend of their city, which was not in keeping with its traditions. The citizens believed industrial advantages and resources were comparatively few, and if the city were to grow and prosper, the accent should be placed on beauty of locale. The Plans and Planting Branch of the Community Arts Association (*see Human Side of a City*), organized in 1922, concentrated on the task of architectural face lifting, while esthetes and editorial writers added their pleas for revival of dormant Spanish-California traditions. "It is up to you . . ." advised one writer, "to save Santa Barbara romantic, and save California's romance in Santa Barbara. . . . Carelessness, ugliness, blind materialism are bad business."

"If every building along each side of State Street, from the wharf to the upper end, were in Colonial Mission, would it be worth anything to Santa Barbara?" the writer continued and then pointed out: "It can't all be done in a week, a month, a year, but some day. . . ."

"Some day" struck the city with appalling suddenness.

At 6:42 on the morning of June 29, 1925, Santa Barbarans were jerked awake by an ominous sound like "an enormous explosion beneath the ground." From La Cumbre Peak, north of the city, an early riser saw the mountains "like the sea tossed by a storm . . . swaying back and

forth like gigantic waves." At the mission, Mass was interrupted by the clamoring bells as the ancient towers were cracked and shattered.

The dam at Sheffield Reservoir gave way and 40,000,000 gallons of water swept down Sycamore Canyon to the sea.

In nineteen seconds, property damage mounted to an estimated total of between ten and twenty million dollars. Because of the early hour only twelve lives were lost.

Many structures had been built in Santa Barbara with no thought of seismological disturbances. Two hotels and one office building were conspicuously damaged. Public buildings, schools, churches, the court-house, and the jail as well as the public library suffered from the shock. The principal loss among residences was caused by the falling of chim-neys and the cracking of plaster. Reinforced concrete buildings, how-ever, showed little evidence of shock.

The catastrophe had one redeeming feature—fourteen blocks of the much-scorned State Street were destroyed. Only a month previous, the city had adopted a new building code and zoning ordinance to pro-

vide for the most modern construction known to engineering science.
Thus armed, the Plans and Planting Branch of the Community Arts
Association, augmented by a Board of Architectural Review and an
Architectural Advisory Committee appointed by the city council, now
guided the work of reconstruction following the earthquake.

All new construction bore the early California stamp of cool white
walls, low-pitched tile roofs, and occasional patios. A new city, designed to capture again the spirit of its early days, arose to replace the
Santa Barbara that had become standardized in the "Main Street"
pattern.

Reconstruction alone was not sufficient for the enthusiastic leaders
of the new building program; new projects began to spring up.   In
1928, agitation for an airport was started.   At last, after many sites
had been considered and rejected as impracticable, Goleta was selected
and the port was dedicated in 1936.   In 1929, a new courthouse (*see
Points of Interest*) was dedicated, and took its place as one of the finer
examples of public building architecture in the United States.   In 1930
Santa Barbara made the ultimate bid for the wealthy tourist trade
with the construction of an L-shaped breakwater, designed to shelter at
least 300 yachts (*see Points of Interest*).   Santa Barbara's latest architectural achievement was the half-million-dollar Federal Building on
May 8, 1937 (*see Points of Interest*), structurally in harmony with the
new plan of the city.   It occupies part of the site where the presidio
was founded in 1782.

While attention was focused on converting Santa Barbara into a
city of beauty, the ever-present problem of water supply, heightened
by the loss of Sheffield Reservoir during the earthquake, developed as a
major crisis.

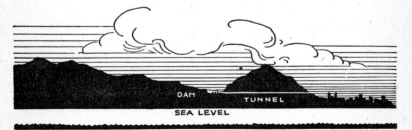

WATER SUPPLY

Santa Barbara's economic expansion depends almost entirely upon
an augmented water supply.   The problem presented by a lack of adequate water, plus insufficient conservation for an increasing population,
has been complicated in the past by divided efforts among civic leaders

towards a solution. Rainfall is Santa Barbara County's principal source of water, and the municipally operated system taps the rain-swollen streams and watersheds over the first range of the Santa Ynez Mountains, north and east, behind Gibraltar Dam.

Principal impounding unit of the system is Gibraltar Reservoir, 7 miles north of Santa Barbara on the Santa Ynez River, a system which drains an area of 219 square miles above Gibraltar Dam. On its completion in 1920, Gibraltar Dam had a capacity of 14,500 acre-feet, but silt accumulation has since reduced its capacity to slightly more than 9,000 acre-feet. From Gibraltar Dam, the water flows through 4-mile Mission Tunnel, where a small additional amount is obtained through infiltration, and continues through supply mains to 6 distributing reservoirs.

Of these, the reservoir now referred to as No. 3, situated near Santa Barbara Mission, reveals the historical beginning of the city's water development. Built in 1806 by the Franciscan padres and their Indian neophytes, the reservoir soon supplied the presidio, and even now is an active distributing unit.

The great drought of 1863-64 closed the era of the vast ranchos; the division of these holdings into small farms and the subsequent influx of settlers brought about a need for more water. Although conservation of rainfall was urged as early as twenty years after the first chartings of the rainfall in 1869, it has been found that the growth of the town itself obstructs the direction of this purpose. Buildings and pavements curtail the absorption areas, and much-needed water rushes away to the sea.

Urged by engineers to impound storm waters of the Santa Ynez River and tunnel them to Santa Barbara, city officials planned to purchase the most strategic site for that purpose. Before the transactions could be accomplished, however, a privately owned water company, members of which disagreed with city officials, purchased the proposed site which included its water rights and all surrounding water-bearing lands. Thus blocked, the city bored Cold Springs Tunnel which saps underground water through infiltration. With continuous boring, this tunnel developed sufficient water by 1897 to warrant a supply main from the tunnel to the city. Civic leaders found the pulse of industry quickening in ratio to the increased water supply.

In 1911 the city purchased complete control of its water system for $150,000, and plans were immediately revived for impounding water from Santa Ynez. The base of Gibraltar Dam was laid in 1913, and in order to meet the urgent need for water the city in 1916 diverted water from the Santa Ynez by means of one of the infiltration tunnels.

The construction of Sheffield Reservoir was the next step. It was built to store water on the near side of the mountains, thus supplementing its intended source of supply, Gibraltar Reservoir. Although the city's population had trebled by this time, its water supply appeared adequate for all needs. In the earthquake of 1925, however, Sheffield Reservoir was shattered and reconstruction was delayed, the burden of supply falling on Gibraltar Dam.

Three successive dry winters resulted in the exhaustion of hitherto dependable reservoirs, and in 1931 an incipient water shortage precipitated feverish emergency well digging. Supply from this source was extremely limited, and in 1934 Santa Barbara's aggravated water shortage was brought to the attention of the Federal Government. No action was taken. In 1936, the city rebuilt Sheffield Reservoir, increasing its capacity to 50,000,000 gallons. The following year a PWA Project, a water-softening-and-filtration plant, was completed, at Mountain Drive and Mission Ridge Road.

Although by 1938, Santa Barbara was credited with having one of the finest *distributive* water systems of any city of comparable size, its problem was still water *supply*. Watershed protection was urged in 1939, when State Forestry Board members suggested changing the deer season from the dry months of early fall to December or January to reduce the hazard of forest fires caused by sportsmen.

By 1940, crops in the low-lying Carpinteria and Goleta Valley districts were threatened seriously by receding water tables and the consequent high cost of pumping. Furthermore, taproots of trees were not reached by surface irrigation, and blight resulted. In both districts, some wells showed saline reaction.

Subject to securing Federal aid, a county-wide plan of conservation and distribution is now in progress. Among specific points considered for the program are the construction of Tequepis Dam, below Gibraltar Dam in the Santa Ynez Valley, with a capacity of 80,000 acre-feet; purchase of Boulder Dam water from the Metropolitan District of Los Angeles; boring of more tunnels in the mountains to draw, by infiltration, underground supplies; construction of another Gibraltar Dam above the present site; increasing the height of Gibraltar Dam to a capacity of 70,000 acre-feet; and immediate construction of a chain of small, strategically placed dams above Gibraltar Dam for the purpose of checking silt in the reservoirs.

THE ECONOMIC SCENE

Administered from the beginning by farmers and businessmen who were neither very rich nor very poor, the Santa Barbara County government has maintained a consistent, progressive plan of procedure for the last forty years. This consistency, rare on the American scene, has assisted in placing Santa Barbara first in the 3,000 United States counties for rural sanitation as well as first in administration standards for relief. Santa Barbara initiated a full-time planning commission prior to any other California county. The county has an adequate number of modern public buildings; its road system is complete; its bonded debt is slight with county indebtedness being only .0025 of assessed valuation.

Assessed valuation and population have grown steadily, doubling each twenty years. The tax rate has been cut from $3.20, in the prosperous times of 1928 to $1.30 per $100 of assessed valuation in recent years. In 1939, Santa Barbara County's assessed valuation was $111,766,935. The county budget for the same year amounted to $2,621,986.22.

Politically, Santa Barbara has become somewhat less conservative during the last few years. Despite the cushioning of wealth which kept a great part of its population from feeling too sharply the economic crash of 1929, the depression hit Santa Barbara as it did other cities.

The State Relief load in Santa Barbara, in proportion to population, is much less than in other cities of the same size, less than 1 per cent of the entire State load being in Santa Barbara County.

Civic affairs of the city of Santa Barbara are administered by an elected mayor. Legislative powers are invested in a council. One councilman is elected from each ward, in which he must reside.

That agriculture is Santa Barbara County's most important industry is borne out by the fact that about 50 per cent of the residents outside the city limits, including the whole coastal plain from the Ventura County line to Gaviota, receive their income from this source. Of the grand total of $17,664,605 realized in 1938 by the agricultural industry of the county, $5,649,698 was derived from vegetable crops, $5,427,489 from the animal industry, $3,917,298 from field crops, and $2,670,120 from orchard crops.

Lettuce, cauliflower, and celery lead the vegetable crops in volume and value. Of lesser importance are such crops as broccoli, carrots, peas, and tomatoes.

Second important industry in the agricultural field in both acreage and dollar volume is the animal husbandry. In value, beef cattle and calves account for a bigger share than do any other items, with dairy products running a poor second.

Other items contributing to the total valuation are hogs, sheep and wool, and poultry and eggs. Santa Barbara County dairies are models of sanitation. Santa Barbara was the first city in California to require that its entire milk and cream supply be obtained from tuberculin-tested, nonreacting cows, and the first city to require that ice cream, ice milk, buttermilk, and cottage cheese be manufactured exclusively from Grade-A milk and cream.

By far the most important of the field crops are beans, with common and baby limas outstripping other varieties by a wide margin. Given a small handful by a sea captain from Peru, a rancher by the name of McAllister first planted lima beans in the sixties. Success of the bean farmers attracted seed growers to the county with the result that, by 1939, 60 per cent of the nation's flower seeds were produced in a few districts (*see Tour 2*).

Lemons account for the greatest share in value of the orchard crops, with a value in 1938 of more than $2,000,000. Of much less value is the walnut crop—$334,755, yet walnuts, initially planted in 1865, were the first crop to be raised commercially in Santa Barbara County. In that year, the captain of a German sailing vessel picked up three sacks of English walnuts from Peru. Sailing up the Santa Barbara Channel, he sold a sackful to a local rancher, who planted them. Today, their by-product, ground shells, is an increasingly important and interesting contribution to the industrial economy of the area, since the powder is used for explosives, insecticides, ceramics, and many other articles. Oranges and avocados also are grown extensively in the county.

Resident labor is employed for all but the pea crop, for which some five hundred migratory workers journey to Santa Barbara County each year. Farm labor is not unionized; the average wage is $3.00 a day, with a minimum wage of 33 cents an hour.

Most recent figures giving an index to the value of farm property are those of 1935, when the average farm was 602 acres with an average valuation of $61.72 an acre. The percentage of lands used for crops under irrigation was 26.6. An adequate solution of the problem of water supply will greatly enhance values.

In dollars and cents value, the "tourist industry" may be considered second in importance only to agriculture in Santa Barbara County, and actually the largest source of revenue in the city proper. While it is impossible to tabulate the exact number of tourists who come yearly to the county by train, bus, air, automobile, and even by sea, a fair estimate for 1937 shows that approximately a half-million tourists, visitors, and convention delegates came to Santa Barbara during that year. They stayed an estimated average of four days each and spent an average of about five dollars a day each, or a total for the year of about ten million dollars.

The development of the oil industry gave Santa Barbara by 1939, a mineral output rating of seventh among California counties. Eighty per cent of the total is made up of petroleum and its by-products. One hundred and thirty-three companies were operating in the county in

1939 in the oil and oil-well supply business with an approximate total valuation of more than twenty million dollars.

Oil was first discovered in the Summerland district, east of Santa Barbara. Seepages of oil on Ortega Hill on the outskirts of Summerland were known as early as 1866, but it was not until 1888 that the community assumed any importance in the State. In that year, a colony of spiritualists was established there by H. L. Williams, who called it by its present name of Summerland, so named because of its year-around equable climate. In 1895, while drilling for water 500 to 600 feet back from the beach, members of the colony struck a vein of natural gas, and, deeper, a heavy, sluggish grade of petroleum. The tracing of producing sands took the hunter under the ocean bed. The Summerland Oil Company constructed wharves into the sea, from which point a conductor pipe was sunk to solid foundation, and drilling operations proceeded through this in the usual manner.

The successful driving of the first well precipitated a scramble for water frontage from which the necessary wharves could be constructed. More than three hundred derricks were installed in the first four years, but subsequent drilling proved the shallowness of the field and activity decreased. While Summerland represents little in the total of California production today, at the time of the discovery it was virtually the third field, in point of time, to come into the California picture.

Production of oil on a large scale did not result in Santa Barbara County until the third decade of the twentieth century, although the liquid had lain within a hundred feet of the surface in places, and drilling had brought forth oil from fields all the way from Summerland in the south to Casmalia in the north. Santa Barbara's boom was ushered in by the discovery of the Elwood field, the first production of which totaled a mere 86,000 barrels in 1927. Three years later it was being hailed in the press for its peak production of more than fourteen million barrels. In 1930, it was exceeded only in production in the State by four other fields. In spite of decreasing production since that time, it remains, among fields discovered since 1927, the largest total producer in the State with the exception of Kettleman Hills.

At Elwood in 1927, drillers again attempted to pump oil through the ocean (*see Tour 3*). The repeal in 1938 of the State Mineral Leasing Act, Chapter 303, Statutes of 1921, prohibits new drilling operations in areas inundated by the Pacific Ocean, but does not affect Elwood wells nor the tideland wells at Goleta. Voluntary curtailment by the drilling companies of California, however, makes it unprofitable to take oil from any of these tideland developments.

Near Lompoc, one of the largest and purest deposits of diatomaceous earth yet recorded has been discovered (*see Tour 3*).

Fishing is one of the major industries of the county. Numerous varieties of fish are caught in the channel and about the Channel Islands. Most prevalent catch is lobster, which one concern exports to points throughout the nation.

The retail trade area of the city of Santa Barbara serves about fifty thousand people and covers a radius of approximately twenty-six miles. As a consumer market, the city rates high, supporting about one retail store for every forty-eight inhabitants. According to the 1935 *Census of Business,* the total amount of retail sales in Santa Barbara County for the one year amounted to $29,841,000 while the payroll of retail distributors in the county was $3,562,000.

Although farm workers are not organized, labor in the city is represented by thirty American Federation of Labor unions and affiliates. These have their own newspaper, *The Union Labor News.* There have been few strikes, none of them lost by the unions. Although the cost of living, including rents, is higher than elsewhere in the southern part of the State, working conditions, hours and wages compare with southern California in general, according to the State Federation of Labor.

Santa Barbara has progressed, yet in many respects the city of a hundred years ago foreshadowed the city of today. In 1842, Sir George Simpson, an English traveler, wrote: "Among the settlements, Santa Bárbara possessed the double advantage of being the oldest [sic] and the most aristocratic." Few would rise to dispute that point today. The city still refrains from the commonplace. Her beaches and festivals never are vulgarized by catch-penny devices. Santa Barbara exemplifies the truth of the statement that life without beauty is but half lived. Nowhere in the State has a higher standard been set and the achievements of this municipality are an incentive to city planners everywhere.

Santa Barbara is old. It was a native *Canaliño* village when the Spanish settled there, and as such, it was ancient even then. Superimposing European culture on the primitive Indian people was a hasty process, as historical time is reckoned. Where once existed the conical huts of the native Indians, now rise the urban structures of twentieth-century industry. Where once the campfires of *Canaliños* lighted the landscape at night, now blazing neon signs brighten the avenues of commerce. Where once natives stalked game in the underbrush, now chain-store clerks weigh out sliced meat behind delicatessen counters.

For Santa Barbara is as new as she is old. Preserving some of the most pleasant aspects of her Spanish traditions, reviving some of the customs of her earliest settlers, she is, nevertheless, as American as Council Bluffs, Iowa. Along her Spanish-Mexican arcades on State Street, her business methods are as streamlined as next year's automobile.

Santa Barbara, born of the Spanish struggle to extend her secular and spiritual empire, tempered by the energy of her American conquerors, matured by the adoption of modern living techniques, has come of age.

Santa Barbara has come of age—yes, but there remains in the community a last link with the prehistoric era. For years, more acute students, not entirely absorbed in the modern scene, believed the *Canaliño* Indians extinct.

Then surprisingly, in 1937, a single, full-blooded descendant of the aboriginal inhabitants was found living in a chicken house on the city dump—near death from a festering, gangrenous injury to his leg.

The survivor was Juan Justo, 82, last of the *Canaliños,* symbol of the dual tragedy of conquest and assimilation to which his race has succumbed.

Had it not been for Dr. Asbjorn P. Ousdal, Santa Barabara physician and anthropologist, this last survivor of the *Canaliños* might have passed on to the obscurity that has veiled the extinction of the rest of his race. Ousdal's trained eye recognized in Justo the physical characteristics of the supposedly extinct *Canaliños.* He brought the old Indian home, dressed his wound, and kept him under medical care for three years. During this time, the doctor attempted to bridge the gulf of incommunicability imposed upon Juan by deafness, failing eyesight, and illiteracy. Locked in this old man's mind, Ousdal knew, were the lore of the *Canaliños* and four-score years of the saga of a dying people.

Gradually, as the two men became better acquainted, Ousdal sketched Justo's life, filled in by more and more details, high-lighted here with a poignant recollection, shaded there by a somber remembrance.

Representatives of the Smithsonian Institution rushed to record the aged Indian's voice speaking the dialect of his extinct tribe.

Juan Justo was born at the Indian village in Hope Ranch, *Cieneguitas.* On page 234 of the second book of baptisms kept at the rectory of the parish church, his birth certificate reads:

1069
Juan
de
Jesús

Año 1858 día 22 Nbre. bauticé solemnemente a un niño nacido el 18 del mismo hijo de Justo y Sisitia* a quien le puse por nombre Juan de Jesús. Padrinos José y Isabel (Indios todos) Averti lo debido.

Jayme Vila, Cura.

1069
Juan
de
Jesús

In the year of 1858 on the 22nd of November I baptized solemnly a child, son of Juan and Sisilia. To this child I gave the name of Juan de Jesús. Godparents were José and Isabel. All were Indians. I instructed them in their duty.

Jayme Vila, Pastor.

* No doubt the mother's name was *Cecilia.* The Indian pronunciation of this name would be sibilant, causing the priest not to recognize it as that of Saint Cecilia, hence his phonetic Sisilia, which in the present transcription has undergone a further change by the "l" being crossed as a "t".

At the age of nine, he fell and broke his leg, thus being permanently crippled. He married but had no children. He was a sheepherder and laborer on ranches in Santa Barbara County before coming to the city in 1889 to work as a street sweeper. He wanted, he said in faltering Spanish, "to wear a felt hat and a uniform so they would know he belonged to the city."

Like many old men, Juan remembers most clearly the younger days, and much that has happened since has faded in the twilight of his years.

Of his portrait which recently hung in an art exhibit in Santa Barbara, a critic wrote: "Aside from its pictorial interest, here is a portrait that is history. Old Juan is the last of the *Canaliño* Indians, the last of his race, that once peopled this region by the thousands . . . his lined face has character and strength, and the poignancy of a last survivor."

Today (1940) Juan Justo awaits the call to the Happy Hunting Grounds, sitting quietly in his dormitory room in the county hospital, curiously untouched and unchanged as the sea itself. He saw his people pass into oblivion, and he remained one of them through all the changes the white man brought.

Out on that very channel his people fished in their strange asphalt-lined canoes. In this shelving valley he lived before the white man's tepees reared steel, stone, and concrete walls to the mellow skies. Capricious nature transplanted him among strange people—and capricious nature dulled his ears to shut out the cacophony of their life, permitting his ancient tongue and his barbaric tribal chants to echo in his memory undisturbed.

Hail! Juan Justo—last of the Canaliños . . . And Hail!
Santa Barbara—la tierra adorada—beloved land.

(Editor's note: Since the above was written, Juan Justo died at the county hospital, Santa Barbara, May 5, 1941.)

Tierra Adorada

SANTA BARBARA (0-850 alt., 34,958 pop.), county seat of Santa Barbara County, and one of the world's most beautiful and wealthy small cities, is situated on the coastal shelf between the Pacific Ocean and the Santa Ynez Mountains, one hundred miles northwest of Los Angeles (*see Backdrop*). It is the all-year-round equivalent of Bar Harbor and Newport in the East, and is chiefly famous for its equable climate, its uniformity of architecture, and its prosperous growth although isolated from any fostering industrial centers. It is a city of many contradictions and each charming, a bit of Old Spain and of New America and of the very heart of California all blended as harmoniously as one of its own magnificent sunsets.

The city has no skyline—in the American sense of the word. Seen from the ocean front, the most conspicuous features are red-tiled or green roofs, white stucco walls, vividly green tropical trees, and everywhere the polychromatic glow of flowers.

Architectural design of public and commercial buildings, even of most of the homes, is of a type now becoming known as the California Style. Many civic bodies in various parts of California have adopted resolutions requesting that all references to architectural types which have become more or less peculiar to California be designated "California Style"—not Mission, Spanish, Mediterranean, nor Latin. This type is that which had its origin in Italy and Spain, was later developed in Mexico and California, and in the last few decades has become typically Californian. The color is generally light in tone. Materials used are plaster, adobe or stucco, stone or artificial stone. Roofs have a pitch seldom steeper than thirty degrees, with a maximum of thirty-five degrees. This uniformity is carried out even in the roundhouse of the Southern Pacific Railroad on the landscaped beach parkway, this building being modeled after the bullfighting arena in Seville, Spain. It is faced with white stucco, has arches for windows, and on Fiesta days is gay with a dozen pennants flying from its parapets.

The County Courthouse (*see Points of Interest*), which contains the jail, is a Spanish castle of rare beauty. It has a sunken garden fringed with exotic palms; giant poinsettias; eucalyptus and acacia trees. The Santa Barbara Street entrance to the jail and to the sheriff's office is a wide sheltered archway suggestive of a great cathedral. The jail tower itself rises to a height of four stories, and is capped by a decorative lookout. On the other sides are Spanish balconies, a *mirador,* delicate ironwork finials, unique in-and-out stairways, historical murals, mosaic floors and an assembly room rich in artistic splendor.

State Street (*Calle del Estado*) is the main business thoroughfare, but there are no blatant projecting signs, no poles nor overhead wires and only two rather high buildings. Through the upper part of the city this street becomes a parkway flanked by beautiful homes, gardens, and churches, and a motorist may drive down its entire length without bucking stop-and-go signals. The pedestrian, however, has the right of way even at mid-block crossings which are indicated by lateral white lines. The lower or ocean end of the street is not so imposing.

Almost all Santa Barbara streets (*see Points of Interest*) retain the Spanish-Mexican tradition of more than a century ago; many of them are honored by old Spanish family names. Others recall Indians, historic names and incidents.

Santa Barbara is not an industrial city, and does not desire to be one. Much of the agricultural and floricultural produce (*see Presidio to Channel City*) for which the county is famous is handled through the city warehouses, but this is almost in spite of herself. English walnuts, lima and navy beans, and the distinctive Santa Barbara lemon are exported in great quantities. The Santa Maria oil fields produce more than 10,000 barrels daily, and the Elwood field averages about 4,000 per day.

Most of the fine stock and show horses, especially the Palominos of which Santa Barbarans are especially proud, are bred within the county.

One of Santa Barbara's characteristic commercial enterprises and the one which is more closely allied with one phase of her great beauty is the exporting of flower seeds—more than 75 per cent of the nation's supply having its source here. In the early summer, thousands of acres of flowers and thousands of gardens, extending in all directions through Guadalupe, Lompoc (*see Tour 3*) and Santa Maria (*see Tour 2*) are aflame with the colors of every flower of the temperate and torrid zones. In the Lompoc Valley more than 6,000 acres are sown to mustard.

Santa Barbara's chief business is simply being Santa Barbara. Her cool, healthful climate, the sea and the mountains attract people of wealth, social position, and leisure. These people have flocked to her outskirts from the East and Middle West, even from the larger cities of California, and have built great landscaped estates; in fact, they have built whole suburbs around the city borders, such as Montecito (*see Tour 1*) and Hope Ranch (*see Tour 3*). Some modern castles with their various formal gardens have been selected by architectural experts as being among the finest homes in the United States.

Of few cities is the old Roman motto so true: "God gave us the country; the skill of man hath built the town." The skill and artistry of man has built this town to fit its beautiful framework of country and sea. No honky-tonk amusement parks clutter its three miles of ocean strand, every foot of which is owned by the city itself; no unsightly structures spoil the hills; few billboards mar the vista from the highways. In keeping with Santa Barbara's aim to safeguard the welfare of its citizens, the city council only recently announced a housing cleanup program in which "demolition or repair" mandates had been issued to landlords—a drive to eliminate approximately 400 unsanitary and unfit houses from the rental market.

Santa Barbara is a wealthy city, a place of polo fields, of trim white yachts and palatial mansions. The breakwater makes her bay one of the most important yachting harbors on the Pacific Coast. In competition with seven thousand other communities throughout the country, this comparatively small city has won the annual Better Homes award every time a presentation has been made during the last sixteen years. It supports community enterprises and public and private welfare agencies which would do credit to any city ten times as large, and is rated by city planners as the most civic-minded community in the West, if not in the entire country.

But Santa Barbara is not merely a show city, not just a resort of suave leisure and play. There are thousands of storekeepers, clerks, stenographers, laborers, taxi drivers, salesmen, agents, and professional men and women, and these make up the average Santa Barbaran, a very regular, ordinary American citizen. He has an automobile in his stucco garage, a radio in his red-tiled bungalow, an orange or avocado tree behind the kitchen, a strip of yellow poppies or rosebushes, giant poinsettias or a pepper tree in the back corner of the lot, and tries to have at least one window that catches a glimpse of the blue ocean or the majestic purple of the mountains.

This average Santa Barbaran and his wife and children are the people who make the city what it is.   They voted the bonds with which to buy the ocean front; they worked for the elimination of billboards; they tend their gardens, keep their lawns looking like green Tientsin rugs, trim their hedges, and keep the corners clean.   They are proud of themselves and of their city.

Backdrop

MOST of Santa Barbara's area of sixteen square miles is included on a narrow coastal shelf which skirts the Pacific where California's coast line assumes a general east-west direction.

The city, thus provided with a highly prized "southern exposure," spreads fanwise from a curving beach, its streets running to low mesa lands on the west, and winding upward on the east and north among wooded canyons and over slopes of the Santa Ynez foothills to points 850 feet above sea level. In the near background are the Santa Ynez Mountains, a rugged ridge extending east and west across Santa Barbara County. One of the tallest peaks, La Cumbre (alt. 3,985), rises directly north of the city.

The bay fronting Santa Barbara is really no more than a graceful curve of the shore, but a breakwater, constructed in 1930, creates an extensive yacht harbor.

About thirty miles south, a string of four Channel Islands (*see Sierras in the Sea*) lying almost parallel to the coast, breaks the destructive force of heavy seas and forms the outer boundary of a deep channel used by coastwise ships. The terrain of the islands is rough, though the degree of ruggedness varies with each island. Anacapa and San Miguel, at opposite ends of the island chain, are dissimilar in topography. Anacapa is rather high, rocky, precipitous, and almost barren of water, while San Miguel is mostly low, with large areas of sand dunes and enough grass to support many sheep pastured there. Santa Cruz and Santa Rosa, largest of the group, are a jumble of picturesque, well-watered canyons, and lofty hills and mountains with altitudes ranging to 2,400 feet. Shore lines of all the islands are jagged and rimmed with bleak bluffs except for a few beaches at the mouths of streams.

No rivers are in the immediate vicinity of Santa Barbara. Nearest is Santa Ynez River which runs from east to west on the other side of the Santa Ynez Mountains from six to a dozen miles inland, and empties into the ocean at the western edge of the county where the coast line reverts to a north-south direction. From this river the city draws most of its water supply by tunnels through the mountains. The creeks on the ocean side of the mountains usually are dry during summer, although in the rainy season water tumbles down their canyons.

Many private water systems derive their water from creeks in the canyons, although wells are the chief source of supply in irrigated areas. At present (1940), only about 25 per cent of land under cultivation in the county is irrigated. The practice, though steadily increasing, is not as essential as in counties farther south, the seasonal rainfall and moist atmosphere augmented by frequent fogs being nearly adequate for ordinary agriculture.

Numerous small farms are scattered among the residential suburbs on the mesa, and between mesa and foothills west of Santa Barbara. Other rich farming areas are Goleta Valley, six miles west, and the Carpinteria district to the east and beyond Montecito. Sandy loam soils predominate in the region, especially in valleys and on surrounding mesas. These soils are well suited for growing English walnuts, lima beans, peas, and all varieties of citrus fruits.

Geology: The thick layer of alluvium, eroded from the mountains and covering the Santa Barbara coastal shelf, and absence of outcropping formations make examination of the lower strata difficult except where oil-well logs are available.

The geology of the Santa Ynez Mountains, however, indicates that the area, in common with most southern California coastal regions, has been submerged beneath the ocean repeatedly. Marine formations of early and later Tertiary age are separated by terrestrial deposits of considerable thickness attesting to the shifting seas of the period. Along the fault lines bounding the Santa Ynez Mountains, and within the range itself, rocks are deformed complexly, indicating intensity of movements of the earth's crust during building of the mountains. A Monterey shale formation, in some places hundreds of feet thick, covers wide areas and is the source of a large part of the county's petroleum output. Along the beach near Santa Barbara the shale is exposed for several miles. In some places large seeps of asphaltum are visible.

Characteristic of the Santa Barbara coastal region are east-west trending faults long associated with local earthquakes. The Santa Ynez thrust fault traverses the northern edge of the Santa Ynez Mountains, and a normal fault, known as the Mesa Fault, runs parallel to it along the southern edge. Since both may be connected far below the surface, the area between—the Santa Ynez block and Santa Barbara itself—probably has the form of a wedge forced upward by tremendous pressure. The severe Santa Barbara earthquake of 1925, caused by slippage along a fault, came after a period of many years during which there were only occasional mild shocks.

The Channel Islands off the Santa Barbara coast are believed to be a submerged east-west mountain range which is rising slowly. Some of the caves that honeycomb the islands are far above ocean level and yet appear to have been cut by the sea itself. That the islands once were connected with the mainland during a comparatively recent period is indicated by elephant fossils found on Santa Rosa.

Fossils: Fossils removed from asphalt beds near Santa Barbara were impregnated with oil and similar in appearance to prehistoric remains taken from La Brea (tar) Pits in Los Angeles, although they were much less numerous. Preserved specimens of Monterey and Bishop pine, Douglas fir, sycamore, manzanita, and redwood reveal that the forest which existed in the Santa Barbara area centuries ago resembled that of the Monterey Peninsula today, a marked contrast to the present native cover around Santa Barbara. Fossils of at least fifty-five living and extinct species of birds were removed from the asphalt beds, half of them similar to fossils from La Brea Pits. Included were remains of the wild turkey, eagle, stork, hawk, and extinct vulture *Teratornis,* and many smaller species; there were also fossils of approximately twenty-five kinds of mammals, among them the extinct grim or dire wolf, gray fox, coyote, antelope, bison, camel, horse, and numerous rodents.

Climate: Santa Barbara's climate is essentially mild, temperatures rarely rising above 90° in summer or dropping below 50° in winter. Mountains present a formidable bulwark against adverse winds from the north and the interior of the State, stopping hot blasts and icy gales alike. Island ramparts on the south perform a similar service by drawing the teeth of the gales which sweep in from the Pacific. Summers are relatively dry, the rainy season extending from October to May with an average rainfall of seventeen inches.

Flora: Semitropical verdure flourishes and both wild and culti-vated trees and flowers abound in and near the city. Native live oaks are particularly numerous, pines are common, and palm, eucalyptus, and pepper trees are part of the landscape. California laurel grows freely in the many canyons. At the foot of San Marcos Pass, twenty miles northeast of Santa Barbara, is the "Laurel of San Marcos" (*see Tour 2*), which has the distinction of being the tallest tree of the species known in the State.

Southern slopes of the Santa Ynez Mountains are covered principally with greasewood, but there is also an abundance of the red-limbed manzanita, one of the most beautiful of California shrubs. Above this cover an occasional yucca plant lifts its white, wax-like crest. Toyon, or California holly, is plentiful along mountain roads, and in spring such shrubs as mountain lilac, deer brush, snow bush, white thorn, and the rare yellow bush poppy cover the mountainsides in a brilliant floral display. Shaded valleys and grassy foothills behind Santa Barbara are also riotous in spring with the gayly colored blossoms of several varieties of lupine, Indian paint brush, Brodiaeas, California poppies, and many rarer blooming plants. On northern slopes of the Santa Ynez Mountains and in the Santa Ynez Valley the live oak is also the characteristic tree. Many varieties are indigenous and many of them attain limb spreads of a hundred feet or more. Along creek beds and the Santa Ynez River, cottonwood, sycamore, alder, and willow trees flourish, while growths of yellow, Coulter, and digger pines stud the higher mountain slopes. As on the seaward side, greasewood and manzanita form the principal coverage. Trees, shrubs, and flowers have been imported from many countries and planted extensively in city parks and private estates.

Santa Cruz and Santa Rosa have considerable vegetation, San Miguel somewhat less, while Anacapa is almost barren during summer because of lack of water. Most of the hills of Santa Cruz and Santa Rosa are clad heavily with brush, and numerous wide areas are covered with cactus. Giant brakes, banked with beds of gold- and silver-backed ferns and other verdure, fill the canyons. Oak, pine, and island ironwood—the latter found only on the Channel Islands—are the most common trees, and to Santa Rosa belongs the distinction of growing one of the two remaining natural stands of Torrey pine known in the world.

Fauna: Of the five hundred species of California birds, about four hundred varieties may be found in the Santa Barbara region. A group of Santa Barbara ornithologists participate in an annual bird-count in which numbers and varieties of birds that come to the area are identified and listed. The Christmas 1939 census revealed 137 species, 2 of them, the Pacific fulmar and the wood duck, new to the area. Commonest among other ducks at census time were the American pintail, lesser scaup, ruddy duck, shoveler, and canvasback. White-fronted goose and ruddy turnstone were reported for the second time. Rare birds were the duck hawk, golden eagle, slender-billed nuthatch, late-staying Phainopola, and dwarf cowbird.

Most common birds found in the city of Santa Barbara are the western mockingbird, California jay, house finch, and several kinds of sparrows and hummingbirds. Western bluebirds and valley quail also are present, but more limited in numbers. Along the beaches gulls, terns, sandpipers, and sanderlings are numerous in winter. Many migrating ducks and geese stop annually upon the lake of Andrée Clark Bird Refuge at the eastern approach to the city. Quail, dove, and wild pigeons are plentiful in the less settled country. Among the nongame birds in the back country are the blue-headed grosbeak in season, the western mockingbird, jay, red-shafted flicker, road runner or chaparral cock, screech owl, bluebird, and the California towhee. The rapidly vanishing California condor is found only in Los Padres National Forest (*see Sanctuary in the Chaparral*) where a refuge closed to all forms of public travel has been established for protection of some fifty remaining condors.

Most common birds on the islands are cormorants, brown pelicans, mourning doves, ravens, and many small birds familiar on the mainland. The island jay, larger and richer in color than the mainland bird, is found only on Santa Cruz Island.

Bobcats, coyotes, an occasional mountain lion, and a few black bears are seen in the mountains back of Santa Barbara, and many deer and small game are taken in season. The only mammals indigenous to the islands are the island fox, the spotted skunk, mice, and bats. The skunk is close kin to the spotted skunk of the mainland; but the island fox's muscular development and dentition are much inferior to those of its mainland cousin. Herds of sea lions and seals visit the islands annually (*see Sierras in the Sea*).

Santa Barbara streams are stocked by the California State Fish and Game Commission with rainbow, eastern brook, cutthroat, and other varieties of trout. Steelhead make their way from the ocean far up the Santa Ynez River during spawning season. The waters of Santa Barbara Channel abound with salt-water fish of nearly every variety; yellowfin tuna, bluefin tuna, marlin, broadbill swordfish, dolphin, amber jack, sea bass, sharks, barracuda, and many other game fish. Among the rocks and in the beds of kelp that surround the islands are starfish, octopuses, crabs, and lobsters.

Sierras in the Sea

B ARREN rocks, semideserts, fertile hills and valleys, and one gem of subtropical beauty, Santa Catalina, all may be found in the Channel Islands of California. Their erstwhile inhabitants long since have disappeared, leaving the isles, with one exception, practically uninhabited. At one time a part of the mainland, they now show differences of flora and fauna that indicate eons of isolation.

Their known history runs the gamut of greed, death, adventure, ruthless exploitation, and a little, a very little, of care for and conservation of the bounties of nature. The white man has driven from them not only the primitive population but also the otter, the sea elephant, much of the fish, and a vast portion of the natural vegetation.

Strange habitants have been introduced—wild boars, buffalo, elk, deer, and domesticated livestock. On their shores live or have lived hard-bitten poachers and smugglers, lonely sheepherders, a female Robinson Crusoe, convict-soldiers, gay pleasure seekers, miners, sailors, aviators, pirates, and plutocrats. The islands are an epitome of four hundred years of conquest and change—only the barren rocks remain as they were when Cabrillo first saw them.

Twenty-five to thirty miles south, off the Santa Barbara County coast line, are four islands, San Miguel, Santa Cruz, Santa Rosa, and Anacapa. These are called the Santa Barbara Islands. Farther south and east are four more islands, Santa Catalina, San Clemente, San Nicolás, and Santa Barbara, and a number of barren rocks.

Of the eight islands, five are the property of the United States government and three are privately owned. Of the five government-owned, one is leased indefinitely to a private individual; another is subject to short-term leasing; a third is used for navy purposes; the fourth and fifth comprise a national monument with the exception of two small areas, each of which is controlled by the Lighthouse Service.

Anacapa is the most easterly of the Santa Barbara group, with Santa Cruz, Santa Rosa and San Miguel extending west along the 34th parallel of latitude in the order named. Santa Catalina, Santa Barbara, San Clemente, and San Nicolás compose the southern group.

Excepting Santa Catalina, none of the islands may be visited without permission of the owner, the lessee, or the appropriate department of the United States government, and to none, again excepting Santa Catalina, is there any regular transportation available for public use.

Veiled in mist is the early history of the islands. Geologically, there is abundant evidence that they were once part of the mainland, the four northern islands forming a structural extension of the Santa Monica Mountains. All contain residues of volcanic activity; some appear to have been submerged totally at one or more periods in the past; some appear to be slowly rising, while others seem to be subsiding. They may have been separated from the mainland independently or in one tremendous cataclysm. Fossil remains of elephants found on Santa Rosa, Santa Cruz, and San Miguel would indicate these islands were connected with the mainland in the late Pleistocene or Ice age.

That they were well populated in the period of colonial exploration is attested by the records of Cabrillo, who discovered the islands in October, 1542, fifty years to the month after Columbus made his first landfall in the Western Hemisphere. Anthropologists have substantiated these records by unearthing numerous large kitchen middens containing such artifacts as fishhooks, cups, ornaments, weapons, and cooking utensils. Many well-filled burial grounds have also been uncovered.

A translation of an account of Cabrillo's voyage written by the pilot, Ferello, who succeeded to command of the expedition on Cabrillo's death, gives some idea of the native population: "The Indians of the islands are very poor. They are fishermen, they eat nothing but fish; they sleep on the ground; all their business and employment is to fish. In each house they say there are fifty souls. They live very swinishly; they go naked."

No reliable estimate may be made of the number of Indians living on the islands, but from the evidence available all the larger ones were populated thickly. With advent of the white man, trouble seems to have descended upon the primitive inhabitants. Some of the islands became the haunts of freebooters and adventurers attracted by reports

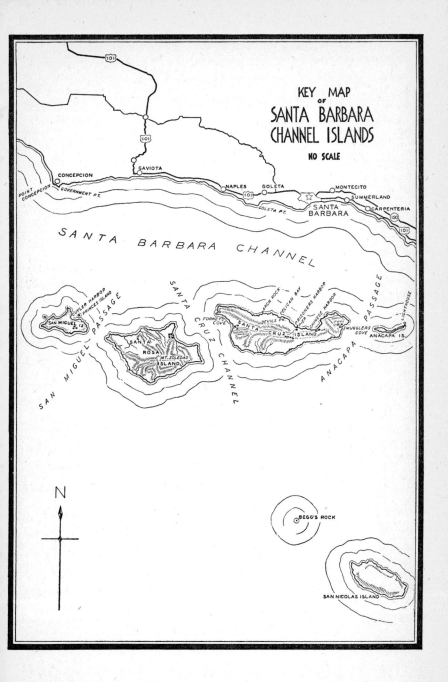

of hidden treasure or by the wealth to be won by slaughtering the otter which abounded in near-by waters.

Some historians state that Russians, accompanied by Aleut fishermen from their Alaskan possessions, periodically raided the islands, established their bases for short periods, and decimated the islands by killing the males and carrying off the women. While raids by Aleuts undoubtedly occurred, there is no reliable evidence of Russian participation.

Very probably the whites also introduced hitherto unknown forms of disease to which the natives' constitutions could offer little resistance. Some of the natives migrated to the mainland; others were removed there to become neophytes of the missions. By 1840, it is probable that the last of the islanders had disappeared from the home of their ancestors.

Of much interest to naturalists are the animal and plant life indigenous to the islands. A dwarf type of fox with a more intensified coloration than the gray fox of the mainland is the largest indigenous mammal. No larger than a house cat, this fox hunts by day as well as by night, and lives off shellfish, mice, lizards, and insects. It is found on all the islands except Anacapa and Santa Barbara. A spotted skunk, as mephitic as its mainland relative, is found on Santa Rosa and Santa Cruz. Mice and tree frogs are on most of the islands, and a night lizard, found nowhere else in the world, inhabits three islands of the southern group. Sea birds and land birds are present in great numbers and variety. Introduced animals include elk, deer, wild boar, rats, wild house cats, and the usual domesticated animals.

Indigenous vegetation is noteworthy for the Santa Cruz pine, found only on Santa Cruz and Santa Rosa, the island ironwood and one of the two surviving natural stands of Torrey pine on Santa Rosa.

ANACAPA

Anacapa, politically a part of Ventura County, is the smallest of the Santa Barbara group and the nearest to the mainland. It lies about 12 miles southwest of Hueneme light and about 32 miles southeast of the city of Santa Barbara. The island is divided into 3 segments separated by narrow channels through which the surging waters rush with tremendous force. The largest of these segments is also the highest, its crest rising 980 feet above the level of the sea and visible, on a clear day, from a distance of 35 miles.

Anacapa, comprising some 700 acres, and Santa Barbara Island, lying about 40 miles to the south and east of Anacapa with its 638 acres, are owned by the United States. Of these areas 538 acres of the former and 581 acres of the latter were, together, set aside in 1938 as the Channel Islands National Monument.

The reason given for creating the monument was the desirability of conserving interesting biological and geological features including fossils of the Pleistocene age. Officially unexpressed was the hope that, by forbidding hunting on the islands, the sea otter and sea elephant which once frequented these shores in vast numbers would return.

Previous to establishment of the monument, part of Anacapa was leased to Ventura sheepmen for grazing purposes, and many yachting parties visited the island. Now permission must be secured from the National Parks Service before attempting to land. However, fishing in the adjacent waters is not forbidden, and the island remains the terminus of the outward leg of the annual yacht race held during *Semana Náutica* (*see Fiesta Land*).

From the sea, the Anacapas look like barren rocks, but, in reality they are rich in small vegetation and offer a hospitable home for insects and small mammals. As evidence of this, a Los Angeles County Museum expedition recently reported that a pair of rabbits introduced on one of the segments in 1935 had in 1940 a total progeny of more than one thousand.

Volcanic rock predominates in Anacapa's formation. The shore line is honeycombed with caves, in the largest of which the traditional pirate of colonial days maintained a hide-out and base of operations. A natural stone arch connecting one of the segments with an outlying hump of rock was until recently a scenic attraction. The arch disappeared in a severe storm about 1936, and has been replaced by a wooden bridge.

Sea lions frequent the rocky shores and the tall cliffs are the home of many varieties of sea and land birds—pelican, gull, bald eagle, western red-tailed hawk, barn owl, the great blue heron, and many others.

There is no water on the island, so animal life is restricted to species which may procure sufficient water from their food or the dew-and-fog-drenched foliage. In addition to the indigenous mice, there are now present the introduced rabbits; black and Alexandrine rats, offspring of those which swam to land from the wreck of the *Winfield Scott* in gold-rush days (1852), and ferocious feral house cats, descendants of domestic tabbies left on the island by fishermen and herdsmen.

Above the outer cliffs on the easternmost segment, towers a lighthouse from which is operated, in addition to the light, one of the government's five Pacific coast radio beacons. Huddled at the base of the cliff are the quarters and workshops of the lighthouse crew, all of whose supplies, even water, must be brought from the mainland. The only other dwellings on the island are four shacks on the west segment, one of which is occupied by an old fisherman who, in return for the privilege of living there, acts as semiofficial unpaid custodian of the national monument.

SANTA CRUZ

Santa Cruz (Sp., Holy Cross), next island to the west, is the largest of the Santa Barbara group. Called San Salvador by Cabrillo, an incident of a lost crucifix and its return is said to be responsible for the present name.

A part of Santa Barbara County, Santa Cruz lies due south of Santa Barbara harbor at a distance of 25 miles. Twenty-three miles in length and from 2 to 6½ miles in width, its 62,000 acres of hills and canyons are well wooded and watered by running streams. The greater part is now owned by Edwin L. Stanton of Los Angeles. The eastern end, comprising some 8,000 acres, is owned by Ambrose Gherini of San Francisco. Sheep have been pastured on the island and, as a result, it is beginning to show severe erosion caused by overgrazing. In order to conserve the natural resources, it is reported, abandonment of sheep pasturage and substitution of cattle are contemplated. No visitors are permitted on the island without permission of one of the owners.

Composed of shales, sandstones and volcanic rocks, Santa Cruz is very rugged with an irregular shore line and many sheltered coves indented in the steeply rising bluffs. Near the center of the island, Picacho Diablo, the highest point, rises to an altitude of 2,434 feet. Two parallel ranges of hills on the north and south coasts enclose a central valley, Arroyo Principal, which is approximately seven miles long.

Resurging tides have gouged numerous caves in the coastal cliffs, among them the Cueva Pintada (Sp., Painted Cave), which has been compared favorably with the renowned Grotto of Capri. Its outer cavern is 60 to 70 feet high, the inner cavern even larger. At low tide small craft may explore the cool interior and view the coloration caused by the action of salt water on the conglomerates that form its walls.

Large portions of the island are covered with groves of Santa Cruz and Monterey pines and scrub oak. The steep slopes of the mountains are thick with chaparral. Indigenous animals are represented by the Island Fox and Island Skunk, several species of reptiles and amphibians, insects, bats, and birds. Of the latter, the Santa Cruz Island Jay, large and noisy, is found nowhere else. Sea lions are numerous along the rocky shore line.

When first visited by white men, Santa Cruz supported a large native population. Their accustomed way of life rudely interrupted by raids of otter hunters and other adventurers, the natives rapidly declined in number, and the survivors eventually migrated, voluntary or otherwise, to the mainland.

SANTA BARBARA MISSION,
THE CATHEDRAL OF EARLY CALIFORNIA

MISSION SANTA INÉS

A PATH OF THE PADRES,
SACRED GARDEN OF SANTA BARBARA MISSION

RUINS OF ANCIENT MISSION AQUEDUCT, SANTA BARBARA

FRAGMENT OF REREDOS (c. 1820), MISSION SANTA BARBARA

FOUNTAIN, MISSION SANTA BARBARA   *Courtesy WPA Art Program*

Soon after winning its independence from Spain, the Mexican government made an unsuccessful attempt to use the deserted island as a penal colony. There is also a story, quite unauthenticated, that later, about 1836, some soldiers, recruited from Mexican prison cells, were sent to Santa Barbara as a garrison. The citizens of the little community, not caring for the presence in their midst of these convict-soldiers, sought to isolate them on Santa Cruz. The island was stocked with cattle in the hope that the marooned soldiers would become self-

supporting, and the garrison was put ashore at the inlet now called, in their "honor," Prisoner's Harbor.

Isolation seemed to hold little charm for the later islanders, for alone or in groups they made their way to the mainland. Legend says one party of twenty built a rude raft of pine and the green hides of freshly killed cattle. On their way across the channel, dogfish sharks, attracted by the green skins, tore the raft apart. The helpless men fell victims to the sea and the sharks, the remains of the raft finally coming ashore south of Santa Barbara with but one of the original twenty staggering to safety.

Santa Cruz formed an old Spanish land grant which, in 1839, under Mexican rule, was transferred to Andrés Castillero. Thirty years later, after passing through other hands, it was sold to Justinian Caire, a San Francisco Frenchman.

In 1854, Martin Kimberly, a San Francisco sea captain, settled on the deserted island as a means of combating a pulmonary illness. He lived there three years with an old sailor who administered salt rubs with a gunny sack as a variant to the daily sun baths which Kimberly had prescribed for himself. Within three years the mariner had regained his health and left the island. According to legend a few domestic hogs which he left behind took to the hills and have provided excellent hunting for many years. However, scientists from the Los Angeles County Museum state that the animals are European wild boars imported many years ago to provide the thrills of the chase. The fact that they are or have been present on the other islands, Santa Rosa, San Clemente, and Santa Catalina, would seem to bear out this explanation of their origin.

Justinian Caire, for the first time since the island came into possession of the white man, tried to realize its potentialities.

In the central valley he built a ranch house, chapel, blacksmith shop, tannery, winery, storehouses, and quarters for one hundred workers. Many of the buildings were of brick, and some are still in use.

He planted a vineyard which, by 1917, was larger than any other in the county and his wines became widely known. From a modest beginning, his flock of sheep grew to number more than fifty thousand. However, the family disagreed and became involved in expensive litigation with the result that the estate finally passed out of the family ownership. Most of Caire's improvements, including the vineyard, have disappeared, and many of the buildings are now vacant. Some years ago an attempt was made by Captain Ira Eaton to establish a resort on the island at Pelican Bay. After operating a few seasons, the enterprise was abandoned.

SANTA ROSA

Santa Rosa, next island to the west, has an area of 78 square miles and contains approximately 50,000 acres. A map of the island suggests a roughly drawn sunfish with an extreme length of approximately 17 miles and a maximum width of over 10 miles. It is a part of Santa Barbara County and lies 33 miles southwest of the city of Santa Barbara. The island is owned by the Vail-Vickers cattle syndicate of Los Angeles and is used by them as a cattle range. Their permission must be secured before visiting the island.

Geologically, Santa Rosa is of much the same formation as Santa Cruz, lacking, however, much of the ruggedness characteristic of the latter. Comparatively low cliffs, not too difficult to climb, form the shore line with numerous little bays and many caves. The highest point is Soledad Mountain, 1,561 feet in altitude with numerous other peaks reaching a height of more than 1,300 feet. The mountains and hills are grass-covered and the canyons are rich in vegetation, including holly, ironwood, greasewood, and other indigenous shrubs and wild flowers. There are several groves of large trees, including island oak, manzanita and a fine stand of Torrey pine. This rare tree is known to grow naturally in only one other spot—on the coast of San Diego County just north of La Jolla. Several canyons on the island contain ample supplies of running water.

Indigenous animal life is represented by practically the same species as are present on Santa Cruz. In addition there are between three and four thousand head of Hereford cattle, some five hundred head of Roosevelt and Tule (dwarf) elk, about eight hundred head of Kaibab Mule Deer and some Siberian snow deer and wild boar, all of which have been introduced.

Santa Rosa is by far the best-conserved island in the upper group. With no sheep and with controlled grazing, the island, excepting the western end, shows little sign of erosion, and the native flora continues to flourish with undiminished vigor.

Along with the other large islands of the channel group, Santa Rosa once supported numerous Indian villages. In the account of Cabrillo's voyage, it is "Los Islas de San Lucas." The primitive inhabitants have vanished, leaving behind evidences of many generations of occupancy. In one sand dune, a Los Angeles County Museum expedition recently discovered an ancient bead factory and collected more than two thousand beads and chert drills. Visible evidence of an even earlier habitant previously had come to light with the discovery, in a deposit of sedimentary rock, of parts of the remains of prehistoric elephants.

Santa Rosa was granted to Antonio and Carlos Carrillo in 1843 by Governor Juan Bautista Alvarado—the largest of the Mexican land grants in Santa Barbara County. The Carrillos built a home on the island that was the scene of many fiestas when friends crossed from the mainland during sheepshearing time. Subsequently the island formed the joint dowry of daughters of Don Carlos, and from them passed through successive changes to its present ownership.

SAN MIGUEL

San Miguel Island, the most westerly of the channel group, lies 26 miles south of Point Concepción and approximately 33 miles southwest of the city of Santa Barbara. Roughly triangular in shape, the island is about 8 miles long and averages 2 miles wide with a maximum width of 4¼ miles. Topographically it is much lower than the other islands of the group and rarely may be seen from the mainland except on very clear days. The maximum elevation is slightly more than 800 feet, and the shores are marked by precipitous cliffs rising from narrow sandy beaches to an average height of 250 feet. At the entrance to the only harbor, Princess Island, a rock some 30 acres in area, rises to an altitude of 288 feet.

When first visited by explorers, San Miguel was described as a well-populated, amply watered land with much vegetation. Cabrillo called it "La Posesión." Today, most of the surface is covered with dunes of drifting sand. Impelled by the strong prevailing winds from the northwest, the drift sand gradually is filling Cuyler's Harbor, the only natural haven on the island's coast, and anchorage is now impaired by the swells which break inside the harbor on rough days.

Sandstone and volcanic rock make up the mass of the island, which is slowly being worn away by action of the wind and waves. Many springs furnish water, but all of it is highly mineralized.

San Miguel is in Santa Barbara County and belongs to the United States. It is administered by the Navy Department and leased to Robert L. Brooks of Los Angeles, who uses it to pasture some 1,200 sheep. Visitors are not welcome on the island without permission of the lessee.

Cuyler's Harbor is reputed to be the burial place of its discoverer, Cabrillo, and the Portuguese Society of America has erected on a near-by hill a granite cross in his memory. Efforts have been made to find the grave, but to no avail. It is quite probable that the site has been worn away by wave erosion, and the bones of the gallant explorer now rest beneath the waves.

Occupancy of San Miguel by the native Indians seems to have terminated about the same period as that of the other islands and probably from similar causes. In 1850, George Nidever bought from a man named Bruce the right to use the island, and stocked it with 17 head of cattle, 45 sheep, 2 hogs, and 7 horses. Twelve years later, procreation had increased his stock to 200 head of cattle, 6,000 sheep, 100 hogs, and 32 horses. From this it is evident that San Miguel at that time was still fair and green, offering excellent pasturage for stock. Nidever states that in the great drought of 1863-64 he lost 5,000 sheep, 180 cattle, 30 horses, and some hogs. In 1870, Nidever moved from the island, selling his lease or rights to Mills Brothers for $10,000.

At one time during President Grover Cleveland's administration, the island appears to have been deserted, since it was seized by a Captain Waters. This intrepid individualist maintained that since the island was not mentioned in the 1847 treaty of Guadalupe-Hidalgo which delimited the frontiers of Mexico and the United States, he as a squatter, had a valid right to it. A personal order from the President finally succeeded in peacefully ousting the squatting captain.

As resident agent for the present lessee, Herbert S. Lester is known as "King of San Miguel." His loyal subjects are his wife, Elizabeth, two young daughters, Marianne and Elizabeth, and one hired hand.

The family resides in ranch headquarters constructed many years ago from material salvaged from the wreck of the schooner *Watson D. West*. A triangular building, with fixed glass portholes set in the outside walls for windows, points into the prevailing north wind. An interior courtyard is surrounded by living quarters, workshops, storerooms, a museum, and a forge. The children attend what is said to be "the smallest school in the world," a building 10 x 12 x 6½ feet, with Mrs. Lester presiding as teacher. Mail and supplies reach the island twice monthly by private transportation, and radiophone communication with the outside world is now installed. In the museum, among other interesting items is the tusk of a Miocene elephant found by Lester.

High winds make the waters surrounding San Miguel dangerous to shipping. Off Bennett Point, the western extremity of the island, lie many wrecks. Among them, according to tradition, is a silver-laden Spanish galleon.

Southeast of the Santa Barbara Islands lie the four islands of Santa Catalina, Santa Barbara, San Clemente, and San Nicolás.

Santa Catalina, in Los Angeles County and owned by the estate of William Wrigley, Jr., is a famed vacation resort, and its manifold attractions have been heralded widely. Combining a balmy climate, luxuriant vegetation, scenic hills and valley, and a splendid harbor with unsurpassed facilities for all the pleasures of the sea, Santa Catalina attracts visitors from all the world. It lies 25 miles southwest of Los Angeles Harbor from which it may be reached daily by ship or by air.

Twenty-two miles long and varying from ¼ mile to 7½ miles in width, the island comprises some 55,000 acres of rugged terrain. Its geology is similar to that of the other Channel Islands, with most of the rocks of volcanic origin. Silver deposits have been found and at one time were worked extensively. The native animals include red fox, ground squirrels and sea lions supplemented by such introduced varieties as wild goats, wild boars, buffalo, black-tailed deer, and Hereford beef cattle. Santa Catalina is especially noted for its birds, of which over sixty species have been classified and for its many flowers and shrubs, some of which are found nowhere else. The island has very little natural water, and is supplied from wells or from reservoirs where rain water is collected.

Santa Barbara Island, approximately 2 miles long and 1 mile wide, juts out of the sea about 40 miles off the shores of Los Angeles County, in which jurisdiction it lies. The island appears from the sea to be a great rock with precipitous cliffs rising 300 feet from the water. The generally rolling contour is broken by two hills, 635 and 562 feet in height.

Owned by the United States, the greater part is now incorporated in the Channel Islands National Monument. The remainder is used by the Lighthouse Service as the site of two automatic flashing lights. There is no water on the island, there are no inhabitants, and no indications that it ever has been inhabited except for short periods. Its formation shows mostly black lava, pumice, and ashes. The rocks and deep kelp beds of the surrounding waters are the home of many species of shellfish. Recently a lone otter was seen upon the shore, characteristically engaged in using a small rock to smash open an abalone.

San Clemente is another government-owned island lying approximately 50 miles south of Los Angeles Harbor and within the limits of Los Angeles County. It is about 22 miles long with a width varying from 1 to 9 miles and an area of approximately 31,500 acres.

The island is being improved by the United States Navy with flying fields and other facilities, and is known as the San Clemente Fleet Training Base. The surrounding waters to a distance of one nautical mile from shore are known as the "San Clemente Island Naval Defense Sea Areas," and are taboo to all water craft unless authorized by the Secretary of the Navy. Visiting the island is not allowed except by special permission.

San Clemente is of mixed volcanic and sedimentary origin with numerous caves in the low chalky cliffs. Much of the terrain is rough and covered with a heavy growth of cactus. There is some water on the island, but none that is potable and the Navy imports its needed water from the mainland.

Island foxes, mice, several species of birds, reptiles, and insects comprise the animal life indigenous to San Clemente. Indian relics indicate that the island was well populated over a long period. A Los

Angeles County Museum expedition recently found in a cave the skeleton of a large dog of an unknown species. The body of the dog evidently had been wrapped in otter skin and given a ceremonial burial. Two chickens which also had been given ceremonial burials were discovered in the same cave. One had been wrapped in cloth, the other in fur, and offerings of seeds in abalone shells were buried with them. Fragments of cloth indicated that the cave was still used by the natives during the mission period.

Farthest removed from its neighbors and most remote from the mainland, San Nicolás Island lies 76 miles southwest of Los Angeles Harbor. It is a part of Ventura County, is owned by the United States, and administered by the Navy Department. Sheepmen have been allowed to lease it on a short-term basis, and its only inhabitants are the one or two herders who tend the few sheep that manage to draw sustenance from the sparse vegetation, and a naval radio operator who maintains the weather station.

San Nicolás is approximately 9 miles long with an average width of 3 miles and an area of something more than 10,000 acres. The shore line is formed by cliffs averaging 500 feet in height, and the interior is a rolling mesa, badly eroded and with little vegetation, mostly coarse grass and a few large bushes. Most of the island is composed of soft sandstone, which is being rapidly worn away by the action of the waves and the strong northerly winds. Shifting sand dunes cover a large part of the land, and while springs are found in many places, the water is highly mineralized, yet potable.

Piles of human bones attest that the island once supported a numerous population. Overgrazing by sheep coupled with the high winds reduced it to its present desolate state.

Charles Frederick Holder says of the island, "I have never felt a more irritating, searching, penetrating wind than this wraith of the spirits of San Nicolás, yet I found this island most attractive from its very desolation—we could not walk one hundred feet without coming across some relic of the ancient people who once lived there—the island seemed to be in the grasp of innumerable sand glaciers which instead of moving up and down were ever shifting in the wind . . ."

In 1835, the ship *Peor es Nada* (Sp., better than nothing) was sent to San Nicolás to transfer the few remaining natives to the mainland. As Captain George Nidever tells the story: "They removed the Indians, some seventeen or eighteen men, women, and children from this island to San Pedro and thence to Los Angeles, and San Gabriel— some one in Los Angeles authorized the removal of these Indians, the last of the inhabitants of San Nicolás, but with what object I do not know and cannot remember that I have ever heard."

One woman (Juana María she was afterwards called) sought permission to go inland and find her son who had become separated from the group. Before she returned, a sudden squall came up, and the ship had to sail away, leaving her on the island. On reaching San Pedro, the ship was sent north at once for a cargo of lumber. It capsized off the Golden Gate, and the intention of its master to return for the marooned woman never was realized. In 1851, Captain George Nidever found traces of the woman on the island. He came back in 1852 and 1853, and finally found her bent with age and half wild.

She was taken to Santa Barbara, but none of her tribe could understand more than three words of the language she tried to speak. By signs she indicated that she had never found the child whom she had left the ship to seek. Juana María died a few months after her rescue, and what is said to be her grave in the mission cemetery at Santa Barbara is marked with a bronze tablet placed there in 1928 by the Santa Barbara Chapter, D.A.R.

Sanctuary in the Chaparral

WITHIN a dozen miles of urban Santa Barbara stretch the solitudes of Los Padres National Forest—where, legend tells, are the lost gold mines of the padres, where man is aiding fifty California condors, world's largest birds of flight, in their struggle against extinction.

Los Padres National Forest, named for the mission padres, is California's largest (more than two million acres), although it makes a lesser splotch on the map than the smaller national forests clustered together in great unbroken stretches in the northern part of the State.

It covers the wild, mountainous half of Santa Barbara and Ventura counties, spills over into Kern and Los Angeles counties, and extends a forked branch northward beyond San Luis Obispo in a gesture of outstretched arms towards its detached upper section in Monterey County.

The United States Department of Agriculture maintains the forest lands for the primary purpose of preserving the vegetation on the mountain slopes as a flood-control and water-conservation measure, but their recreational value as a factor in public well-being is fully recognized. Use of national forests for recreation is free of charge, but subject to regulations for fire-prevention and preservation of plant and animal life (*see What, Where, When, How*). Regions of greatest fire hazard and watershed value are open in the dry season only to bearers of special forest-service permits. In Los Padres Forest, two other areas are closed altogether to public travel and use throughout the year. One of the forbidden reserves is the Juncal watershed, which protects the water supply of Montecito; the other is the Sisquoc Condor Sanctuary. More than 250,000 persons a year vacation in Los Padres Forest. Some rent cabin lots at nominal yearly fees from the Forest Service, and on these have built permanent summer homes. There are no hotels nor automobile camps in the forest, but cooking facilities, water, and other simple conveniences are provided at public camps and State and county public parks within the forest boundaries. The recreation grounds at Mount Pinos and Frazier Mountain, near the boundary line between Kern and Ventura counties, are being developed for snow and ice sports and summer recreation.

Several good county roads and two State highways traverse parts of the forest in Santa Barbara County. State 166 winds through the Cuyama River district, at the northern edge of the county, from Santa Maria (*see Tour 2*) to a junction near the Kern County line with US 399, which passes through the Ventura County district on its way from Ventura to Bakersfield. State 150 crosses the Santa Ynez Mountain district through San Marcos Pass (*see Tour 2*), north of Santa Barbara. In the pass is a junction with State 150 and El Camino Cielo (*see Tour 2*), one of the most spectacular scenic drives in the forest.

Those who make a study of national forest conservation observe that, without the government program of watershed protection, southern California could not increase nor even maintain its present population. Here occasional rains come from fall to spring with long, warm months intervening. Most of the streams go dry in summer, and late in the season vegetation becomes intensely inflammable. Denuding of mountain slopes by fire causes winter rains to run off very rapidly, carrying away topsoil and reducing the fertility of the land so that succeeding cover is slow-growing, inferior, and less effective as watershed protection. On one hand the rapid runoff silts municipal reservoirs with its burden of precious topsoil, reducing storage capacity and thereby shortening the water supply. On the other, it pours into streams which roar down the valleys, flooding crops and communities as they go, and rushing to waste in the sea. Such streams become dry far earlier in the season than those which drain well-clothed watershed areas.

Droppings of vegetation form a natural mulch on the ground which prevents rapid runoff of rain and melting snow, and keeps the soil underneath in condition to absorb water. A well-covered watershed holds about 84 per cent of the water long enough for it to seep through the soil into underground drainage channels. These feed wells and springs in the valleys upon which many farms and towns are totally dependent the year round.

The value of the mountain cover and its extreme susceptibility to fire in the dry season make fire control and prevention the first concern of the Forest Service. Statistics show that 85 per cent of the costly annual forest fires in California are caused by negligence and accidents among smokers and campers, and these notwithstanding the elaborate fire-precaution regulations in effect for users of the forests (*see What, Where, When, How*).

During the dry season, normally between the first of June and the middle of November, extra lookouts, guards and patrolmen are added to the regular force. Speed in detecting and reporting fires to head-quarters is essential because of the rapidity with which a blaze spreads through the dense, dry cover. Twenty-three lookout stations on high peaks in Los Padres Forest give a direct visibility coverage of about one-third the forest area. The rest is patrolled by forest guards. Most of the lookout and guard stations are connected by telephone with the rangers' headquarters, from which men and fire-fighting equipment are dispatched to fires. Isolated lookouts and patrolmen communicate with headquarters by short-wave radio.

Fire trucks are stationed at intervals in the forest, but the principal fire-fighting equipment—trucks, tools, portable kitchens, food supplies, and other fire-camp paraphernalia—are kept at a central warehouse. Saddle horses and pack mules are kept for carrying food, water, and equipment to fire camps in parts of the forest not accessible by auto-mobile.

Crews fighting large fires, which may burn for several days and eat over many square miles of forest, communicate with the base fire camps and the supervisor's office by radio. A radio unit at the base camp provides a communication center for fire messages. Airplane patrols have been used in reconnaissance of large fires and to drop supplies to fire fighters. In great emergencies, citizens in the area may be drafted to help fight fire. Normally, the Forest Service handles even the larg-est fires with the help of the usual crews of paid fire fighters and C.C.C. workers.

Consumption of forage plants by livestock works a double good— it reduces fire hazard through trimming surplus foliage, which would become extremely inflammable at the end of its annual growth. This vegetation also is a very valuable source of feed for the livestock indus-try. Local ranchers pasture more than six thousand cattle and horses in the forest every year by permission of the Forest Service. Grazing allotments are regulated to perpetuate forage resources and to reserve sufficient feed for saddle and pack stock of campers and for wild deer.

Other resources of the forest besides water, recreation, and grazing are not important. About eighty thousand acres are in timber, prin-cipally pine, fir, redwood, incense cedar, and native oak. Much of it was taken from the forest in early days, but now the only trees cut are those removed in forest-improvement work, for the timber is considered of greater value for recreation use and watershed protection than for lumber. The wood of old and defective trees removed from the forest is used for fuel in the forest camps and stations, and any surplus is given to campers or sold at cost of handling to residents of adjacent regions.

In the Cachuma and Gibraltar reservoir areas are a few deposits of cinnabar, an ore which yields mercury. Several small cinnabar mines operate in the Cachuma district. Twenty-five per cent of the revenue from grazing fees, timber sales, cabin-lot rentals, etc., is given to the State for distribution to the public school and highway funds of the counties within which the forest lies. The Forest Service uses an additional 10 per cent in building roads and trails within these counties.

First move toward government control of forested areas in California was made in 1891, when Congress authorized the President to set aside reserves from public lands to protect native timber and insure favorable conditions of water flow. Several mountain areas in San Luis Obispo and Santa Barbara counties were designated for such purpose during the years from 1898 to 1906. In 1908, they were combined and named Santa Barbara National Forest. Civic and county organizations asked for the name Los Padres National Forest, and the change was granted in 1936.

In earlier days, church and family picnics and buckboard outings were sufficient to the general need of outdoor recreation, and remoter haunts were left to hunters and the hunted. But the claiming of more and more urban land from nature for agricultural and industrial enterprises, and the cramped and complicated existence in large population centers have developed a taste for recreation in absolute wilderness solitude which is repelled, rather than to any degree satisfied, by the picnic and auto camp sort of outing. Family-type camps accessible by automobile within Los Padres number scarcely more than sixty, but the preference for "roughing it" in genuinely primitive surroundings is such that nearly three hundred trail camps in isolated forest areas have been made to meet the demand. More areas of the forest are being made accessible as rapidly as need increases. Development of trails and camps has been speeded up by the Civilian Conservation Corps and other emergency fund work and there are now more than sixteen hundred miles of trail.

A special 75,000-acre preserve, the San Rafael Wild Area, is for enjoyment by those who prefer packing light and sleeping on the ground in the open. It is to be kept free of motor roads and any other development incompatible with its primitive condition, but still, in the interests of sanitation and fire precaution, there are trail camps. However, these are provided only with the simplest and fewest facilities.

The San Rafael Wild Area lies along the headwaters of the Sisquoc River with its southernmost tip less than fifteen miles north of Santa Barbara as the crow flies. At its northern end is a region locally called the Hurricane Deck Country because of the fierce winds that sweep across its lonely and extremely rugged fastnesses. In this region, infrequently penetrated by man, lives a dwindling band of lean, long-horned wild cattle, last remnants of the once numerous and more widely ranging descendants of stock which strayed from the missions and *ranchos* in the Spanish, Mexican and early American periods.

In the Hurricane Deck Country are supposed to be legendary gold mines of the padres, from which the missionaries are said to have obtained gold for making religious vessels.

More than legend are the painted Indian caves found in many places in the forest, for one of them has been studied by scientists from the Smithsonian Institution and is open to tourists (*see Tour 2*).

In Los Padres are several areas set aside as game refuges within which all forms of wild life are offered safety from predatory man. Outside these areas many animals are hunted in season under the regulations of the State fish-and-game code. The Forest Service assists in stocking the streams with trout fry every year, and several good fishing spots are accessible by automobile. Most plentiful of the hunted animals are deer—southern black-tailed and California mule deer—which are estimated at more than thirty-thousand head. Quail, doves, and wild pigeons are sufficiently plentiful to provide good hunting during the limited open season for game birds. Small animals such as foxes, raccoons, rabbits, and others are of good number, but major fur-bearing animals are not. Black bears and cougars are present, but rare. More numerous are coyotes. The predators, which are not considered a menace to users of the forest, are hunted at any season of the year, but only on special permission, for shooting and trapping of predators are regulated to maintain a complete and balanced wild-life community.

The SISQUOC CONDOR SANCTUARY, a twelve-hundred-acre reserve in the southern half of the San Rafael Wild Area, is closed to all forms of use in an effort to preserve the natural conditions necessary to the existence of the California condor (*Gymnogyps californianus*). This remarkable creature is not only the largest existing bird of flight (average wingspread between nine and ten feet, maximum eleven feet), but also the only one of its kind in North America.

The condor tribe has but one other representative in the world, the Andes condor of South America. Condors and common turkey buzzards constitute a family related to that of the Old World vultures. All are characterized by dull blackish or brownish plumage and naked heads. A few California condors are thought to be living in Lower California, but except possibly for those, the birds do not exist anywhere outside the region centered in Los Padres National Forest.

The Sisquoc sanctuary was set aside by the Forest Service in 1937 after alarm at the condor's dwindling numbers became widespread among wild-life conservationists. A subsequent search throughout the bird's habitat in the mountains of Santa Barbara and Ventura counties disclosed that only six were living there. The condor depends upon carrion for food, and in the days when predatory beasts and the animals they preyed upon were plentiful, the bird had little trouble finding abandoned carcasses to eat. Even in the early days of extensive cattle and sheep ranching, when the stock was valuable for its hide but almost worthless for meat because of lack of markets, there was plenty for the condor to eat, for carcasses stripped of hide were left lying, and animals dead of natural causes were not removed.

The condor cannot turn to preying on living animals for food, for he is not equipped by nature for catching and killing. The condor's toes lack sufficient strength to carry weight of any consequence, and his claws are not developed into talons. In pioneer days there were tales about condors carrying off small children to their lairs, but the absurdity of such stories scarcely needs further pointing out. The condor is also too ponderous to depend upon taking live prey for food. He rises from the ground into the air with great difficulty, and always seeks a high spot from which to do so. Only the most desperate hunger would drive a condor to a carcass in a thicket or gully, where he has insufficient free space to put his great wings into action, and is therefore subject to attack and death at the fangs of any prowling beast of prey. Even when feeding on ground only slightly depressed, he eats hurriedly and then walks at once to the nearest high open spot, where he can get off the ground quickly if need be.

The bird's ability to remain in the air for hours at great heights, enabling him to keep many square miles of ground under observation with his extraordinarily far-seeing eyes, makes it possible for him to depend to a certain extent upon the prowess of nimbler creatures better equipped than he to catch and kill for food. Cougars, wolves, and coyotes are able to kill more than they can eat at once, so the condor watches their movements from the sky, and when one of them brings down its prey, he watches until it has eaten its fill and departed, then he descends to finish the remains. In pioneer days, when the giant birds ranged throughout California, Oregon, and Washington, many were killed for their wing-feather quills, in which miners carried gold dust.

Likewise, the bird's slow and spare reproduction contributed to near extinction.

Breeding data are anything but ample, because the birds have withdrawn farther and farther up the most inacessible peaks as man extended his hold on the countryside. It seems that condors do not nest every year, and when they do, they produce but one egg. A twelve-year record of one pair showed they nested only three times during that period. The newly hatched bird's head is bare like that of his parents, but his body is covered with white down. He is a baby perhaps longer than any other creature in birddom; he does not begin to use his wings until he is six months of age. Probably condors do not breed until they are much older than other birds, and are considered in the prime of life at twenty. Their length of life has been estimated at thirty years.

Human Side of a City

SANTA BARBARA bears the imprint of four different cultures. The rudimentary folkways of the Indians, the Old World culture of the Spaniards, the Aztec heritage of the Mexicans, and the American influx of Yankee sailors, nineteenth-century settlers, and latter-day tourists have combined to cast the city's present mold.

Many traces of the Indian culture remain. Today, the shelves of national and international museums house vast stores of the *Canaliño* Indian artifacts, including ornaments, weapons, and utensils, although their folk patterns have been obliterated by more dynamic cultures.

Few of the customs of the Spanish and Mexican settlers survived American rule in Santa Barbara. A small residue of Mexican folk art and legend, however, exists in a scattering of homes about three blocks from the water front where more than three thousand Mexicans preserve some of the folk patterns and beliefs of their forebears despite intensive efforts by educators, civic leaders, and clubwomen to "Americanize" them.

Throughout the various cultural evolutions, Spanish influence has dominated Santa Barbara. A hundred years ago, although Monterey led somewhat in prestige as the capital of Alta California, the inhabitants of the presidio of Santa Barbara "acknowledged no peer anywhere in the point of Castilian aristocracy." The Spanish imprint on the city's social and cultural life remains deep today despite frequent erosion by American enterprise.

The huge waves of immigration which descended on other California communities following discovery of gold in 1848 failed to penetrate Santa Barbara. Travelers from Mexico, following the coast route to the gold fields, added little or nothing to cultural expansion during their rush northward. Then, in the late sixties Santa Barbara began to feel the effect of newcomers from the east. These new settlers possessed enterprise; and though somewhat subdued, their Yankee commercial instincts were not stifled wholly by the somnolent and carefree atmosphere. The tiny outpost became decidedly *gringo* in its desire for commerce; in a short time it assumed the appearance of almost any other western city of the period, with little interest in any form of cultural activities.

But Santa Barbara's destiny was not in the field of commerce. Climate and location decreed otherwise, attracting increasing numbers of retired business people, semi-invalids, artists, and writers. After the turn of the century these people adopted Santa Barbara as their own and began to expand the city's social and cultural outlets. Little by little they revived old Spanish traditions, recognizing that on these is based much of the city's natural charm.

The Old Spanish Days Fiesta (*see Fiesta Land*), a four-day celebration featuring the pageantry of episodes from Santa Barbara history, was inaugurated in 1924 and has become a yearly event. Fears of old Spanish families that the wholesale assumption of *sombreros, mantillas,* and *serapes* by twentieth-century settlers might be a travesty on revered Spanish customs, have been allayed by rigid prohibition of commercialism and banality.

EDUCATION

The progress of education in Santa Barbara has varied accordingly with the city's several governmental regimes. In 1793 attempts were begun by the presidio to conduct primary departments for the few children in compliance with an order by King Charles IV of Spain. These first attempts were none too successful, since few pupils were enrolled. Later even less stress was laid on book learning: "For a boy to be a polished gentleman and expert horseman; for a girl to embroider nicely, sing sweetly, and be gay" was enough. Under early American rule, first-grade curriculum in a school at Anacapa and Cañón Perdido Streets in 1851 consisted of a single song:

"Todo fiel Cristiano
Está obligado a tener devoción"

("Every faithful Christian
Is obliged to have devotion"),

which the pupils sang over and over. Four years later, public school lessons, entirely in Spanish, were held for about forty pupils in the presidio church. The teacher, examined for his proficiency, answered the query, "What is the largest river in the world?" with the unhesitating reply, "The Santa Mariá" (an insignificant stream in Chile).

Hearing of the need of the recently Americanized city for a school that would teach English speech and assist in the establishing of American standards of education, a small band of five nuns, Daughters of Charity of St. Vincent de Paul, set out from the Atlantic seaboard and arrived in Santa Barbara during Christmas week, 1856, after sailing the Gulf of Mexico and crossing the Isthmus of Panama on mules. Early the following year, they established St. Vincent's School, which later became a home for orphan children, and a center for charitable work.

By 1868 there were five school districts within the county, and 1,627 pupils. In 1870 a $16,000 two-story brick school was built in Santa Barbara, but desultory attempts to foster education during the next few years were thwarted by a combination of Mexicans who wanted no schools, and Americans who were afraid to entrust the Board of School Commissioners with the necessary money. In 1875 a scant 796 pupils were receiving instruction in the city, 62 of them in the Santa Barbara College (founded in 1869).

Today, Santa Barbara's school system, in a State which maintains an exceptionally high standard of education, is in the vanguard. The city's schools are governed by a Board of Education which has jurisdiction over both elementary and high-school districts. Nine kindergartens, nine elementary, two junior, and one senior high school are housed in recently erected modern structures.

Study courses are based on an integrated curriculum, and an excellent health program is carried through various clinics and the Moore Dental Foundation. Short motion-picture films of travel and similar themes are used in regular classroom work. Organizations formed for development of visual education on a research basis provide for use of these films. Santa Barbara's school system is one of three in the United States to receive such an appropriation. The Adult Education Department of the city schools maintains both day and evening classes regularly.

Santa Barbara State College (1940 enrollment, 1,750 students) is an outgrowth, not of the old Santa Barbara College, but of the Anna S. C. Blake Normal School established in 1908. A forty-six-acre tract of land, purchased in 1932 and situated on a headland above the Breakwater, is being developed as a new site for the college. Since that time additional land has been secured so that the site will be adequate for 4,000 students.

RELIGION

During Santa Barbara's early years the accepted religion of all inhabitants was Roman Catholic. Yankee settlers became Catholics as a prerequisite to owning land under Mexican rule, and the religion of the Franciscan padres continued its hegemony until well in the sixties. By 1867, enough Protestants had arrived to found the Trinity Episcopal Church in March, and the Congregational Church the following September. Various churches were erected during the next three decades as population increased. Today, almost every major religious belief and racial division has its place of worship. Forty-seven churches, including the ancient Santa Barbara Mission, represent thirty-two denominations. Among the buildings are samples of some of Santa Barbara's finest architecture, and the clergy includes men who rank among the leaders of their profession.

RACIAL GROUPS

Racial minorities provide a fertile field for group activity. At the hands of Santa Barbara clubwomen, schoolteachers, and social workers, first-generation immigrants receive basic training in American citizenship. Among Santa Barbara's 9,000 foreign-born and foreign-descended, there are only 682 illiterates. The community passion for organization is reflected within the minority racial groups themselves, and there are some 30 clubs—8 Scandinavian, 7 Mexican, 5 Italian, 4 Negro, 2 Chinese, 2 Japanese, 1 Greek, and 1 Filipino. Mexicans make up the largest foreign group, with 3,279 individuals. Since many of these are descendants of the Mexicans who lived on the land before it came into possession of the United States, not all can be termed foreigners. But the Mexicans appear to be the particular focus of Santa Barbara's paternalism. A special educational program provides visiting teachers who organize classes in homes and teach American customs and the English language to Mexican mothers. The Spanish Parent-Teachers' Association gives talks on health and social welfare. A Mexican garden club encourages the pastime of floriculture by holding an annual show of gardens cultivated by local Mexicans.

Two-thirds of the Negro population of 525 (1930) live in the area bounded by East Haley, East Montecito, State, and Garden Streets, and the rest are scattered. About one-fourth of them own property, and several are in various professions and businesses, but most are day laborers or domestic servants. There are two churches, the Colored Baptist and the African Methodist-Episcopal. Negroes have their own program in the Adult Education department of the schools. The small Oriental population of approximately 500 Japanese and Chinese is concentrated in a congested square block not far from the city's most exclusive shopping district.

The Japanese have two churches, a Buddhist and the Japanese Congregational. They have organized two clubs—the Santa Barbara Citizens' League for the Issei (first-generation Japanese), and the Santa Barbara Japanese Association for the Nissei (second-generation Japanese). Every year they celebrate the birthday of Buddha on April 1, the Emperor's Birthday on April 30, and the Annual Doll Festival on March 3. A Japanese class held in the Buddhist Temple teaches traditional flower arrangement, Japanese social customs, and the Japanese language. Most of the Japanese are domestic servants, gardeners, truck farmers, or storekeepers.

The Chinese have one church, the Chinese Presbyterian Mission, and two clubs—the Benevolent Association for the older Chinese, and the Sun Wah Association for the younger group. Chinese Independence Day is celebrated annually on October 10. Most of the Chinese are employed in private homes, or in laundries or restaurants. A few are merchants.

CLUB ACTIVITIES

That Santa Barbara is a fertile field for development of clubs and organizations is evinced in 230 groups which comprise the city's organized forces. Some of these groups promote civic betterment and preservation of Santa Barbara's early relics and historic landmarks. Many others maintain rigorous campaigns through cultural activities in an effort to keep Santa Barbarans intellectually alert.

The Community Arts Association often has been called "Santa Barbara's greatest asset." Formed in 1920 and composed of artists, writers, and friends of the fine arts, the group exerted tremendous influence for civic betterment and cultural expansion. It was one of the largest organizations of its kind in the country at one time with as many as 1,200 to 1,500 members contributing their time and efforts in its four branches: Plans and Planting, Music, Drama, and School of the Arts.

Spearhead of the post-war emphasis on civic improvement was the Plans and Planting branch. From a nucleus consisting of several adobe buildings of early years, among them the De la Guerra house, the Plans and Planting unit under the guidance of Bernard Hoffman in 1924 created the De la Guerra Studios—antique and specialty shops, tea rooms, and art studios, and demonstrated that it was possible for Santa Barbara to develop an architecture of her own.

The 1925 earthquake gave further opportunity for architectural "face-lifting" (*see Presidio to Channel City*). Above the ruins of the old business section the Plans and Planting branch supervised the erection of interesting new buildings. Under the tutelage of an Architectural Advisory Committee, a Better Homes Committee, and a privately established Community Drafting Room, Santa Barbarans became architecture conscious. Markets, furniture stores, motor company buildings, and cafeterias were designed with balconied façades, and equipped with heavy copper-colored sun curtains.

After successful application in the business section, the project was extended to private homes and public buildings. Familiar Eastern and Midwestern types of architecture were supplanted gradually by a synthesis of Latin types, fusing Spanish, Italian, and Mexican design considered appropriate to climate and terrain—the new "California Style" (*see Tierra Adorada*). Today, modernity and tradition have combined to win many prizes for Santa Barbara in national small-homes contests. Following civic reconstruction, the Community Arts Association continued its crusade to promote the general culture. A yearly grant of $25,000 from the Carnegie Foundation was obtained in 1922, and nearly $1,300,000 was spent on cultural activities during a period of ten years. A school of the arts, teaching painting, decoration, architectural design, and language, was established. A music branch was formed by the association to conduct choruses, support fellowships in the School of the Arts, and present a series of concerts each year. A drama branch sponsored monthly plays with nonprofessional actors, and offered prizes for original plays. Cessation of the Carnegie grants in 1930, with the beginning of the depression, curtailed activities of the association during the ensuing decade, but Santa Barbara's interest in the arts began to rise again during the later 1930's.

MUSIC

Music, in particular, has been fostered by Santa Barbarans eager to preserve what they feel to be their city's peculiar musical heritage. The *Canaliños,* unlike many Indian tribes, greeted their first white visitors not with arrows but with flutes—whose "weird noises," according to Father Crespi, kept Portolá's weary company of explorers awake "all through the night." These bowl flutes and pipes were made of several whistles tied together. The Spanish brought folk music antedating that of both the French-Canadian and the Negro on this continent. Still later, hardy music lovers braved the damp of Santa Barbara's first adobe theater to hear Nordica, Schumann-Heink, Kubelik, and Paderewski.

Today, symphony concerts are given by the Southern California Music Project and sometimes by the Los Angeles and San Francisco Symphony Orchestras on tour. The Santa Barbara County Bowl in

Quail Canyon, a WPA project, is considered one of the finest outdoor amphitheaters of its size in the country.

Musicians, eminent in their respective fields, find Santa Barbara inspirational background. Composers living in the city include Henry Eicheim, violinist-conductor, who has led the playing of his own compositions with symphony orchestras throughout the nation; Klyne Headley, winner of a scholarship given by the widow of Edward Mac-Dowell at Peterborough, New Hampshire; Antoni van der Voort, violinist-arranger, who recently won first prize in a national competition sponsored by the St. Louis Symphony Association for symphonic composition; Roderick White, violinist; and Arthur Bliss, Joseph Mac-Manus, and Walter Buchanan.

Leopold Stokowski, long-time conductor of the Philadelphia Symphony Orchestra and more recently celebrated for his successful tour of South America with a youth symphony orchestra, owns a home in Santa Barbara. Other celebrities in the musical field who live in Santa Barbara at least part of the year include John R. Britz, conductor and cellist; Philip Abbas and Marcel Guerman, cellist; Grace Kaplun, Paul McCoole and Mildred Couper, pianists; Eleanor Mellinger, harpist, and Raymond Eldred, violinist; Lotte Lehmann, internationally famed concert soprano, lives in Santa Barbara.

DRAMA

Although early Santa Barbarans exhibited the usual frontier enthusiasm for offerings of small itinerant theatrical troupes, only sporadic, halfhearted efforts were made to develop drama talent or appreciation until well past the middle of the nineteenth century. Then, a musician, turned tavernkeeper, José Lobero, came to Santa Barbara in 1859, and five years later opened a saloon which served to finance most of his extraordinary talents.

He organized a band, an orchestra, and composed and sang his own music. Soon he included theatrical performances in his activities, recruiting local casts, writing and directing plays, and occasionally acting in them.

Then he secured additional financial backing from Colonel William Hollister, and at Cañon Perdido and Anacapa Streets, started the first Lobero Theater in a rebuilt adobe schoolhouse. The theater was dedicated February 22, 1873. The first play offered was an opera written and directed by Lobero, and even its scenery was painted by the versatile Italian.

Although Lobero himself met with reverses, his contributions to the culture of the community are still remembered. He last appeared with his band at a funeral in the middle eighties. Ill and bankrupt, he lost both theater and tavern, and later shot and killed himself.

The old Lobero Theater continued to be the fashionable theatrical center of Santa Barbara until the turn of the century when it was supplanted by the then new and modern Potter Theater. For almost two decades the Potter Theater held virtual monopoly over Santa Barbara's theatrical fare.

In 1910, the American Film Manufacturing Company acquired a quarter of a block at State and Mission Streets, and there, under the "Flying A" trademark, began to produce reel after reel of comedies, thrillers and serials. Santa Barbara's beach front served as both desert and South Sea strand. The most famous of the serials was *Diamond From the Sky,* directed by William Desmond Taylor, who later became the victim in an unsolved murder mystery of Los Angeles in 1921. The first chapter of this serial was released in March, 1915. Lottie Pickford was featured because of the exploitation value of her name. Her sister, Mary, had become "America's sweetheart."

In 1920, stimulated in part by the rising national interest in the Little Theater movement, the Community Arts Association's drama branch began to produce and present plays enacted by amateurs. For several years, ten plays were given annually at the Potter Theater.

The success of this venture led to purchase by the Association of the old Lobero Theater. On its site, a picturesque new theater was built, architecturally reminiscent of buildings in Majorca, Spain. Retaining the historic name, the new Lobero Theater opened in August, 1924, with presentation of *Beggar on Horseback.* Since its opening, the new Lobero Theater has offered both professional and amateur productions. Recently the house became county owned. The Lobero Foundation guides its destiny and broadens its activities.

Producers of new plays frequently try them out in Santa Barbara before formal presentation in Los Angeles or San Francisco.

The Little Theater movement still thrives in Santa Barbara. Two theaters, the Alhecama, owned by Mrs. Max Schott, and the Playbox, managed by Klyde Kraft, feature presentations which are produced, directed, and enacted by nonprofessionals.

Prominent in the dramatic world are such residents of Santa Barbara as Robert E. Jones, designer and producer; Colin C. Clements and Marion C. Wentworth, playwrights, and Irving Pichel, director and actor. Ronald Colman owns San Ysidro Ranch, and lives there part of the year. The late Warner Oland owned a home in Carpinteria. The late Salisbury Field, playwright, made his home in Carpinteria and his widow, Isobel, stepdaughter of Robert Louis Stevenson, is an author in her own right. Martha Graham, leading American dancer, went to school at Santa Barbara.

LITERATURE

Although it is not a writers' colony, Santa Barbara has become the home of many authors who have fled congested, commercialized conditions of metropolitan life. A number of writers of national reputation have been drawn to Santa Barbara from other States, but a great many are indigenous—these, however, are mostly semiprofessionals who have been impelled by the color of their environment to produce articles, pamphlets, or books on the local scene. Since Father Crespi, historian of the first California exploring party, described the region's native populace in 1769, Santa Barbara's growth, terrain, and personalities have been limned in dozens of histories, romances, and biographies.

Santa Barbara's prehistoric man has been studied and described by David B. Rogers, formerly Curator of Anthropology of the Santa Barbara Museum of Natural History (*see Presidio to Channel City*); resident chroniclers of Santa Barbara's early development include H. H. Sheldon, Father Zephyrin Engelhardt, John S. Southworth, Michael Phillips, and W. A. Hawley, and early mission days live in the writings of several Franciscan friars. Richard Henry Dana's (1815-82) visit during the 1830's was described in his *Two Years Before the Mast,* and Alfred Robinson (1806-95), whose marriage to a De la Guerra is one of the high lights of the Dana book, later presented his own picture of early Santa Barbara years in his *Life in California* (1846).

Among the 200 writers claimed by Santa Barbara is Margaret Cameron, whose *John Dover* (1924) contains scenes laid in the old Massini Adobe. The late Marguerite Wilkinson's second book, *By a Western Wayside* (1912), was written in Santa Barbara. Stewart Edward White completed several of his works in Santa Barbara. The late Kate Douglas Wiggin and Rebecca N. Porter spent their childhood days in the city.

Among contemporary writers living in Santa Barbara at least part of the year are Caroline Hazard, former president of Wellesley College; Frank Hilton, western-story writer; Hobart C. Chatfield Taylor, author of a Molière biography used as a textbook; Robert W. Hunter, writer on sociological subjects; Donald Culross Peattie and Louise Redfield Peattie, who collaborate on novels and articles; Raymond Moley, editor of *Newsweek;* Eleanor Wilson McAdoo, biographer; Phyllis Bottome, Eleanor Hoffman, Edith S. Clements, T. E. Ripley, William Ellison, Charles Perkins, and Harry Hervey.

The late Ernest L. Thayer, author of "Casey at the Bat," and Robert Cameron Rogers, author of the poem, "The Rosary," spent the last years of their lives in Santa Barbara. Rob Wagner, writer, artist, and editor of *Script* magazine, published in Beverly Hills, California, was at one time a resident of Santa Barbara.

Among several scientists and research workers who have written books are Dr. W. D. Sansum, director of the Sansum Clinic; George Coleman, formerly at the Pasteur Institute in Paris, who now lives in Montecito; Dr. Harry Devighne, and Dr. Logan Clendenning, physician; Dr. A. P. Ousdal, physician and anthropologist, and William Dawson, Ralph Hoffman, and Seldon Spaulding, ornithologists.

ART

Among the earliest art celebrities to find Santa Barbara an inspirational home were Henry Chapman Ford, Alexander F. Harmer, and Thaddeus Welch. Ford arrived in 1875. Notable are his series of etchings of California missions. Harmer made his home in Santa Barbara in 1893 and thereafter devoted his palette to the paintings of early-California scenes. Welch, whose later years were spent in the county, painted the familiar canyons and mountains of the western landscape.

Not the least among those who came to Santa Barbara in more recent times, are the cowboy artists, Charles Russell and Edward Borein. Both have made permanent records of the Old West and depicted the life of the range.

Cecil Clark Davis, noted for her exquisite portraiture, has been a resident of Santa Barbara for many years. She is the widow of Richard Harding Davis, novelist and reporter.

Art exhibits from many countries have been held in the Faulkner Memorial Art Gallery, which was designed by Myron Hunt and H. C. Chambers and built in 1930 as a wing of the Public Library. It was decided from the first that a gallery of this sort, with limited space, could best serve the artistic life of the community not by gathering at great expense a small permanent collection, but by keeping it for changing exhibitions of pictures from different countries as well as various art centers of the United States.

Changing exhibitions of pictures from cosmopolitan art sources have embraced a panorama of canvases and sculpture from pre-Renaissance to modern. These exhibitions have included groups of old masters; collections of modern Spanish, French, Hungarian, German, Polish, Japanese, Guatemalan, Mexican, Balinese art works and ancient Tibetan, regional American, and American Negro collections. Individual features have included works of Arthur B. Davies, Dean Cornwall, Stowitts, Russell Cheney, Charlotte Berend, Gleb Illyin, Lockwood de Forest, N.A., Archipenko, William Ritschel, N.A., Belmore Browne, A.N.A., Guy Rose, Paul Sample, Karoly Fulop, Conrad Buff, Nicolai

Fechin, Alfredo Ramós Martínez, Elmer Schofield, N.A., Ernest Fiene, Ben Ali Haggin, Thomas Moran, N.A., Carl Hofer, Frederick Taubes, Kay Nielson, Erica von Kager, Maurice Sterne, Cornelis and Jessie Arms Botke, and sculpture by Isamu Noguchi, Lovet-Lorski, Anna Coleman Ladd, José de Creeft and Alice Carr de Creeft, and Matéo Hernández.

Representative canvases have been shown of Santa Barbara artists, including Clarence Hinkle, Italo d'Andrea, Carl Oscar Borg, William S. Bagdatopulos, and the late Fernand Lundgren. Jack Gage Stark and the late Colin Campbell Cooper are two whose works have furnished one-man exhibits for the gallery.

Murals by Dan Sayre Groesbeck present a pageant of early Santa Barbara history in the new County Courthouse. Also among the city's permanent art decorations are those executed by John Marshall Gamble for the Fox Arlington Theater. Santa Barbara's legacy of art is not confined to the city; in Santa Inés Mission (see Tour 2) are the finest paintings of any of the missions. Among them is one attributed to Murillo.

A number of Santa Barbara artists were represented in San Francisco's Golden Gate International Exposition. Among these were the painters Douglass Parshall, Clarence Hinkle, Walter Cheever, DeWitt Parshall, Charles Cabot Daniels, Eunice C. McLennan, Clarence Mattei, Blossom Owen, Edith Catlin Phelps, Ann Louise Snider, and G. B. Troccoli. Sculptors represented were David Gray, Anna Coleman Ladd, Helen M. Seegart, and David Swanson.

Purchase by the county of Santa Barbara's old post-office building in 1939, to be used as an art museum augmenting the Faulkner Art Gallery, will make possible the establishment of a permanent art exhibit for Santa Barbara. It is expected the new museum will afford both space and lighting for seven large galleries of adaptable size and adequate lighting. Gifts of painting, sculpture, and other art as well as generous sums of money have assured this project of successful continuance in the community.

Among the artists who reside in Santa Barbara or whose works have played a part in the cultural life of the community are Allan Cram, marine and figure painter; Rico Lebrun, New York mural painter; Lilia Tuckerman, whose panoramic backgrounds appear in the Museum of Natural History; S. E. Vaughan and Joseph Knowles, whose murals decorate the Veterans' Memorial Building; Mr. and Mrs. Albert Herter of the Herter Studios, New York; Margaret Ely Webb, illustrator and designer of bookplates; Dudley Carpenter, portraitist; Frank Morley Fletcher, English artist; Paul Julian and Campbell Grant, selected by the United States Treasury Department to paint murals for the Federal buildings in Santa Barbara County; Wright

Ludington, William L. Otte, Mary Coulter, Marian Hebert, Standish Backus, Jr., John B. Hamilton, Roy Lawhorne, Channing Peake, Lyla M. Harcoff, Richmond Kelsey, Ella Snowden Valk, Francis Sedgewick, Ethel B. Wack, Frank Post, Thomas E. Ripley, Stanley Edwards, Ann Louise Snider, and James Bodrero.

PRESS AND RADIO

Newspaper history in Santa Barbara dates from 1855, five years after California was admitted to the Union. B. W. Keep, a printer, and R. Hubbard, a writer, came to the community to start the *Gazette,* a 4-page, 5-column weekly with one page printed in Spanish. The *Gazette,* after almost seven years of prosperity, offended city leaders in a tactless editorial. A boycott by advertisers brought Santa Barbara's first newspaper to an untimely demise in 1861.

Eight years elapsed before Santa Barbara's second newspaper, the *Post,* was founded by E. B. Boust who arrived from the Mother Lode country with a press brought from the Atlantic coast. The *Post* was acquired by J. A. Johnson, and its name subsequently was changed to the *Press.* In 1871, it came out as a daily paper.

In the meantime, Boust started another paper in 1870, the *Times,* which, after a five-year struggle, ceased publication. Subsequently, five papers were started in Santa Barbara, only to meet the same fate as the *Times.* They were the *Index,* the *Daily Republican,* the *Santa Barbaran,* the *Advertiser,* and the *News.*

The *Democrat* was launched in 1878 by Keep (formerly of the *Gazette*), Boust (formerly of the *Post* and *Times*), and F. A. Moore. It proved a more enduring publishing venture than many of the others. For about six months it continued as the *Democrat,* and then Moore purchased the interests of his partners and changed the name of the paper to the *Independent.*

On January 1, 1900, Thomas M. Storke, descendant of Captain José Francisco Ortega, who came to Santa Barbara with the Portolá expedition in 1769, purchased the *Independent.* Thirteen years later he acquired the *News,* which had been revived in 1895. Thus, in 1913, Storke combined the two papers under the name of the Santa Barbara *Daily News.*

The consolidation left Santa Barbara with two papers, the *News* and the *Press.* In 1932, these were merged as the *News-Press,* with morning, evening and Sunday issues. In 1938, Storke was appointed to fill the unexpired term of United States Senator William Gibbs McAdoo, resigned.

From its humble beginning seventy-seven years ago, the *News-Press* has grown to the largest single business institution in Santa Barbara

County, with almost three hundred names on its pay roll. From a 4-page, 3-column newspaper with a circulation of only a few hundred, the *News-Press* has expanded until its daily editions range from 14 to 28 standard 8-column pages. Its circulation in Santa Barbara, Ventura, and San Luis Obispo counties totals about sixteen thousand. Three major press services are employed—the Associated Press, the United Press, and the International News Service.

The *Union Labor News,* a weekly, is published by union labor of Santa Barbara.

Of all the journalistic pioneers of Santa Barbara County, the Lompoc *Record* alone has had an uninterrupted career under the same name. Founded by H. H. Broughton, April 10, 1876, this weekly had, by 1940, a circulation of 1,180. It is now published by Ronald M. Adam.

In Santa Maria, the daily *Times,* with a circulation of 2,578 (1940), is published by R. K. and S. C. Hancock, who also publish the Santa Maria Valley *Vidette,* a weekly founded in 1882. Another weekly, the *Courier,* is edited and published by E. R. Trebon, with 1,960 subscribers.

Other weekly newspapers published in Santa Barbara County are The Santa Ynez Valley *News,* Solvang, Walter L. and Mella Hanson, publishers; the Goleta Valley *Leader,* Marshall Selover, publisher; the Carpinteria *Chronicle,* published by Mrs. Ann W. Riley, and the Carpinteria *Herald,* edited and published by Arthur M. Clark.

Associated with the Santa Barbara *News-Press* is radio station KTMS, also under the ownership and management of Storke, the publisher. The initial broadcast was sent over KTMS on October 31, 1937. Since that date, the station has been affiliated with the Blue Network of the National Broadcasting Company. Programs emanating from Santa Barbara heard nationally over this system have included the Mission Choristers singing from Santa Barbara Mission.

KDB Radio Station is considerably older than KTMS, having been established in 1925. In 1931, the station came under the control of the Don Lee system and, through this arrangement, released Columbia Broadcasting Company programs until December 25, 1937. Since that date KDB has been a member of the Mutual Broadcasting System. Originating from KDB over the Mutual system are such programs as local popular orchestras and the Easter and Christmas broadcasts of the services at the Old Mission.

Fiesta Land

NESTLING at the foot of the chaparral-clad mountains in the heart of the American Riviera, the playland that is Santa Barbara looks out over the sun-capped wavelets of the channel which bears its name—out to where the rugged peaks of the Channel Islands break the smooth line of the horizon, and endless leagues of the vast Pacific roll betwixt this smiling land and the storied shores of the Orient.

Fair and pleasant is this land, gracious and hospitable always have been its people. The aboriginal inhabitants, the Indians, welcomed the first Spanish explorers with demonstrations of friendliness, with feasts gathered from the sea and with fanfares from their primitive horns. Present-day residents carry on early-California traditions of gaiety and devotion to the joys and amenities of life.

Spanish California—in nostalgic memory, "Spanish Arcadia"—during its halcyon days was the scene of innumerable festivities. Not only were all the accepted occasions utilized, but many of the more difficult tasks of daily life were lightened by the holiday spirit in which they were undertaken by the community. Cattle branding, wine making, and even the washing of linen afforded opportunities for festivity. Domestic anniversaries, arrival of new officials from Mexico, advent of a stranger or ship, even presence of a prisoner of state furnished sufficient incentive for a fiesta of some sort.

Food and drink, music and dancing were the concomitants of a fiesta, as they are in all isolated communities. The more spacious adobe homes included a large room especially built for dancing. Here Californians, from adolescent to octogenarian, swayed to the rhythm of guitars and castanets.

Las Posadas, an observance which preceded Christmas, lasted nine days. Each day closed with a *tertulia* (Sp., party). *Cascarone* balls were an integral part of the carnival week which always preceded Lent. *Cascarones,* from which the dances took their name, were prepared carefully, often months in advance. They were made by filling empty eggshells with perfumed confetti, gold tinsel, and occasionally with gold dust. They were invaluable aids to shy swains and others, who won favor by breaking them over the dark tresses of their velvet-eyed *inamoratas.* The old Spanish dances required grace and skill, and solo dancers of the gentler sex often were showered with the jewelry of the onlooking *caballeros.* However, these spontaneous tributes usually were returned to the impetuous donors in the course of a few days by the dancing *señorita's* personal maid.

The end of the Mexican rule and the influx of Americans did not disturb this spirit of *dolce far niènte* (It., delightful idleness). Rather did the newcomers absorb the prevailing atmosphere and join heartily in the accustomed life of the community. While many of the old customs have been abandoned and some of the more primitive forms of amusements have vanished, the spirit of gaiety, romance, and color of "Spanish Arcadia" has been perpetuated and thrives unrestrainedly in the Santa Barbara of today. This rich heritage has been crystallized in three annual fiestas which now attract visitors from far and wide. These events are the Old Spanish Days Fiesta, the ride of *Los Rancheros Visitadores* (Sp., the visiting ranchers), and *Semana Náutica* (Sp., nautical week), of which more anon.

Santa Barbara offers much in addition to fiestas for the entertainment of residents and visitors. This region has many natural advantages for all kinds of sport and recreation. Smooth, sandy beaches which stretch for miles; an island-protected sea channel for fishing and yachting; mountains with game; trout streams—all these in a climate where the temperature seldom reaches higher than 90°, nor goes lower than 32°—make Santa Barbara the year-round recreation center of many of America's leading citizens, and a favorite vacation spot for thousands of modest-circumstanced visitors.

In the realm of sports there is no evidence of any preoccupation with the city's Spanish-Mexican heritage. Golf, tennis, badminton, baseball, and other games of skill and brawn are as popular in Santa Barbara as in other American cities. Facilities for virtually all recreation familiar to the average American are provided, but proof of the presence of substantial wealth lies in the emphasis given such financially restrictive activities as yachting, polo, and the annual horse and dog shows.

Shielded by a 2,364-foot breakwater, the harbor is the home port for more than 250 pleasure craft, ranging from small sailboats to luxurious steam and Diesel-powered ocean-going yachts. The city's southern exposure has made the channel waters a marine festival ground for yachting enthusiasts. A cruising area of ninety miles, protected by the Channel Islands, provides one of the smoothest yacht-racing strips on the Pacific coast. Biennially the Southern California Championship Regatta is held at Santa Barbara with some 250 boats competing in 25 classes. The harbor also on several occasions has been the starting point for the biennial California-Hawaii race. The combination of balmy climate and protected channel serves to make the joy of yachting continuous throughout the year.

Polo ranks with yachting as one of the city's most colorful sports. In spring and summer, games are played with top-ranking teams from other parts of the country. Contests are held every Sunday during the season and practice games are played daily. The Santa Barbara Polo Association has had many internationally famous players on its teams and practically every year one or more members was placed on a national team or a Santa Barbara team represented the United States in international matches against teams from England, India, Australia, Mexico, or the Argentine (before the war).

At the annual Fair and Horse Show, outstanding on the city's social calendar, the equine blue bloods hold the center of the stage. Horse breeding has become so popular, both as an industry and as a hobby, in Santa Barbara and vicinity that the show, held in Pershing Park, is now ranked as the most important event of its kind in the West. More than a hundred equine entry classes include sleek Arabians and Royal Golden Palominos bred on neighboring ranches in addition to representatives from major stables throughout the United States.

Less imposing in scope and number of entries, but almost as important in the eyes of society is the All-Breed Dog Show. An annual event for many years, the show usually is held during the first week of August at the Santa Barbara Riding Club. Here, amid a setting of rolling hills, trophies are displayed, tables are set and refreshments served, while spectators view the open-air exhibition rings from awning-shaded benches.

Miles of broad, clean sandy beaches fringe the coast line of Santa Barbara County. Between the city of Santa Barbara and the sea lies the three-mile municipally owned beach with its new $80,000 outdoor plunge, open day and night during the summer months. No commercializing of this city property is permitted. Lying behind the Breakwater, the western part of the beach, inside the harbor, is frequented by those who like to swim or frolic in calm, smooth water. More vigorous swimmers prefer the eastern end and the long, curving beach west of the Breakwater, where combers break upon the sandy shore. Several species of trout are found in the Santa Ynez, Manzana, and Sisquoc Rivers in the mountains of Los Padres National Forest. These include rainbow, eastern brook, Loch Leven, steelhead, and cutthroat. Some black bass are also taken from these streams. The Santa Ynez and Manzana Rivers are accessible by automobile, but the Sisquoc may be reached only on foot or by pack train. At intervals these rivers are stocked with young trout by the authorities. A State fish hatchery is maintained within the forest.

Although sea fishing is not so good off Santa Barbara as elsewhere on the Pacific coast, game fish of many kinds are caught in the waters between the city and the Channel Islands. These include barracuda (in the fall), channel rockfish, black rockfish, striped rockfish, halibut, mackerel, chilipepper, bocaccio, Pacific cultus cod, California corbina, short-fin sea bass (commonly called sea trout), sole, whitefish, half-moon, sculpin, sheepshead, and garibaldi. Occasional catches of the bigger game fish such as broadbill and marlin swordfish, yellowtail, yellowfin, albacore, and other species of tuna are reported.

In Los Padres National Forest, game, in season, challenges hunters. More than a quarter of a million vacationists seek the sylvan seclusion of the forest each year (*see Sanctuary in the Chaparral*).

Horseback riding is available to those who cannot afford to own one of the beautiful mounts seen in such numbers around the city and its environs. Numerous riding academies are adjacent to the trails that lead north, east, and west from the city. Here horses may be hired at nominal rates, riding instruction is given to novices, and conducted horseback tours are offered daily.

In the realm of games, golf, tennis, badminton, archery, bowling, etc., are available to the person of modest means (*see Places to Play*). Although most of the golf courses around Santa Barbara are owned by clubs which restrict their use to members and guests, many of these clubs offer short-term memberships and there is an excellent public golf course.

More than a score of public tennis courts are scattered about the city in the playgrounds and parks and on the beaches. Free tennis instruction for beginners is provided by the City Recreation Commission. Similar provision is made for such activities as badminton, archery, cricket, croquet, lawn bowling, baseball, softball, basketball, golf putting, fly-casting, pinochle, bridge, checkers, chess, bicycling, and others. All of these courses, courts, or other facilities are open to residents and visitors alike without admission charge (*see Places to Play*).

Always there are some who visit vacation spots purely for relaxa-

RIBBON OF CONCRETE THROUGH ROCKY GAVIOTA PASS

ANACAPA ISLAND (*LEFT*) AND SANTA CRUZ ISLAND
(*RIGHT*) AS SEEN FROM THE MAINLAND AT VENTURA

ARCH ROCK, SANTA CRUZ ISLAND

PELICAN BAY, FAIR ANCHORAGE AT SANTA CRUZ ISLAND

FORNEY'S COVE, BLEAK HABITAT OF SEA
LIONS, WEST END OF SANTA CRUZ ISLAND

A BROKEN SHIP MAST MARKS THE GRAVE OF
BENJAMIN FOXEN, SANTA BARBARA COUNTY

MORTON BAY FIG TREE, GROWN
FROM A SAPLING OF THE 1870'S

tion; who do not wish to indulge in any sport—whose greatest exertion is sightseeing. To these Santa Barbara offers many interesting trips. For decades the community has boasted of its beautiful gardens, many of which are on the magnificent private estates which adorn the city and its environs. Since 1926, the Santa Barbara Garden Tours annually have attracted many visitors and have enabled them to enjoy and study carefully cultivated plants and flowers which are native to this region. Personally conducted automobile trips to ninety or more of the luxurious gardens are available at certain seasons of the year.

Other conducted tours are made to the museums, the historic adobe buildings of the early Spanish settlers, to the famous flower farms northwest of the city, and to the three old missions—Santa Bárbara, Santa Inés, and La Purísima Concepción. Boat trips to the Channel Islands are made during some seasons, either powerboats or sailing vessels being available for these excursions.

For those who wish to combine improvement of the mind with other vacation activities, the Santa Barbara Nature School provides stimulus for a variety of interests. Summer classes are offered in tide-pool and desert life, tree, bird, and garden study; physical and biological science; popular astronomy, meteorological observation. Field trips include the Santa Barbara Botanic Gardens, the Andrée Clark Bird Refuge, the Natural History Museum, and other points of cultural interest.

Stressing the Spanish background of Santa Barbara and serving to call attention to the city's playground facilities and its gracious manner of life are the three annual celebrations—the Old Spanish Days Fiesta, the *Semana Náutica* and the ride of the *Rancheros Visitadores.*

Beginning with the August full moon and continuing for four days, the Old Spanish Days Fiesta is celebrated by the entire community. Newspapers, newsreels, and national radio broadcasts publicize the event and attract thousands of visitors who join wholeheartedly in the festivities. It is the city's most democratic festival—men, women, and children from all walks of life donning Spanish costumes and participating in the gaiety. It had its inception on the occasion of the opening of the tradition-surrounded new Lobero Theater in 1924 and, except in 1925, when the earthquake intervened, has been an annual affair ever since.

The old Lobero Theater was the center of the social life of Santa Barbara for several decades. In 1924, the Community Arts Association completed the new structure on the historic site of the original. This achievement and the restoration of the near-by Casa de la Guerra (*see Points of Interest*) constituted an initial civic accent on the pageantry and charm of the pueblo of remembered yesterdays.

It was desired that the entire populace should participate in the dedication. A celebration, appropriate to the occasion, and at the same time general in character, proved difficult to conceive, but the suggestion of turning back the clock to the "leather dollar" era—those Arcadian days when Spanish *dons* waxed rich from the sale of hides and tallow to the Yankees—happily won the approval of all the members of the committee in charge.

To inspire the confidence of the more conservative elements of the community, proponents of the fiesta stressed simplicity and a revival of genuine hospitality with a simultaneous banning of the tawdry or purely commercial. Thus reassured, the whole citizenry mobilized to make the event memorable. All endeavored to contribute something of lore or of moment to the occasion. Certainly no other California community could provide a more beautiful or more atmospheric setting, more gaily caparisoned steeds nor more inherent love of the traditional fiesta spirit.

A latent longing for the less prosaic was found everywhere under the surface of the casual, and it soon found expression in the task of re-creating the romantic yesterdays. In every home there were preparation and anticipation. All-but-forgotten melodies and dances were revived. Charming ladies had learned them in their long-gone youth and, though their years bordered on the century mark, they graciously and skillfully taught them to eager new generations.

The city was draped in scarlet and gold, the old royal colors of once mighty Spain. Precious heirlooms, unearthed from family chests, again graced proud forms—quaint, ruffled frocks, gay shawls, and high, gracefully carved combs. Silver braid, bright sashes, and broad sombreros emboldened the most retiring citizens as they embarked on the synthetic adventures of other days and other ways.

This was the atmosphere of the first old Spanish Days Fiesta in 1924, and the same spirit has characterized every subsequent renewal.

The fiesta begins with a reception and pageant on the steps of the Santa Barbara Mission. There the throng of residents and visitors, most of them in costume, are blessed formally by the Franciscan friars and are invited to participate in the festivities. On the second day an historical pageant passes down the main streets. In this procession are oxcarts, covered wagons, stagecoaches, and flower-bedecked floats, bearing musicians and gay *señoritas*. Marchers and riders are dressed as characters of early Santa Barbara history—as *caballeros* and their ladies, as soldiers, Indians, Franciscan padres, Yankee trappers, and miners.

Fiesta nights are featured by street dances, the singing of old Spanish songs by strolling troubadours, entertainments in the sunken garden of the County Courthouse, and by a pageant in the Santa Barbara County Bowl, portraying episodes in the history of the city under Spanish and Mexican rule. Children's parades, a flower festival, and a rodeo in the old Spanish style are other attractions of the four-day celebration (*see Public Invited*).

Horsemen come from far and near to attend the fiesta, and each visiting rider or driver is given stable facilities for his mount or his team without charge. Santa Barbara enjoys its fiesta, and the number of visitors it attracts from all over the nation steadily grows with each succeeding renewal.

Another important celebration in harmony with the city's history is the annual ride of the *Rancheros Visitadores*. It is a natural out-growth of the friendships engendered during the Old Spanish Days Fiesta.

A desire to promote the wholesome camaraderie of the past led Edward Borein, Santa Barbara's western artist and enthusiast, to sug-gest a revival of the annual ride of the Spanish *dons* from rancho to rancho. In those days it was the custom to cut out the strays in the herds on the open ranges and brand the calves which had been born since the last roundup. Contests of skill, followed by feasting, invari-ably marked the close of the roundup at each rancho. Borein's sugges-tion was greeted with applause by the horsemen of Santa Barbara County.

In May, 1930, some sixty-five riders assembled for the first caval-cade. Golden Palominos and proud Arabian thoroughbreds, carrying silver-mounted tack, brushed stirrups with shaggy mustangs from the range. Emerging from the heavy gray mist of a reluctant day, they cantered with casual grace down the old familiar trails of the Santa Ynez, to converge in the plaza of Santa Barbara, Queen of the Mis-sions. Here, amid the tolling of bells, the tinkling of trappings, and the whinnying of horses, the brown-robed friars blessed them and bade them *"Vayan con dios"* (Sp., "Go with God"). This was the start of the first revival of the annual ride of the *Rancheros Visitadores*.

The modern affair is actually a glorified camping trip, although it retains the color and spirit of the original. After receiving the blessing of the friars, the horsemen ride northward following, whenever possible, the routes pursued by the original *rancheros*—over hills, through can-yons and across streams. A chuck wagon, a wagon loaded with refresh-ments and another with bedding, accompany the riders, who camp out between visits to the *ranchos*. Swivel-chair caballeros, either too tired or too timid to ride the spirited steeds and skittish cow ponies, follow in lumbering old stage coaches.

The original *rancheros,* once they arrived at a *rancho,* proceeded with the work of the roundup, after which they engaged in riding and roping contests and other sports which grew out of their work with cattle. This exhibition of skill, now called a rodeo, was followed by a fiesta.

Today's *rancheros* proceed at once with the sport and fiesta phase of the visit, immediately upon arrival, there being no actual roundup work to do, even if the riders were so inclined. Rodeo sports consist of roping goats, bulldogging calves, and playing polo with broomsticks and tennis balls. After several days' riding, the cavalcade arrives at the Santa Inés Mission, where they are given a benediction by the friars. The climax is a final fiesta given by the Native Daughters of the Golden West.

Although stressing good-fellowship and healthy recreation, the *Visitadores* sincerely have wished to emulate, in some concrete form, the unselfish service of their predecessors. This desire is being realized, in part, by the acquisition and restoration of the Covarrúbias and "Historic" adobes (*see Points of Interest*). One of these adobes is now used as a museum and serves as general headquarters of the organization. Other valuable civic objectives in memory of the colorful past are planned for the future.

The original group of sixty-five has grown steadily until, at present, more than five hundred members and their guests comprise the annual cavalcade. Thus, although the limitless cattle ranges are no more, and the dashing *vaqueros* of other days have been sleeping these many years, they are not forgotten. When spring flings her gay colors over the hills and valleys in the years which lie ahead, the *Rancheros Visitadores* will ride with them again—in spirit—down the old trails of the Santa Ynez.

High light of the summer yachting season is the *Semana Náutica,* or nautical week, third of Santa Barbara's colorful celebrations. Usually this begins on July 4th and ends with an immense fireworks display on the night of July 7th. Open to public participation are sailboat and outboard-motor races, street dances, aquatic sports, tournaments, and a parade of the flotilla.

Vessels of the United States Navy participate in the gala event. In recent years, as many as five battleships with a complement of more than five thousand officers and men have honored a single nautical week. At least one warship, open to visitors, is anchored offshore each year. Navy officers and their wives are feted with teas, dinners, and balls. The *Rancheros Visitadores,* in honor of the officers, hold a primitive barbecue at the Juan y Lolita Rancho, owned by Lieutenant Commander John J. Mitchell, U.S.N.R., and the only *presidente* the organization ever has had. Nor does Santa Barbara overlook the enlisted men; every form of recreation and entertainment is arranged for their benefit.

Climaxing the festivities is a spectacular illuminated marine pageant, followed by a dance in the huge new Santa Barbara armory. This celebration is devoted entirely to hospitality, pleasure, and marine sports; business takes second place, and the carnival spirit reigns.

Santa Barbara is not always in the throes of a gigantic civic celebration. But there is no closed season for pleasure seekers, and every day in the year finds a surprising number of visitors enjoying quietly the peace and relaxation that are so great a part of Santa Barbara's charm.

Part 3

Points of Interest and Tours

Points of Interest

1. SANTA BARBARA COUNTY COURTHOUSE (*open 9-5 Mon.-Fri.; 9-12 Sat.*), bounded by Anacapa, Santa Barbara, Anapamu, and Figueroa Sts., is a two-story, white-stucco structure, built in a spacious U about a large sunken garden reached through a giant archway which opens on Anacapa Street.

The courthouse, with its towers, loggias, exterior stairways, balconies, grillwork, and gardens, is one of the most exotic public buildings in the nation. Reflected in its architecture are the sentiment and tradition associated with the city's past. Its design is regarded as the ultimate achievement of that community expression which, since the 1925 earthquake, has brought about rebuilding of the city with harmonizing Mediterranean and California type structures.

The Anacapa Arch, facing Anacapa Street, is considered the most impressive of the courthouse's several entrances. Its height and width are enhanced by heavy stone facings. Adjoining the arch, the *mirador* (Sp., observatory), a clock tower with an observation balcony, rises seventy feet above ground level. On one side of the arch is the Hall of Records, on the other, the main building housing offices, courts, Board of Supervisors' assembly hall, and the county clerk's quarters. Between is the Service Building. All are connected by a bridge.

The supervisors' hall, which is furnished with seats and desks of carved oak covered with leather and studded with large brass nails, is decorated with murals painted by Dan Sayre Groesbeck. They depict the arrival of Cabrillo in 1542, building of the Santa Bárbara Mission, coming of the Americans, etc. Other rooms and offices of the courthouse are furnished and decorated in Spanish style. Much tile and mosaic is used in corridors, galleries, and stairways.

The building was designed by William Mooser. It was completed and dedicated in 1929. The cost was almost one and a half million dollars.

SANTA BARBARA HISTORICAL SOCIETY MUSEUM (*open 2-4 Mon.; free*), in the courthouse tower, contains among its relics what is alleged to be the *cañón perdido* (Sp., lost cannon), which gave its name to a Santa Barbara street. It was the cause of events memorialized in two other street names and symbolically pictured in the design of the city seal. The American brig *Elizabeth* was wrecked near Santa Barbara in the winter of 1847-48. Among the articles salvaged was a small brass cannon, useless because its carriage was missing. It was left on the beach after everything else had been removed, and lay there for six months. One morning it was missing. According to some accounts, a band of *Barbareños* made off with it in the night and buried it in the sands of the *estero* (estuary), the mouth of Mission Creek, east of the present pier. The commander of the army post at Santa Barbara, one Captain Lippett, was known as a highly excitable man. He believed not only that the *Barbareños* had taken the cannon, but also that they were planning a revolt, and intended to use the gun against the Americans. When the *Barbareños* did not deliver the cannon at his order, he immediately dispatched a hysterical account of the situation to Colonel Richard B. Mason, military governor at Monterey, not stopping to take up the matter beforehand with his superior officer, Colonel J. D. Stevenson. Governor Mason took Captain Lippett at his word and at once levied a military tax of $500 on the town, to be collected through an assessment of $2 on every male citizen more than twenty years of age. He dispatched Colonel Stevenson to Santa Barbara to collect the tax, and upon his arrival the colonel conferred with Don Pablo de la Guerra, an influential citizen who thoroughly understood the temperament of the native people. At Don Pablo's suggestion, the colonel collected the tax to the soothing strains of the regimental brass band brought to town for the occasion.

Soon thereafter, Governor Mason, who may have begun to feel that Captain Lippett had undue cause for alarm at the disappearance of the cannon, ordered the $500 turned over to the little city to be used in building a jail. What actually became of the money from that point is more of a mystery than the true fate of the *cañón perdido*. Some sources say that the native officials refused the money and that it was at length given to the American authorities in the city for building the jail. According to another account, the prefect of the pueblo of Santa Barbara, a native *Barbareño,* accepted the money from the governor but would not give it up when his office was supplanted by the newly formed city council. The prefect reminded them that the money had been entrusted to him for the building of a city jail, and declared that until the jail was built he would not release the money. Acting in faith, the city then built the jail, and once more asked for the $500. But the prefect still withheld it, this time on rather obscure grounds. Some reports are that the money had disappeared over the gaming table in an effort to increase it to a sum considered sufficient for jail building. The city council proceeded to bring suit to recover the money, and because it was a well-known fact that the former prefect and the judge of the district were relatives, the case was heard in San Francisco. In some unaccountable way, the papers in the case were lost, and the whole litigation lapsed. Santa Barbara had nothing to show for all its trouble except a new city calaboose and a growing stock of legends about the $500 and the *cañón perdido*.

In 1850, a survey of the city was made and three streets were given names commemorating the affair: *Quinientos* (five hundred) Street, *Cañón Perdido* Street, and Mason Street (after the governor). In a last gesture of fine *Californiano* humor, the council chose a design for the city seal showing a cannon statant encircled by the words *"Vale Quinientos Pesos"* (Good-by Five Hundred Dollars).

Then ten years later, the cannon turned up again. On a stormy night, Mission Creek became a raging flood and swept away some of the estuary banks, cutting a new channel and thereby disclosing the long-lost cannon. It was hauled up State Street to the Cañón Perdido Street intersection, where it stood for some time on an improvised carriage. Then again its history became blurred. It was sold to a junk dealer for $80, and there are those who say it met its end in a San Francisco brass-foundry furnace, but other sources are equally confident that the cannon now at the head of the museum's winding stairway is the original, genuine *cañón perdido*.

Other displays in the museum are a collection of Indian relics and artifacts, and saddles and branding irons from Spanish, Mexican, and early American ranching periods.

2. SANTA BARBARA PUBLIC LIBRARY (*open 9-9 weekdays; 2-5 Sun.*), SW. corner Anapamu and Anacapa Sts., is a Spanish-Renaissance structure of one and one-half stories with an ornate, arched entrance. Over the door is a polychromed wood carving, bearing the city's coat of arms. The central device is surrounded by shields of four famous libraries: Italy's University of Bologna, Paris' Bibliothèque Nationale, Spain's University of Salamanca, and Oxford's Bodleian Library. Within the building are an open reading court and a large reading room.

The building is a restoration by Carleton M. Winslow, who designed the overdoor decoration. Original architects of the structure, built in 1917, were Francis W. Wilson and Henry Hornbostel of New York. The building was damaged by the 1925 earthquake.

The library was incorporated in 1882, and since 1910 has extended its services throughout the county in twenty-two community and forty-six school branches. The book collection is 133,000 volumes.

FAULKNER MEMORIAL ART GALLERY (*open 10-5 Mon., Thurs.; 9-9 Tues., Wed., Fri., Sat.; 2-5 Sun.*), a wing of the library building, contains two top-lighted galleries for exhibition of paintings and prints. The choice and hanging of visiting exhibitions are under supervision of a committee of local artists appointed by the Library Board.

The gallery wing was given by Mrs. William P. Gould in memory of her sisters, the Misses Anne, Abby, and Emily Faulkner, and was designed by Myron Hunt and H. C. Chambers, Los Angeles architects, to harmonize with the main building. It was dedicated in 1930.

3. On the SITE OF THE CASA DE AGUIRRE are the Mihran Studio Building and the Little Town Club, 17-21 E. Carrillo St. Don José Antonio de Aguirre, a wealthy Spanish-French merchant and shipowner, built the original *casa* (Sp., house) in 1841 for his bride-to-be. It was built of adobe, with a score of apartments arranged in a quadrangle around a paved patio. Its wide corridor-roof was supported on hand-carved posts. It was a contemporary of the near-by Carrillo Adobe, and ranked among the most famous of the Spanish-California homes of that day.

4. CARRILLO ADOBE (*open 9-5 weekdays*), 15 E. Carrillo St., a one-story dwelling of thick, tan-gray adobe walls, with a long, red-brick-paved piazza across the front, was built about 1828 by Daniel Hill, who gave it the first wooden floor used in town. The house was the birthplace in 1833 of Isabel Larkin, first child born in California of parents who were both Americans. In the 1840's the house was conveyed to Captain John D. Wilson. The charm and graciousness of his Spanish wife, Ramona, placed it among the glamorous and well-loved early California homesteads which welcomed many a pioneering stranger from the United States. Doña Ramona's son by a former marriage, Romualdo Pacheco, became a governor of California after it was admitted to the Union.

Some time in the 1860's the house came in possession of Guillermo and Joaquín Carrillo, cousins and brothers-in-law. It is said that the adobe was frequently the meeting place of the Santa Barbara City Council in the 1850's, Don Joaquín having granted free use of one of his rooms for its sessions.

Major Max C. Fleischmann acquired the property in recent years and gave it to the Santa Barbara Foundation to be preserved as a landmark. The organization uses it as its headquarters. Most of the original structure remains, and additions have been made at the rear of the house.

5. FEDERAL BUILDING (*open 8-6 Mon. to Fri.; 8-1 Sat.; lobby always open*), SE. corner Anacapa and E. Canon Perdido Sts., a two-story reinforced-concrete structure of modified California design, is one of the rare instances in which the United States Post Office Department defers to local architectural trends and deviates from its

predilection for classical lines. With its low-ground-floor walls, a second-story setback overlooking the sloping, brown, shingle-tile roof of the first story, and small roofed wings projecting at either end, the exterior is in harmony with the city's predominant architectural style (*see Human Side of a City*). The architect was Reginald D. Johnson, designer of the Santa Barbara Biltmore Hotel and several Montecito homes. The building was dedicated in 1937. It occupies land once a portion of the Spanish presidio grounds, and adjoining it is one of the original presidio buildings.

6. Abutting the east patio wall of the Federal Building is EL CUARTEL (Sp., the barracks), 122 E. Canon Perdido St., the oldest adobe in Santa Barbara. It was erected on the presidio grounds by Captain Francisco de Ortega in the 1780's. The little building, a one-story, two-roomed structure with a red-tiled roof, is shut off from the street by a six-foot-high wall, and further hidden by the semitropical trees and shrubbery of a tiny patio. The building's eastern section is a few inches lower than the western. Expert appraisers of early-California architecture consider El Cuartel an excellent example of adobe construction.

All traces of the first buildings erected in the presidio when it was established in 1782 have disappeared. The larger structures, of which El Cuartel was a part, were built around a courtyard 80 yards square. A false door, 9 feet wide and roofed over, was probably intended to mislead attackers; the actual entrance was 12 feet wide. The buildings included the quarters of the commander—a four-room suite, a kitchen, a *despensa* (storeroom), and corral; the quarters of the *alférez* (second lieutenant)—a 3-room suite, kitchen, *despensa* and corral; the chaplain's 2 rooms and corral; church and sacristy; sergeant's house; guardroom and barracks; 33 family houses, 2 extra *despensas* and an additional corral. The soldiers' wages were paid in grain grown at the presidio. A small iron cannon, 2 brass pieces and a brass 6-pounder constituted the armaments of this military outpost, which had jurisdiction over Los Angeles during that city's infancy. In Santa Barbara's pueblo days, after California had come under Mexican rule, *El Cuartel* was used as the *cárcel* (jail).

7. LOBERO THEATER, 33 E. Canon Perdido St., is a white concrete structure rising in 3 tiers from a 1-story, tile-roofed, arcaded entrance foyer on the Canon Perdido Street façade. The auditorium is a 2-story-height section, and the stage unit behind it is 5 stories high. The building is an adaptation of the Spanish-California style. It was designed by George Washington Smith, Santa Barbara architect, and erected in 1924 by the Community Arts Association.

Once it produced amateur community plays exclusively, but now its repertoire consists principally of foreign films, legitimate dramas and concerts, with occasional community presentations.

The playhouse is named for José Lobero, who opened the original Lobero Theater in 1872 (*see Human Side of a City*). Lobero, an Italian musician who became a tavernkeeper, lost the fortune made in the 1860's and 1870's, by sponsoring grand operas and local-talent musical plays. A surviving feature from the old theater is its Ship Curtain, dated 1869, which is supposed to have been painted in the east for the Maguire Opera House of San Francisco. Shortly after the curtain's arrival in San Francisco, however, the Maguire Theater was razed and the curtain was then obtained by Lobero for his new theater. The curtain shows a view of San Francisco Bay, with the clipper ship *Western Continent* being towed into the wind by a tug, and is considered a masterpiece of scenic painting of the middle nineteenth century. It is still hanging in the Lobero Theater, but not on display.

8. Market buildings now stand on the SITE OF THE THOMPSON HOUSE, 809 State Street, where the Stars and Stripes were raised over Santa Bárbara by Lieutenant Colonel John C. Frémont two days after Christmas in 1846. Frémont and his ragged troops, who had spent Christmas Day in a hazardous descent from the summit of storm-lashed San Marcos Pass (*see Tour 2*), entered the tranquil little channel town while its inhabitants were at morning Mass and, without bloodshed, took possession for the United States. Frémont established his headquarters at the home of Captain Alpheus B. Thompson, an early-American resident of Santa Bárbara, and put his soldiers up in tents in front of the house. The national ensign was run up on a pole before the tents every day.

The Thompson house was a hip-roofed, adobe-walled, two-story pillared structure bearing a wooden-railed balcony or piazza which extended continuously about its four sides at the second-story level. Captain Thompson built it in 1835 for his wife, Doña Francisca, one of the Carrillo daughters. After the Thompsons' time, the house became the St. Charles Hotel for many years. It was the last adobe on State Street, but the present passion for preserving historical landmarks came too late to save it. In 1929, the Native Sons of the Golden West affixed a bronze marker to the wall of the market building erected on its site. The plaque bears an embossed reproduction of the old house.

EL PASEO (Sp., the promenade), bounded by State, De la Guerra, Anacapa, and Canon Perdido Sts., is a block of distinctive little shops, studios, and offices in Spanish-type structures arranged about shaded patios and passageways. The buildings have red-tiled roofs, hand-hewn wooden balconies, casement windows, wrought-iron grilles, and tiled stairways. Art objects and craftwork are sold at the edges of miniature plazas shaded by acacias, eucalypti, and fruited orange trees. The little Street of Spain, which goes into El Paseo from De la Guerra Street, is stone paved.

El Paseo and its structures were designed by James Osborne Craig for Bernard Hoffman, who began the work in 1923, at the time he was starting the restoration of the Casa de la Guerra.

9. Enclosing the south side of El Paseo stands the 122-year-old CASA DE LA GUERRA (Sp., de la Guerra House), 15 E. De la Guerra St. (*adm. by application*), built with Indian labor by Don José

Antonio de la Guerra y Noriega, fifth *comandante* of the Spanish presidio. The *comandante* and his wife, a daughter of the Carrillo family, were the social arbiters of Santa Barbara for more than three decades. The big U-shaped house, which was eight or nine years a-building, stands with its back against El Paseo, and faces De la Guerra Plaza across a sleepy patio garden. A wide, tile-paved piazza with a tile roof supported on square wooden posts extends around three sides. One of the adobe bricks of the front corridor bears the date 1826, the year the building was supposedly completed. The ceiling beams, however, did not reach Santa Bárbara until 1827. They were carried to port in a ship of the French navigator, Duhaut-Cilly.

The east wing of the house is now the residence of Miss Delfina de la Guerra, a descendant of Don José Antonio. The spacious chambers of the north and west sections are partitioned into shops and studios. *La bodega* (the wine cellar), now an art shop, is in the northwest corner. The rear patio is occupied by the shops and courtyards of El Paseo. In Don José Antonio's day it was surrounded by buildings which included a great oven larger than an ordinary room; a flour mill; a two-story building for storing supplies bought from sailing ships; a carriage shed; and the *bodega,* in which not only wine, but potatoes and olives, were stored.

Don José Antonio was *comandante* of the presidio between 1815 and 1839. He was one of the post's most influential commanders, and after leaving office retained an authoritative and respected place in the community, although his Castilian birth cast a slight shade of prejudice against him after Mexican rule set in.

In 1836 and again in 1859, the year following Don José Antonio's death, the author, Richard Henry Dana, was a guest in the *casa,* and in his famous *Two Years Before the Mast* he described the festivities and graciousness of the De la Guerra household.

10. OREÑA ADOBE (*open 8-6 daily; 9-12 Sat.*), 27-29 E. De la Guerra St., is the central unit of a three-building structure housing business offices, studios, and an antique shop. The house, which in its early days stood alone and is still a fundamentally independent structure, was built by Don Gaspar Oreña in 1849, shortly after the beginning of the American regime. The building on the right is said to have been one of the structures belonging to the De la Guerra family. An Oreña descendant has bought it within recent years and a door connecting it with the Oreña Adobe has been cut in the side wall. The aperture between the Oreña house and the building on the left, a brick structure with an asphalt shingle roof and tall French windows, has been plastered over lately.

11. The two-story concrete CITY HALL, SE. corner E. De la Guerra St. and De la Guerra Plaza (between State and Anacapa Sts.), is one of the few public buildings in Santa Barbara which survived the 1925 earthquake. The modified Spanish design blends harmoniously with the uniform architecture of the city's post-earthquake buildings. A wide arcade along the lower part of the façade is surmounted by a

balcony across the upper central section. An ancient pepper tree and shrubbery shade the front of the building. It faces west across De la Guerra Plaza, a public square set aside in 1855 by the city council, before that body had a hall of its own in which to hold sessions.

12. The Neighborhood House, 800 Santa Barbara St., occupies the SITE OF THE ARRELLANES ADOBE, built by Don Teodoro Arrellanes in 1795, scarcely a dozen years after the *presidio* had been established. It was the first home of consequence built outside the *presidio* grounds. The adobe was destroyed in the 1925 earthquake, but seven carved wooden porch pillars, brought around Cape Horn in a sailing vessel in 1800 and added to the house when the porch was built, were saved from the ruins and incorporated in the piazza of the Neighborhood House (a community social service center).

13. The so-called "HISTORIC" ADOBE, 715 Santa Barbara St., a one-story, five-room house, was built about 1836 near State and Carrillo Streets and moved to the present site in 1922 to make way for the erection of a modern structure on the original site. It was built for Concepción Pico de Carrillo, sister of Pío Pico, one of California's Mexican governors. It has not been determined whether this or the Covarrúbias Adobe was the meeting place of the last congress under Mexican rule in California. The congress was held in 1846 and conducted by Governor Pico. The 1925 earthquake, which destroyed many of Santa Barbara's biggest and newest buildings, did no damage to the "Historic" Adobe. It is now used as a historical museum and is filled with early California relics.

14. COVARRÚBIAS ADOBE, ten feet south of the "Historic" Adobe, is a big L-shaped house, one of the two adobes said to be the meeting place of the last Mexican Congress. The house was built in 1817 by Don Domínguez Carrillo. It has four lofty, spacious rooms, and its *gran sala* (Sp., great room, parlor) is fifty-five feet long. Tar paper replaces tiles which covered the roof originally, but the beams, rafters, and adobe walls remain. Only one of the three massive buttresses at the south wall is the original; the others, of burnt brick, were built later.

Don José María Covarrúbias came in possession of the house in 1847, and it was his home thereafter for about fifty years. Don José went east in 1852 to deliver the State's first electoral vote—for Franklin Pierce, fourteenth President of the United States. It was said that when Covarrúbias arrived at the New York port, all of Tammany Hall was there to welcome him, and he spent $10,000 for wine and dinner parties on the visit.

The old house is now the headquarters of *Los Rancheros Visitadores* (*see Fiesta Land*), who purchased and are now (1941) restoring both this and the neighboring "Historic" Adobe.

15. THE NATIONAL GUARD ARMORY, 700 E. De la Guerra St., is housed in tile-roofed, one- and two-story buildings of white concrete, dominated by a square tower rising left of the great arched entrance. It is designed according to War Department specifi-

cations for armory buildings, but modified in exterior lines to conform to the architectural standard of the city. Edwards and Plunkett designed the structure, which was built by the Works Progress Administration in 1938 at an approximate cost of $165,000. The land, which consists of an entire block, was donated by the city. A flood-lighted parade ground is on the property. The spacious armory floor where the guardsmen engage in their weekly drills is also used for dances and various athletic games. The armory houses the Second Battalion of the 144th Field Artillery, California National Guard.

16. SAILORS' SYCAMORE, NW. corner of Quinientos and Milpas Sts., is an aged and failing tree which in its prime was used by sailing-ship captains to take their bearings when bringing their vessels into the port of Santa Bárbara. It was a landmark visible for many miles along *El Camino Real* (Sp., the royal highway) in the mission-founding era. Its age is estimated at five hundred years. The city park department is undertaking (1940) an experiment in which sycamore saplings planted at the old tree's base will be topped and grafted into the ancient trunk after their roots have become well developed. Tree surgeons in charge of the experiment hope to save the life of the patriarch by thus giving it a new root system.

ANDRÉE CLARK BIRD REFUGE (*always open*), E. end of Cabrillo Blvd., is a 49½-acre municipal wild-fowl preserve created on reclaimed salt marsh land. On an island-tufted lake paralleling the boulevard, geese, ducks, swans, and other water birds live. A bridle path encircles the lake and a parking place (*free*) is on the east shore. At the northwest corner of the Bird Refuge, on the adjoining property and conveniently near the Southern Pacific right-of-way, are the HOBO JUNGLES where itinerants cook and sleep in the open as the guests of Mrs. John H. Child, whose wooded, landscaped hills rise along the western borders of the park. The "knights of the road" have made Mrs. Child's benevolence known among their fellows throughout the country.

South of the Bird Refuge is the estate of Mrs. Anna E. Clark—widow of William A. Clark, former Senator from Montana—who gave the land and money for the Bird Refuge.

CABRILLO BOULEVARD extends westward from the Bird Refuge, following the gentle inward curve of the shore to the harbor. PALM PARK extends along the seaward edge from the bathing pavilion at East Beach, east of the junction of Cabrillo Boulevard and the foot of Milpas Street, to the wharf at the foot of State Street. It is a palm grove with lawn, picnic tables, and seats.

17. Standing in Palm Park is the CABRILLO MONUMENT, four blocks east of the junction with Milpas Street and Cabrillo Boulevard, or midway between that and the wharf at the foot of State Street; it is a large sandstone boulder with a bronze tablet marking the spot on which Juan Rodríguez Cabrillo, first mariner to sail the waters of the northern California coast, is supposed to have landed in 1542. There is nothing in Cabrillo's log to indicate that he actually went ashore here.

The yacht-dotted waters of SANTA BARBARA HARBOR, west from Stearns Wharf at the foot of State Street, lie behind the sheltering arm of a long stone breakwater projecting from the shore east of Castle Rock Bluff, on which the earliest *Barbareños* built a stone fortress to guard their landing place against the invasion of pirates.

If it is true that ghosts of long-extinct craft return to haunt former anchorage, the trim pleasure boats bobbing in Santa Barbara Harbor today rub sides with puffing paddle-wheelers, tall-sailed Yankee clippers, Spanish caravels, matting-sailed junks, plank canoes chinked with native asphalt, and pitch-daubed boats made of hides or tule stalks. Hundreds of years before the Spanish explorers came, the harbor—nothing more than a lovely curve in the coast line—offered a sheltered spot for the ingenious plank canoes of the *Canaliños,* and ages before them, the tule-stalk rafts of more primitive Indian aborigines. Nobody knows how often a crew of frightened, almond-eyed sailors may have nosed a tub-like junk into the harbor with sighs of relief, but China's most ancient manuscripts hint of more than one unplanned trans-Pacific voyage made by crafts caught in the grip of the powerful Japanese current.

It was not until long after its discovery nearly 400 years ago by Cabrillo that the harbor of Santa Barbara really became a harbor. All during the early history as the port of the pueblo of Santa Bárbara, it was merely a landing place, and in the season of the "southeasters" every ship rode the swells beyond the kelp beds with slip-chains on its anchors, ready to sail if a blow came, and ride out the storm in the lee of Santa Rosa Island. Traders and travelers were brought ashore from ships by surfboats and carried to dry land on the backs of sailors until 1865. In that year movements to build a wharf finally came to a head in the formation of the *Compañía del Muelle de Santa Bárbara* (Sp., Santa Barbara Wharf Company) by a group of early-American and British civic leaders. The wharf they built, which extended from the foot of Chapala Street, was so fragile that no craft of more than a hundred tons dared make fast to it, and seven years later John P. Stearns, a prominent pioneer, built a better wharf at the foot of State Street which served the city until the present modern wharf was built in its place in 1928. This wharf, named for Stearns, was also erected by Santa Barbara civic benefactors, among whom was Major Max C. Fleischmann. He contributed two-thirds of the cost of harbor improvement.

The Breakwater at the harbor's west edge, which extends 1,800 feet from shore in an obtuse-angled L, is designed to shelter 300 yachts. It is 150 feet wide at the bottom and 18 feet wide at the top, along which is a lighted promenade. The jetty is made of Santa Cruz Island rock. Its deflection of ocean currents has caused sand to accumulate along the water front on both sides, increasing the beach area by some seven acres. The rock arm also renders the water off the beach placid and excellent for surf bathing and swimming. The entire area, called West Beach, has been developed as a public beach park and playground.

Just west of the Breakwater, on top of Castle Rock Bluff, circular rock formations mark the SITE OF A SPANISH FORTRESS built between 1780 and 1790 to guard the Santa Barbara roadstead against the invasion of pirates.   Though no records remain to substantiate the fact, the fort is believed to have been erected by soldiers of the Santa Bárbara *Presidio*.   History does not record any military engagement calling forth broadsides of cannon balls from this mesa fortress, or of any buccaneers having entered the roadstead in defiance of it, but evidence of its existence arouses romantic conjectures of stirring scenes in the days when the pirate Hippolyte de Bouchard and his cutlass-bearing contemporaries landed at different points along this coast to sack and burn *haciendas* (estates) of the Spanish *rancheros*.   Castle Rock used to project from the coast line, but in the interest of public safety it was shorn level with the bluff several years ago.   One of the cannon formerly used in the old fortress stands on the lawn of T. Wilson Dibblee, 2232 Santa Barbara Street, former owner of the ocean-front property which includes Castle Rock.

North and west of Castle Rock and West Beach is the new 43-acre campus under development for the Santa Barbara State College.   An athletic stadium is among the improvements already made on the new site.

BURTON MOUND, encircled by Burton Dr., is a little knoll rising in the middle of the area of residential drives and homes bounded by Yanonali, Chapala, Mason, and Bath Sts.   Nothing about its appearance today indicates its history, but beneath its surface archeologists have found evidence that three distinct Indian cultures, the earliest extending into antiquity, have existed on the site.

At the foot of the mound, where today Chapala Street and Cabrillo Boulevard meet, was the old Puerto de Santa Bárbara, landing place for the mission and presidio.   The land was then owned by the mission, but after secularization it was granted by the Mexican government to James Burke, an American settler.   He sold it to Joseph Chapman, young American.   Chapman conveyed the land to Benjamin Foxen, the English *ranchero* who showed Lieutenant Colonel John C. Frémont the path through San Marcos Pass (*see Tour 2*).   The property continued to pass from hand to hand through the years, and one of the owners— some sources say Chapman—built a massive adobe on the knoll some time before the 1840's.   The dwelling stood on the mound for seventy years, the most conspicuous landmark on the Santa Barbara water front.   During the tenancy of one of its occupants, Lewis T. (Don Luis) Burton, who died in the house in 1879, it came to be known as the Burton Adobe.   Later the knoll was called Burton Mound after the house.   By the turn of the century, the old house was gone, and in 1901 the Potter Hotel was built on the mound.   Landscaped gardens covered the site of the ancient Indian villages.   In 1921, the hotel, then known as the Ambassador, burned down, and the site was released for archeological investigation.   In 1923, the excavations revealing the existence of the Indian cultures were made by the Museum of the American Indian, Heye Foundation, of New York.

Evidences were that the last village had covered the entire knoll and spread to fringes of the marsh then surrounding it. It had clustered about a fresh-water spring on the eastern slope, one of many sweet and sulphur water springs on the mound and around it. A huge cemetery covered the southwestern slope. Artifacts and utensils from the mound show that the later inhabitants took a great deal of pride in making articles of perfection and beauty. Buttons from Spanish uniforms, glass beads from Venice, and old liquor bottles marked the arrival of the invading whites.

18. At Chapala and Montecito Sts. stands the huge and beautiful MORETON BAY FIG TREE affectionately called "the old rubber tree" by Santa Barbarans who have known it since its youth. It is now sixty-three years old, and its measurements (height 62 ft.; branch spread 135 ft.) surpass those of other trees of its kind in the State. The city engineering department estimates that the branches cover an area of 12,712 square feet, and that 9,500 persons can stand under the tree's shade at noon. The tree's size compares favorably with the best specimens of Moreton Bay, in eastern Australia, where the species originated. The Santa Barbara tree is apparently watered by underground springs. Part of one of its roots is visible in a wall 120 feet southwest of the trunk.

The tree yields neither edible fruit nor rubber, but it is related to the trees which produce the market fig and to those which produce rubber commercially. Also, it is akin to the Banyan tree. The large, leathery, shining green leaves of the Moreton Bay Fig are very like those of its popular relative, the rubber plant, sometimes called the rubber fig. This is the plant that grew in pots in hotel lobbies in the early part of the century, and still enjoys favor with many.

19. SANSUM CLINIC, 317 W. Pueblo St., is housed in a separate unit of the Cottage Hospital, which stands directly across the street. It is the headquarters of Dr. William David Sansum and his staff, specialists in the diagnosis and treatment of stomach ulcers and diabetic ailments. Dr. Sansum's clinic, which was originally housed in the main building of the Cottage Hospital, was the first diabetic clinic in the United States. In 1935, he and his associates began using an improved insulin compound in the treatment of *diabetes mellitus,* commonly called sugar diabetes.

The hormone called insulin is a secretion of certain cells in the pancreas (a large gland placed behind the stomach in man, and present in all mammals and fish). This hormone promotes utilization of sugar in the body, and failure of the secretion causes loss of control of the utilization of the sugar, so that the condition known as *diabetes mellitus* exists. Excessive hunger, thirst, and progressive emaciation attend the disease, and if not successfully treated, death usually results. Existence of the hormone has been known since 1889, but it was not isolated until 1921. In that year Dr. F. C. Banting, who was working with Dr.

C. H. Best under the direction of Dr. J. J. R. MacLeod at the University of Toronto in Canada, discovered insulin—the hormone—in extracts of partially degenerated pancreas. The first use of the insulin compound they made for treating diabetes was in the case of a Toronto boy in 1922.

20. SANTA BARBARA MISSION is distinguished by the twin bell-towers of its church from its sister missions up and down the State, which have single-towered churches. Architecturally it is the finest and most graceful of the missions, and in its regal position overlooking the evolving town on the plain below, it came to be called Queen of the Missions. The façade of the church, flanked by the square, three-tiered towers, is chastely ornamented by six slender engaged columns of modified Ionic order; these are surmounted by a pediment bearing three seated figures and, in the tympanum, a niched sandstone figure of Saint Barbara. Above the pediment is a stepped gable cresting supporting a cross. Design of the entire façade is based on details of the classic Ionic order as illustrated in an old Spanish edition of a volume of the Roman architect Vitruvius, which was among the mission properties, and which still reposes in the mission's library. In designing the church, Padre Ripoll modified the Ionic details with a blend of Spanish and Moorish architectural features. The six-foot-thick walls, of dressed stone and mortar, are painted ivory. The broad-stepped stone platform across the church front is that which stood before the entrance of the original church built on the site. (The present edifice was built in 1815.)

The arched entrance is deeply recessed and has double-paneled doors. The interior of the long narrow nave is finished in plaster and has small splayed windows in the side walls. Ionic pilasters painted in imitation of veined marble are surmounted by a painted dentil cornice. The flat wooden ceiling is embellished with painted and carved rosettes. The original statues of the saints brought from Mexico by the first padres, and the stations of the cross which came later, in 1797, still stand in place in the church.

This is the only California mission in which the altar light has never been extinguished since the founding. The main altar in the present church is screened by a painted and paneled reredos with Roman Doric columns. On the Epistle side is the tomb of Father Francisco García Diego y Moreno, first Bishop of California. In a vault under the sanctuary is the body of José Figueroa, fifth Mexican governor of California.

Near the center of the nave are two small doors set opposite each other in the side walls; that on the right opens to the cemetery where the bodies of 4,000 Indians and 500 whites are buried in graves under the shade of bamboo, willow, cypress, palm, and olive trees. Old Spanish-California names are cut above the stone slab entrances to the burial vaults. A large crucifix of pale wood stands against a dark cypress bower. In a vault with the bodies of other mission padres is that of

Father Sánchez, the "Father Salvierderra" of Helen Hunt Jackson's romantic California novel *Ramona*.

The door on the left side of the church opens on the Sacred Garden, a patio about which the U of the monastery combines with the church wall to form an enclosure. Admission to the garden is denied most men from the outside world, and all women except visiting royalty and the wife of the President of the United States. In the court hangs a bell which is rung for the hours of daily offices and for secular duties. When a friar dies, the attending brother immediately strikes this bell.

Old relics and treasures of the early days of the mission are in the cloisters, the library, and the monastery's curio rooms. Among them are several pages of church music in which the padres printed the notes in various colors to make it easier to teach them to the Indians. Treasured possessions are old paintings which were shipped from Spain and transported across Mexico to California on the backs of pack animals. The canvases still bear creases from their journey. Research is being carried on in an effort to determine whether one of the paintings is Murillo's original *Assumption of the Virgin*.

Beyond orchards and fruit and vegetable gardens in the northwest (rearward) part of the mission's twenty-acre grounds is the new building housing St. Anthony's Seminary. In this college, which was founded in 1901, young men are trained for the Franciscan order. It was included in the formal organization in 1915 of all Franciscan monasteries, convents, and Indian missions of California, Oregon, Washington, and Arizona into one province under the patronage of St. Bárbara.

The mission community is partially self-supporting. Seminary students and friars co-operate in cultivating oranges, lemons, grapes, olives, walnuts, and vegetables in quantities sufficient for half the year. The lives of the friars are substantially the same as those of their predecessors when the mission was young, except that today they conduct more than 25,000 sightseers a year through the church and grounds. All the friars rise at five o'clock in the morning, and after religious service and breakfast, work until noon—some in the kitchen, garden, or shoe shop, some at the business of the parish, and novices at studies in preparation for priesthood. The noonday meal is followed by a rest period, after which work and studies are resumed until dinnertime. A recreation period follows dinner, then the friars study until bedtime at 9:30 p.m. In the old days in California the friars wore gray habits, but in 1897 Pope Leo XIII decreed that brown was thereafter the only official color of the Franciscans' attire. The order was founded by St. Francis of Assisi, an Italian friar, who died in 1226. The friars of the order live a life of self-denial and modest simplicity patterned after and consecrated to the life and tenets of the founder.

Santa Barbara, tenth in the mission chain, was founded in 1786 (*see Presidio to Channel City*). The first structures built on the site were temporary living quarters, storehouses, workshops, and a chapel of poles, clay, and thatch. As in the building of the other missions, these were replaced with tile-roofed adobe structures within the following half-dozen years. Meanwhile the Indian neophyte population increased to more than four hundred. The *Canaliño* Indians, like most of the tribes in the Southwest, led a half-starved, struggling existence in their native condition. When the missions were being built, many of the Indians came willingly into the fold: *atole* (Sp., gruel), *pozole* (Sp., stew), and rations of beef and wheat in the mission fare held urgent appeal. They readily learned the obligatory Christian doctrine in Castilian Spanish and in their own native tongue. They labored in the fields and gardens, tended the stock, helped with building construction and maintenance. Their women did the weaving and other domestic work. Sister missions supplied cattle, sheep, goats, horses, mules, corn, beans, barley, and wheat until Santa Bárbara's own stock of these things could become established.

Within the twenty years following the founding of the mission, construction projects of a scope unusual in mission building were carried out. Two reservoirs, one of them of masonry, and a dam which impounded water that flowed into the other through an aqueduct were built. The masonry reservoir east of the mission was built in 1806. Today it is still in regular use as one of the distributing basins of the municipal water system. The dam was built farther away, up the canyon of Mission Creek. It still stands in what is now the Santa Barbara Botanic Garden. Still in their places on the mission plaza are the octagonal stone fountain built in the twenty-year period, and the washing trough where Indian women knelt and washed their clothes, slapping and pounding the wet garments on the flat stones as they laughed and gossiped in the sunshine. During that period also, the long, arched corridor across the front face of the monastery was erected—primarily for protecting the wall against rain, and incidentally for the sake of beauty.

The earthquake of 1812 interrupted this steady growth. The church, which had been rebuilt once or twice before, was demolished. A new church, which is the one standing today, was built in 1815, apparently over and around the remains of the previous structure.

Completion of the towers several years later was celebrated with days of ceremony and merrymaking. The left tower held six bells of Peruvian and Mexican manufacture, and while they rang, the Indians, soldiers, and settlers feasted and drank. Booths of flower-decked boughs were placed before the doors of the Indian houses, which stood in four long rows running eastward from the mission. Companies of Indians from other missions came, singing and dancing, and the Santa Bárbara neophytes poured seeds upon the ground for their guests to walk upon.

When the Hidalgo revolt broke out in Mexico (1811) the Franciscan College in that country became unable to provide the friars' annual stipends, and the goods on which the missions had depended to a large extent. The pay of the territorial soldiers and mission guards ceased, and they all looked to the mission for support for themselves and their families. The Indians, whose labor produced this support, were abused often by the soldiers. A great unrest grew among the neophytes of the missions, and finally the Indian Revolt of 1824 broke out, following the flogging of two or three neophytes by soldiers at Santa Inés Mission (*see Tour 2*). The Santa Bárbara Indians were coerced by those at Santa Inés, they said, and were afraid not to join in the uprising, but they promised to do no harm if only the soldiers were sent away permanently. The guards prepared to withdraw under the fathers' orders, but the Indians demanded that they surrender their weapons. On refusal of two of the soldiers, the Indians attacked them. The commander of the presidio, Captain José de la Guerra y Noriega, was enraged at this and sent troops to the mission to put down the rebellion, and subsequently several Indians were killed. After the troops went back to the presidio, many of the Indians fled into the hills. That afternoon the troops returned to the mission and, above the protests of the padres, killed the remaining Indians in revenge. Those who had fled retreated farther into the hills and refused to return. After several months of threats and persuasion from padres and presidio officers, and many minor conflicts, the Indians were returned to the mission.

Occasional feasting and gaiety continued to break the monotony of mission life as in the past. An always diverting occasion was the greeting of vessels as they put in to shore, events in which both the mission population and the Santa Bárbara community joined. The settlers wanted rice, sugar, tobacco, knives, calico, and silk mainly; the Indians wanted red handkerchiefs and beads.

Further departures from everyday routine were the religious processions from the church to the beach in times of drought, for the purpose of praying for rain. A figure of the Holy Virgin was carried—ornamented with finery from the chests of everyone in town—and verses were chanted to accompaniment of flutes and violins. The procession was repeated over and over until rain fell.

In the early 1830's the government of Mexico began secularization of the California missions. In the ensuing chaos, the Indian became brutalized with disease, poverty, disorder and—as liquor was freely sold to them—drunkenness. Some of the fathers, heartsick at seeing the work of years in ruin, returned to Mexico.

Within a few years it was apparent even as far distant as Mexico City that the missions were dying. With pledges of financial and other aid from the government, Fr. García Diego y Moreno, California's first bishop, took up his episcopal residence at Santa Bárbara Mission in 1842 and entertained hopes of building a cathedral and palace there, but he died four years later without having received any aid from Mexico and with all hope of cathedral and palace building abandoned.

Meanwhile (1843) Governor Manuel Micheltorena ordered control of the missions returned to the padres, but by that time it was too late to revive the properties. Governor Pico offered Santa Bárbara Mission and its lands for rent to seculars in 1843, retaining the principal building for the bishop and padres.

During the following decade the number of friars dwindled from the 150, who had brought the first civilization to California, to the four stationed at Santa Bárbara. These four sustained themselves with donations, and gifts from benefactors. But no lay brothers entered the fold, and no recruits were available from either California or Mexico. The domestic affairs of the big monastery were neglected from shortage of personnel, and it seemed that the mission community had at last drawn its final breath. In 1852, the four missionaries appealed to heads of the Church in Rome, and the Superiors-General empowered the Commissary-Prefect of the Missions to make Santa Barbara Mission a hospice as prelude to establishment of an apostolic college for the education of novices.

California was now part of the United States, and eventually the mission churches, monasteries, cemeteries, and gardens were returned to the Catholic church, and Santa Barbara Mission received nearly three hundred acres, with a patent signed by Abraham Lincoln in 1865. History of the mission from that year is without notable event until the 1925 earthquake, which demolished much of Santa Barbara and damaged the mission buildings. Their repair was undertaken that same year, and on completion of the restoration in 1927, the mission held the final requirements it needed to be eligible for consecration. Its wooden altar had been replaced by one of stone that was immovably united with the foundation of the building; the building itself was a permanent structure of stone; and the mission church was free of debt. Santa Barbara, the first mission in California to be consecrated, celebrated with a three-day festivity in which the consecration ceremony was held on the first day, a Pontifical High Mass and observation of St. Bárbara's Day on the second, and a Pontifical Requiem Mass on the third.

21. SANTA BARBARA STATE COLLEGE, fronting on Alameda Padre Serra and Lasuen Road, occupies three main buildings and several smaller structures compactly grouped on a fourteen-acre hillside campus overlooking Santa Barbara, Goleta Valley, and the Pacific Ocean. A dominant Spanish-Moorish tone is revealed in the exterior form and pattern of the structures, the majority of which were designed under supervision of George B. McDougall, former State architect (1912-39).

Ranged along Gaucho Road, which traverses the campus from east to west, are Ebbets Hall, the Quad, and the Administration Building. EBBETS HALL, the first on the east end, next to the Alvarado St. corner, is a two-story, cream-colored concrete building of Spanish design. It houses the classrooms, laboratories, and dietetic kitchens of the home economics department, and the school cafeteria. A spacious wing at the northwest corner, designed for home economics students, is known as Practice House. Linked to Ebbets Hall by a covered passageway is the U-shaped, cream-colored QUAD BUILDING, its cloistered walls enclosing three sides of an oblong patio. It is of poured concrete construction, and has facings of dark red brick around the cloisters to the height of the doorways. Both cloister roof and main roof are of red tile. Trumpet vines trail up the cloister columns and pergolas, and an oblong pool reflects boughs of eucalyptus and cypress trees. The building contains classrooms and laboratories of science and art departments, offices of the Associated Students, the Associated Women's clubroom, and the college bookstore.

The two-story ADMINISTRATION BUILDING, L. of the Quad, is of stuccoed concrete and has a second-floor setback with a balcony. It houses the library, auditorium, and offices of the College President, Deans, Registrar, Recorder, and Comptroller. The library includes a collection of Lincolniana and materials of the Civil War and Reconstruction periods. The massive wooden doors of the building's main entrance open into a foyer, with a grand staircase headed by lofty studio windows which look out on the Santa Ynez Mountains.

Behind the Administration Building is the GYMNASIUM, a cream-colored stucco unit, facing east. It is approached by a shallow rise of stairs and a three-arched portico somewhat similar in design to the main entrance of the Quad.

North and west of the gymnasium are the five buildings housing the Industrial Education division of the college. Most of these will be occupied by classes and laboratories of other college departments when the Industrial Education division moves into the new plant now under construction on the future college site northwest of the harbor break-water. The buildings of the Industrial Education division, first unit to be constructed on the new campus, have a total floor space of 70,000 square feet. Among courses offered in this division are: architectural landscaping; drafting and design; radio and electricity; airplane construction and pilot training; transportation; mechanics; building construction; printing; visual education (including cinematography and use of motion pictures as visual aids in public school education); woodworking; machine-shop practice (including manufacture of tools and instruments); stagecraft; painting, decorating, upholstery; industrial chemistry; and industrial science (including principles of air-conditioning and various other aspects of science in their application to industry).

One-story RIDGE HALL, a greenish-black-roofed structure of wide siding painted cream color, stands in conspicuous isolation on a rocky ridge overlooking the two- and one-half-acre athletic field at the far western end of the campus.

Among smaller temporary buildings of bungalow or cottage style are PINE HALL, a low, white-walled, board and batten structure with varnished pine interior decoration, containing general classrooms; and MUSIC HALL, a long stuccoed bungalow built in one- and two-story heights on a hillside, housing music-class practice rooms and offices of instructors.

The college is an outgrowth of the Anna S. C. Blake Normal School founded in 1908. In 1921, a legislative enactment changed the name to State Teachers College of Santa Barbara, and in 1935, by a similar act, the name was changed to Santa Barbara State College. Present enrollment (1940) exceeds 1,800 and all departments of the college are severely crowded. However, the new college plant is designed to accommodate a maximum of 4,000 students. The nucleus of the new tract, which lies on elevated ground sloping to the edge of beautiful West Beach, was purchased in 1932.

22. SANTA BARBARA MUSEUM OF NATURAL HISTORY (*open 9-5 weekdays; 10-5 Sun.*), Puesta del Sol and Mission Canyon Rds., housed in low, white Spanish-type buildings picturesquely grouped in two acres of wooded canyon grounds, exhibits specimens of plant and animal life indigenous to Santa Barbara County, natural habitat groups of animals, and Indian artifacts. It operates departments in anthropology, paleontology, botany, ornithology, mammalogy, and entomology, with collections in each division displayed in a series of communicating exhibit halls. Particularly interesting are the Rogers anthropological collection, a cactus garden with more than 1,000 plant specimens of 350 species, the botanical department collection of 8,000 sheets of pressed flowers, and the Hazard collection of mounted birds and 40,000 birds' eggs. In the new lecture hall, completed in 1938, is a collection of seventeen Indian blankets representing the work of tribes of the southwestern States, Mexico, and Alaska.

Through the museum's department of education, nature classes for children are held, pamphlets on natural history and geology are issued, and weekly natural history programs are broadcast over a Santa Barbara radio station.

The museum is maintained by endowments, gifts and memberships. Its first building was erected in 1922 on land donated by Miss Caroline Hazard.

SANTA BARBARA BOTANIC GARDEN (*open 8-6; free*), 1289 Mission Canyon Rd., is a twenty-five-acre arboretum of plants and trees native to California, and has special sections devoted to species indigenous to Santa Barbara County. Labeled specimens are divided in ten sections and grown in characteristic plant associations, such as desert, mountain, foothill, canyon, and waterside groups. Within each section, individual species are gathered in family groups. The large succulents division is particularly attractive. Purpose of the plantings is to determine the adaptability of the various species to cultivation.

Large and small sandstone rocks of the Eocene period are strewn about the grounds.

The garden was established in 1926 by Mrs. Anna Blaksley Bliss as a memorial to her father, Henry Blaksley. The grounds are owned by the Santa Barbara Museum of Natural History.

23. Below a promontory in the Botanic Garden overlooking the bed of Mission Creek is the OLD MISSION DAM, built in 1807 by Indians under direction of the Franciscan fathers of Santa Bárbara Mission. The Indians were Christianized members of the *Canaliño* tribe living in a village on the hillside above the canyon in which the Botanic Garden now lies. Rock used in the dam, which is 110 feet long, 19 feet high, and 17 feet wide, was taken from near-by deposits. The tiles on its top were made from red soil found in the canyon and fired

in improvised Indian kilns. The mortar is said to have been made from burned sea shells and animal bones recovered from Burton Mound. Parts of the stone aqueduct which carried water from behind the dam to the reservoir of Santa Bárbara Mission still exist along the road leading from the Botanic Garden. Several well-preserved sections of the aqueduct are also standing along the road from the reservoir to the mission grounds. As late as 1912, the reservoir was a serviceable part of the city's water system, and once in recent years, when the supply line of this system was damaged, Santa Barbara turned back to the Old Mission reservoir for emergency water supply.

Tours

The following three tours cover the most frequently visited and most accessible parts of Santa Barbara County on the principal highways within its boundaries—State 1, State 150, and US 101. So that each tour may be taken independently of the others, the starting point of all three is Santa Barbara City Hall, and the mileage figure given at this point is 0 *m.* The mileage figures along the main route of any one tour then accumulate from this starting point, and are given in miles and tenths of miles, thus: "MONTECITO, 4.2 *m.*," (four and two-tenths miles from Santa Barbara City Hall).

Wherever points of interest lie at a distance from the main tour route (which usually follows a numbered State or Federal highway throughout), a side tour is made. The mileage figures on a side tour do not affect those of the main tour, and accumulate only from the point at which the side tour leaves the main route, thus: "CARPINTERIA, 11.3 *m.*, . . . Carpinteria County Park, 0.4 *m.*" (four-tenths mile from Carpinteria). The text of a side tour is printed in small type so that it may be readily identified as such, and eliminated at will from the itinerary without confusing tourists who wish to stay on the main route.

Wherever the road taken on a side tour continues to another junction with the highway on which the main tour is routed, this fact is stated at the end of the side tour. Other side tours must be retraced to the main route.

The mileage on side tours is not included in the total main tour mileage figure given in the introductory material to the tour. To compute the total trip mileage, the mileage of side trips to be taken must be doubled to account for retracing, and added to the main tour total.

The abbreviation R. and L. are used for "right" and "left" in tour directions. Where necessary to avoid confusion with text, they are enclosed in parentheses.

All population figures are those of 1940 U. S. census.

Tour 1

MONTECITO AND THE SOUTH COAST REGION

Santa Barbara—Summerland—Carpinteria—Montecito; 26.5 *m.*
State St., Cabrillo Boulevard, Ánimas Rd., Channel Drive, Olive Mill
Rd., US 101, Linden Avenue, State 150, Sycamore Canyon Road.
Concrete- and asphalt-paved roadbed throughout.

Southern Pacific R.R. parallels route between Santa Barbara and Carpinteria.
All types of accommodations between Santa Barbara and Carpinteria.

This is a short circular tour which goes out along the shore with
its fine beaches, passes the "oil derricks in the sea" at Summerland and
the polo fields and exclusive riding schools on its outskirts, and turns
about at Carpinteria to return to Santa Barbara by a meandering offshore route among the canyons and foothills at the base of the Santa
Ynez Mountains. Magnificent glen-and-hillside estates and the village
center of Montecito are on the return route.

Southwest from Santa Barbara CITY HALL, 0 *m.,* De la Guerra
St. and De la Guerra Plaza, on De La Guerra St. to State St.; L. on
State to Cabrillo Blvd.; L. on Cabrillo Blvd.

Passing the seashore grove called Palm Park and Cabrillo Pavilion at East Beach (*see Points of Interest*), Cabrillo Boulevard bends
inland to follow the curve of a lake, the Andrée Clark Bird Refuge
(L), 2.3 *m.* (*see Points of Interest*).

The junction with Ánimas (Sp., souls) Rd. is at 2.8 *m.* The main
route is R. on this road, past a triangular flower plot in the center
of the intersection.

The shady green of SANTA BARBARA CEMETERY (R) lies along Ánimas Road, which traverses its north side and turns seaward along its east side. The Santa Barbara city boundary line runs along the cemetery's north and west sides, placing the property outside the city limits. Within the cemetery is a Crematorium designed by George Washington Smith, architect of Santa Barbara's Lobero Theater. Murals on the Crematorium's interior walls are by Alfredo Ramos Martinez.

The cemetery lies on land once the burial ground of the ancient Canaliño village of Swetete, which stood on the promontory now occupied by the estate of Mrs. Anna E. Clark, west of the cemetery. As Ánimas Road approaches the oceanside and turns abruptly left, it becomes Channel Drive, which follows the curve of the shore line.

John Percival Jefferson's estate (L) MIRAFLORES (Sp., view of flowers), 3.4 m. (not open), is notable for the residence designed by Reginald D. Johnson, architect of Santa Barbara's Federal Building (see Points of Interest) and the Biltmore Hotel (see below). Johnson's Miraflores house was awarded the American Institute of Architects' exhibition medal for domestic architecture in 1922. The house is characterized by plain wall surfaces relieved by wrought ironwork at windows and balconies, and by concentrated ornament at the main entrance. The grounds of the estate are sometimes included in the annual Garden Tours (see What, Where, When, How), but sightseers are not admitted under other conditions.

The SANTA BARBARA BILTMORE HOTEL (L), 3.8 m., presents to the sea the white concrete faces of its various wings and annexes. The simple design of the building, enriched by the multiplicity of façades and low-pitched tile roofs, allows the appropriate landscaping of the grounds to play an integral part in the total architectural effect. The structure was designed by Reginald D. Johnson, architect of the Miraflores house (see above) and other notable Santa Barbara buildings.

As Channel Drive curves inland (L) upon passing the Biltmore Hotel, it becomes Olive Mill Road.

At 4.4 m. is the junction of Olive Mill Rd. with US 101. Right on US 101, now the main route.

Parallel with the highway along this section are local roads, one on either side, which bear more leisurely traffic. US 101 is known as Coast Highway to residents of the regions through which it passes on its way along the Pacific seaboard from Baja California to Puget Sound.

At 4.9 m. is a junction with San Ysidro Road, which proceeds left 1.1 m. to the village center of MONTECITO (see below).

As the highway achieves the crest of Ortega Hill at 6.2 m., the ocean view expands, and looming above the surf are a few oil derricks on piers, remainders of Summerland's once-famous "oil wells in the sea" (see below).

Backed by scattered frame dwellings, the frame business buildings of SUMMERLAND (32 alt., 300 pop.), 6.8 *m.*, string out on either side of US 101. On the site of Summerland a small settlement called Fenton stood in the 1870's, and was renamed Ortega after the coming of the railroad in 1874. In 1888, that part of the old Ortega Rancho in and around the settlement became the property of H. L. Williams, a Spiritualist, who subdivided his rather extensive holdings as lots, 25 x 60 feet in area, and generously sold them to settlers for only $25 apiece. Williams' spiritualist camp meetings drew many interested people from all over the country. The colony maintined a seance room which was kept always full of flowers. As a rule, these meetings were augmented by feasting and dancing, all of which added a somewhat lively note to the little community scene.

At first, all the newcomers lived in tents, but they soon built homes in the new community. Williams donated land for a school, the Temple, and four parks. He also renamed the old townsite Summerland because of its year-around equable climate.

Throughout the late 80's and the early 90's an occasional shaft was sunk for oil, and in 1895, when the Summerland oil pool was fully exploited, large companies rushed in and reached hungrily into the sea for "black gold." Long wharves with derricks jutting up from them were built over the surf, and the wells were bored deep into the ocean bed. They were the first oil wells ever to be drilled into the ocean, and the railroad, in a drive to popularize rail travel between Los Angeles and Santa Barbara, advertised them with the catch-phrase, "See the Oil Wells in the Sea." The spiritualist colony was shouldered aside by the excitement over oil, but those who sold their land received many times the $25 they had paid for it. Heavy gales have now swept away most of the old piers which supported scores of derricks in the 1920's, but production had already begun to dwindle as early as 1910. Stumps of piers are still visible in the water offshore about Summerland. Several wells with steel derricks supported on concrete offshore abutments draw from a deeper stratum of the subsea pool.

Rolling, cultivated hillsides characterize the landscape southeast of Summerland. On the right the ocean is almost constantly in view, and on the left, beyond stretches of country broken by clumps of various kinds of shade trees, vineyards drape the more distant slopes in mats of green.

Part of the estate of Major Max C. Fleischmann, Santa Barbara civic leader and benefactor, is visible to left at 7.8 *m.* At 8.2 *m.* a column of young eight-foot-high live oaks stands on either side of the highway, memorials to Santa Barbarans who met death in active service in World War I. The columns are continuous to the western boundary of the Fleischmann Polo Field, 8.8 *m.* Beyond this, lemon groves and vegetable fields appear in neat rectangles along the approach to Carpinteria Valley, an important lima bean growing center. English walnuts were among the earliest crops grown in the valley. In the 1880's oranges and lemons were introduced and rapidly supplanted the walnuts. Today enough lemons are grown to keep the valley's two

THE RUIN OF A CLOISTERED CORRIDOR (1900)

MISSION LA PURISIMA CONCEPCION

THE CORRIDOR RESTORED TO ITS ORIGINAL CONDITION (1941)

RUINS OF LA PURISIMA MISSION (PRIOR TO 1935), LOMPOC VALLEY

LA PURISIMA MISSION UNDER RECONSTRUCTION

THE RESTORED CHAPEL, LA PURISIMA MISSION

A CCC WORKER IN LA PURISIMA MISSION WEAVES
TULE STALKS WITH RAWHIDE THONGS, EXACTLY AS
DID THE NEOPHYTES WHEN THE MISSION WAS BUILT

citrus packing plants (*see below*) busy. Two other packing houses in the valley handle the produce of the bean and truck crop growers.

The little Bougainvillea-covered frame houses of CARPINTERIA (Sp., carpenter shop), 12.1 *m.* (11 alt., 1,000 pop.), cluster about the intersection of US 101 and Linden Ave., the wide main street of the town. Modern business buildings of reinforced concrete stand among venerable brick landmarks of the 1870's and 1880's. Carpinteria was established in 1863 as the trading center for the increasing farm population in the surrounding area. Land, which the new city council in Santa Barbara was selling hand over head at rock-bottom prices, was purchased by Carpinteria settlers at twenty-five cents an acre.

The town is still the valley's trading center and farm-produce shipping point. It is named after a Canaliño Indian village which stood in 1769 near the spot where the town lies today. The village was visited in that year by Don Gaspar de Portolá and his expeditionary party. They named it La Carpintería because they had watched the aboriginal "carpenters" building a canoe there (*see Presidio to Channel City*).

The avenues of Carpinteria, which run northeast-southwest between US 101 and the water front, are named for various kinds of trees. Near the northwest corner of US 101 and Walnut Avenue is the THOMAS WARD TORREY PINE, a specimen transplanted from Santa Rosa Island in 1890 and believed to be the largest of its kind (height 96 feet, branch spread 114 feet). It was brought from the island as a seedling and planted in its present location by Thomas W. Ward. When thus artificially propagated in deep, fertile soil, where constant ocean winds do not strike it, the Torrey Pine grows straight and tall. But in its natural habitat on rocky ocean bluffs it is dwarfed and scraggly, and bent far to leeward under the drive of incessant winds. It occurs naturally only in a small area north of San Diego, and on Santa Rosa Island (*see Sierras in the Sea*).

Facing southeast on Palm Avenue, just south of its junction with US 101, is a citrus grove in which stands the GIANT EUGENIA TREE, said to be the largest of its kind in the State (height 76 feet, branch spread 51 feet). It stands about 25 feet off Palm Avenue. This tree (*Eugenia myrtifolia*) is a native of Australia and is known also as the Australian Brush-Cherry. Its fruit resembles small dark-red cranberries and is sometimes made into jelly. The family to which the tree belongs (*Myrtaceae*) is large, and embraces the guava and other genera which bear fruit made into jellies; it also includes the genus *Pimenta* and various yielders of spices (pimento, cloves, allspice). The wood of some varieties of Eugenia is hard, and valuable in manufacturing various articles. The dense, glossy foliage and uniform shape of *E. myrtifolia* make it a handsome ornamental and shade tree for streets, parks and gardens, and it is sometimes trimmed for use in formal gardens, or as a hedge.

Age of the Carpinteria specimen is not known, but seedlings from it were planted along a road from the town to the foothills in 1905 by S. F. Shepard, an early resident. Since *E. myrtifolia* does not begin to bear seeds capable of germination until it is about seven years of age, the Carpenteria Eugenia cannot be less than forty-two years old.

Carpinteria's two lemon packing plants are between Sixth Street and the Southern Pacific Railroad, one and two blocks southeast of Linden Avenue, in the southern part of town. At Sixth Street and Maple Avenue is the Carpinteria Mutual Citrus Association's SUNKIST PACKING PLANT (*open 9-4 Mon.-Thurs. during spring and summer season, infrequently open in fall and winter; free*). One block east of this establishment, at Sixth and Walnut Avenue, is the CARPINTERIA LEMON ASSOCIATION PACKING PLANT (*same conditions of admittance*).

Santa Barbara County's three-million-dollar annual lemon crop is produced on about eight thousand acres, virtually all of which lie in the southern part of the county. Goleta Valley, Hope Ranch (*see Tour 3*) and Carpinteria Valley are the principal centers of production in the region. Lemons are picked at regular intervals the year around, but the heaviest crops come between February and June. The growers do not gather their fruit themselves. All operations from the time the fruit is ready to pick until it is shipped to market are in charge of packing-house managers chosen by the growers through their co-operative organizations.

Lemons are picked by size while most of the fruits are still green in color. Some are tree-ripened when the pickers make their rounds of the orchards about every six weeks, but the best-grade lemons are dark green when cut from the tree. The pickers carry a metal ring of standard size and clip only that fruit which is too large to pass through the ring.

Field boxes of lemons are brought from the groves in trucks and trailers, emptied into the washer at the packing house and given a quick hot bath at 115 degrees Fahrenheit. Soap powder and soda ash clean and disinfect the fruit. Then it is taken on a conveyer belt with rubber fingers to 24 sets of scrubbing brushes, from which it emerges shining clean and dry, to be segregated according to the various stages of ripeness indicated by the color of the rind. Then it rests in curing rooms from a week to three months. Ventilators admitting air through floors and ceilings are closed in the daytime and opened at night. Refrigeration, artificial air-conditioning or other control of temperature is unnecessary in this region, for temperatures do not vary greatly from 56 degrees, or humidity from about 85 per cent. Free circulation of ocean air is ideal for lemon curing.

When the fruit is cured to a bright yellow, it is sent to the packing unit of the plant and separated according to size, which indicates quality. The shape of lemons prevents their being handled entirely mechanically, as oranges are, and therefore more handwork is necessary. Women attend the rotary bins, which are designed to separate the lemons according to size by dropping the smaller ones first and the larger ones last. As in oranges, the best lemons are a uniform large size, and the few oversize and all the undersize are less desirable. After the lemons are packed into boxes, each grade to itself in a box, the lidding machine stamps on the box the number designating the size of the lemons inside, and clamps the lid into place. The boxes are then loaded into freight cars waiting on the railroad siding. Each car holds 406 boxes, and the year's crop fills about 3,500 cars.

In Carpinteria is the junction of US 101 and Linden Ave.

South (R) from US 101 on Linden Ave. 0.5 *m.* to CARPINTERIA BEACH COUNTY PARK (*children's playground, picnic facilities*), a sloping, half-moon-shaped beach facing a small inlet.

At Carpinteria Beach County Park is the junction with a hard-surfaced road; L. here.

At 0.6 *m.,* reposing in a covered enclosure near a small tile-roofed house about 200 yards off the road (L), is the dead trunk of the GREAT CAR-PINTERIA GRAPEVINE about which conflicting stories center and year by year resolve themselves into legend innocently perpetuated as fact. There were at least two, and possibly more than two, "great" Carpinteria grapevines, and the histories of these have become more entangled than the twisting ten-drils of the vines themselves in the days when they covered trellises scores of feet square and bore tons of fruit each year. There were also two such vines in Montecito (*see below*), and all are beginning to be remembered in a hazy way as "The Big Grapevine."

In 1850, a grapevine in Carpinteria was already famous for its size, and it is said that the first election in Santa Barbara County, held in that year, was conducted under the shade of its monster branches. It was cut down and exhibited at the Chicago World's Fair in 1893, seventeen years after one of Montecito's mammoth grapevines was sent to the Philadelphia Centennial Ex-position. But another immense vine remained in Carpinteria to carry on the town's claim to the "largest grapevine in the world." In 1904, it was growing over a trellis more than 100 feet square; in 1913, its trunk had attained a reputed girth of nearly ten feet, and its branches bore six to twelve tons of grapes a year. The vine is said to have been planted in 1846, but a legend ascribes the date of planting of one of the vines to 1809, the year of the birth of so many great men (Lincoln, Darwin, Tennyson, Poe, and others). In 1914 or 1915, the vine was uprooted in a flood precipitated on the valley by a cloudburst, but its trunk was saved. It is supposed by some to be the one now on exhibition within the enclosure, but others believe this to be the relic of the one sent to the World's Fair in 1893.

At 1 *m.* is CARPINTERIA STATE PARK (*camping prohibited; use of picnic facilities 25¢*). Among its provisions for outdoor sport are an ocean fishing pier and an archery range. Within the grounds is a recreation hall, a two-story building of California architecture, equipped for dancing, playing badminton and ping-pong (*25¢ a game*), and other indoor sports.

Southeast of State Park, the road is narrow and very rough, but possible to drive on.

At 1.2 *m.* is the OLD ASPHALT PIT (R), now exhausted and being filled in with dumps of city refuse. The last of the asphalt was taken from the pit in recent years, but even scientists have not ascribed a date to the earliest use by man of the deposit which lay here. They believe that the first human arrivals in the region had been attracted by the pitch that oozed from the sand, and had settled at its borders. A dense bed of kitchen midden, four feet in depth in places, fills the subsurface space lying between the railroad tracks and the cliffs. Marked stratification of this bed of camp refuse indicates that the lower layers are of much greater age than the upper. Beneath the kitchen midden strata is a sandy structure through which asphaltum seeps at irregular intervals, and beneath this is a heavily impregnated layer in which Pleistocene plant and animal remains are embedded.

No graveyard and only a few artifacts have been found among the camp debris, which gradually came to cover the last vestiges of surface asphaltum on the site. In later ages, when a higher type of Indian peopled the spot, the only remaining evidence of asphaltum there was the seepage from the face of the cliff (R), below the level of the kitchen refuse. This seepage still exists, and is known as the Indian Pitch Spring (*see below*).

At 1.4 *m.*, on the cliff face (R) below the surface level and not visible from the road, is the INDIAN PITCH SPRING. Although an iron hydrant is placed over the seepage, the black liquid pitch still trickles down the cliff. The little tule-grown *barranca* (Sp., ravine) between the cliffs, and the wind-swept cypresses on the further point of the cove below are little different from the scenery familiar to the Indians who took pitch from this and other asphaltum springs on the coast in this region, daubing their baskets, tule-stalk boats, and plank canoes with it.

North of this spring and the exhausted asphalt pit, and separated from them by a large section of earth bearing no remains, is another extensive deposit laid down by prehistoric Indian occupation. The deposit is on the Higgins Ranch between US 101 and the Southern Pacific Railroad, on the southeast edge of Carpinteria. The asphalt deposits here are still worked occasionally, and from them fossils of prehistoric plant and animal life similar to those found in Los Angeles' La Brea Pits have been taken. Santa Barbara Museum of Natural History has been given sole rights to anything of scientific interest found in the pits, and usually has representatives there watching the work when the asphalt is being mined. Fossilized shells of many ocean mollusks indicate that the entire deposit once lay under the sea, but that the asphalt pools later lay on the surface of the land for ages is shown by the presence of land plant and animal remains. Artifacts of the Hunting People (*see Presidio to Channel City*) are among the human remains from these pits. Tokens of much earlier ages include cones of Bishop and Monterey pines; hind foot of *Equus occidentalis,* the extinct Western horse; bones of the dire wolf and of an early stork; and partial remains of *Neogypo errans,* of the Vagabond Vulture, and of the *Teratornis*—all three extinct birds of the vulture type, and the latter the largest bird of flight ever known (probable wingspread, 18 feet).

In Carpinteria, L. (north) from the junction of US 101 and Linden Ave. on Linden Ave., which leads to the alternate return route to Santa Barbara.

At 12.7 *m.* is the junction with State 150. Left on State 150, the return route.

The way proceeds through farming land with walnut orchards on the left and lemon groves on the right. Bean fields cover several little hills to the very top. The ocean, seen in occasional glimpses beyond the orchards, lies now at the left. The Santa Ynez Mountains along the right present views of verdant canyons between outthrust ridges.

At the rear entrance of the FLEISCHMANN POLO FIELD, 15.6 *m.,* passed on the main route along US 101, the State highway turns sharply right and climbs into the foothills between rows of Monterey Cypress. The range of this tree, which here is artificially cultivated, is even more restricted than that of the Torrey Pine which grows naturally only near San Diego and on Santa Rosa Island (*see Sierras in the Sea*). The Monterey Cypress is indigenous to but one spot in the world—the seacoast at the mouth of the Carmel River near Monterey. The Monterey Cypress, like the Torrey Pine (*see above*), grows straight and tall (up to eighty feet) when planted in deep soil in localities protected from constant winds. But on their native sea-cliffs both trees grow in wind-flayed, grotesquely twisted attitudes of torment which painters and photographers have endlessly portrayed since the early days of California's exploitation by brush and lens. The resemblance of many specimens of Monterey Cypress to the classi-cal Cedars of Lebanon has been remarked more than once, and may have given rise to the rather widespread impression that the two trees are the same. They belong to entirely different families of conifers.

The Monterey Cypress, the Torrey Pine, and other plants indig-enous to the California seacoast and islands are thought to be sur-vivors of a vast Pleistocene forest that grew in the valley which once lay between the mainland and the islands, and in a later age subsided into the ocean, taking the forest with it and leaving only a thin margin of growth along both edges.

With the feathery branches of Monterey Cypress overhanging it, the highway winds through the hills across a corner of the national forest (*see Sanctuary in the Chaparral*), and at 18.7 *m.* passes into the district of wealthy estates about Montecito.

On the list of Montecito estate owners are such nationally known family names as Fleischmann, Du Pont, Pillsbury, Armstrong, Stetson, Gould, McCormick, Spaulding, and others. Names of the establish-ments are often fanciful, sentimental, humorous or pretentious, and although some of them are Latin, Italian, or mongrel, most of them are Spanish. A few of the names: "St. Veep's Heights," "Riven Rock," "Pompeiian Court," "At Ease" (major general's home), "Quien Sabe?" (Sp., who knows?), "Horafeliz" (happy hour), "Case del Sueño" (house of the dream, or dreamhouse), "Casa Nuestra" (our house), and "Casa Mia" (my house).

The plant material and floricultural conditions in the region about Santa Barbara are similar to those in parts of the Mediterranean shores, South Africa and New Zealand, so that many exotics natural to tropical areas are grown successfully in the luxurious gardens and magnificently landscaped grounds of the big estates. More than ninety of the estab-lishments are visited on the summer and winter Garden Tours which have been conducted every year since 1926 by the Plans and Planting Branch of the Santa Barbara Community Arts Association (*see What, Where, When, How*). None of the estates are open to sightseers under other conditions, except Featherhill Ranch and El Fureides (*see below*), which are open on application.

The RANCHO SAN CARLOS (*not open*), 18.8 *m.* (R), is the estate of Charles H. Jackson, Jr., dog fancier and polo player of inter-national repute. On the estate are his Kerry Blue kennels, and stables containing some of his polo ponies.

State 150 continues, between various small estates (R) and the

227-acre RANCHO LAS FUENTES (Sp., ranch of the fountains) along the left (*not open*).

The ESTATE OF MISS AMY DU PONT (*not open*), 20.3 *m.*, is NW. of the junction with Buena Vista Lane (R). Miss Du Pont is a member of the nationally known Du Pont de Nemours family of Delaware.

VILLA REPOSA (*not open*), 20.9 *m.* (L), the estate of Mr. and Mrs. Robert Edmond Jones, is a reconstruction of the famous villa of that name on Lake Como, in Italy. Opposite the entrance is a circular fountain with a figure by the English sculptor, Gilbert Bayes. The six-hundred-foot avenue of cypress ends at a white stuccoed Greek studio building with a recessed porch and black-and-white marble floor. Within a pink-walled garden, wide-spreading trees cast their shadows over grass and moss inlaid with glistening white stones which give the effect of fresh-fallen rose petals. Every variety of rose in California is growing on the estate. The "rose-petaled" villa of Lake Como is re-created in the pale pink stuccoed house with its roof of deeper pink tiles; a rare, pale pink Bougainvillea clambers over it. Climbing roses and white wistaria cover the outer-garden pergola, which has pink stucco pillars and a floor of rose tile. Pines from all over the world are growing on the grounds.

The estate is sometimes included in the Garden Tours (*see What, Where, When, How*), but is not open to sightseers under other conditions. Jones is a designer of theater sets, and Mrs. Jones is the sister of Walter Huston, motion-picture character actor.

CONSTANTIA (*not open*), 21.1 *m.* (L), estate of Arthur Meeker, has a house designed after the type of architecture developed by the Boers in South Africa. Shells made of cement border the paths.

A few small tile-roofed buildings of stucco or concrete, half-hidden among trees, compose the village center of MONTECITO (Sp., little wood), 21.3 *m.* (250 alt., 2,000 pop.); the red-tiled roofed building of the Fire Department faces a little store, the Community Hall, and other buildings across East Valley Road (State 150). The community surrounding the village center spreads over a wide area in the rolling foothill and canyon country. It is almost rural in aspect. There are no commercial establishments and few sidewalks, winding roads are shaded by fine old trees, and big houses are placed far back from the roads and concealed by dense foliage. The prevailing architectural style is Californian, but the influence of unrelated forms of architecture is apparent in some of the homes.

The site of Montecito was originally part of the Santa Bárbara pueblo lands (*see Presidio to Channel City*), of which allotments were given to soldiers when their enlistments at the presidio expired. From earliest times it was a region of exceptional beauty, with its leafy canyons and its forested valley, and the Spanish called it *El Montecito,* the little wood. Even today it is not infrequently referred to as "the Montecito." Quail, deer, bear, and strayed cattle still roamed the valley in 1847, by which time a small settlement had developed, consisting of a few little ranches with the houses not more than a quarter-mile apart. Open land was planted to corn and wheat and tilled with wooden plows drawn by oxen. Don Nemicio Domínguez set aside an acre of his farm in 1855 for the building of a schoolhouse.

Americans did not begin settling in "the Montecito" in numbers until the 1860's, although Wilbur Curtiss settled there in 1855 and Newton M. Coats in 1858, and in 1859 two or three other Americans were among the valley's thirty souls. In 1863, John Coats bought a tract of land in the Montecito at the current price of seventy-five cents an acre. In the late 1860's the first of the Montecito estate builders had erected a fine old-fashioned Southern home on Hot Springs Road and made the first landscaped garden in the valley. This was Colonel W. A. Haynes. With others soon to follow Haynes' lead, bears were still so common in the region that a $50 bounty was set on every one taken within the limits of the settlement, and horse thieves and highwaymen were using the Montecito as a hide-out. But the intimate and wooded little valley held such strong appeal that notwithstanding this double menace, Colonel Haynes soon had a number of distinguished neighbors whose lush gardens grew all sorts of exotic plants and trees. In the 1870's the bears gradually retreated into the Santa Ynez Mountains and the freebooters all met one form of justice or other, leaving the future of Montecito tottering for awhile between those who wished to keep its natural beauty for homes and estates, and a few hustling Americans who wanted to make it a health center by exploiting the hot springs which had been discovered there in 1801 by an Indian wandering in the foothills.

Estate builders mingled with the mixed Spanish and American upper society of Santa Barbara from the first. In 1874, the Santa Barbara *Times* referred to Montecito as "what we may call the fashionable neighborhood of Santa Barbara." "Montecito Day," the sixteenth of July, was a festive occasion from early Spanish times and was celebrated with picnic and *fandangos* as late as 1886.

During the boom of the 1880's the Montecito Land Company subdivided the Forbes property, a four-hundred-acre tract with ocean frontage lying just east of the Santa Barbara city boundary line, and sold plots for $100 an acre and more. The present layout of Montecito began to take form in the early 1900's, as larger numbers of wealthy Easterners came to California to build homes in ideal settings.

CASA DEL HERRERO (Sp., house of the blacksmith), 21.6 m. (*not open*), is the home (L) of Mrs. George Steedman. Imported Spanish tiles used in the magnificent garden are a notable feature of the grounds, which are sometimes included in the Garden Tours (*see What, Where, When, How*), but are not open to sightseers under any other conditions.

The CHURCH OF OUR LADY OF MOUNT CARMEL (*always open*), 21.8 m., was designed by Ross Montgomery after the

Pueblo Indian architecture of the Rio Grande country in New Mexico. Exterior walls show wide expanses of stucco tinted in antique ivory to resemble the adobe work of the Pueblo Indians. Protruding beams at the roof line and leaning ladders at various levels emphasize the motif. Light and shadow effects are achieved by architectural masses and plantings of cacti. The interior is chastely simple, with a floor of stone and a ceiling of half-hewn logs laid in the herringbone pattern of old Franciscan ceilings. Contrasting colors in sanctuary and nave relieve the simplicity. Pairs of engaged spiral columns in off-shade pink and blue stand at either side of the altar, which is primitive and essentially Indian in conception. The altar and reredos are of stone. On the steps and the predella of the altar lies a Navajo rug in black, white, gray, and ruby red. The crucifix above the altar is of silver inlaid with black enamel. The Indian motif appears again in the wall decorations by Charles and Sebastian Maas. Doors are of hand-hewn wood. Sanctuary lamp, candlesticks, and tabernacle are of repoussé silver.

The church was consecrated in 1938.

The little houses of the OLD SPANISH SETTLEMENT, 21.9 *m.* (R) are those in which the earliest residents of Montecito lived (*see above*).

PARRA GRANDE (Sp., great grapevine) LANE (R), 22 *m.*, runs past the site of the garden in which the grapevine that gave the road its name was planted by Doña Marcelina Feliz de Domínguez some time between 1796 and 1815. La Parra Grande, as this vine was known locally throughout its years of fame as "the largest grapevine in the world," had attained enormous proportions by 1873, when there were two or three estates in Montecito established by wealthy Americans. Its trunk circumference was nearly five feet, its branches covered a trellis 100,000 square feet in area, and it bore 8,000 to 10,000 pounds of grapes a year. In 1876, it was taken up and sent to Philadelphia to be displayed in the California section of the Centennial Exposition. Memories of La Parra Grande, the Great Grapevine of Carpinteria (*see above*), and one or two other prodigious grapevines in Montecito and Carpinteria are confused in the minds of many old-time residents.

Right from State 150 on Parra Grande Lane to EL FUREIDES (*open on application*), 0.3 *m.* (L), one of the loveliest country seats in America, and known to many tourists as "the Gillespie place." It is the estate of J. M. Gillespie, who built his big Mediterranean-type house with advice from Bertram Goodhue, famous architect. Elements of Roman, Pompeiian, Persian, Arabian, and Spanish design influence the character of the house, which has severely simple white cement walls on three sides, relieved only by the iron grilled windows. On the garden façade a row of Ionic columns, and bas-reliefs depicting characters of the Arthurian legends, break the plainness. Mr. Gillespie explains that the name El Fureides may be constructed to mean "pleasaunce," which can only be translated into English as "pleasure garden."

More than 125 varieties of palms grow on the grounds, and many rare plants of other kinds. The estate's thirty-three acres are divided between the gardens and a wood. Four terraced pools are the axis of the Persian garden.

State 150 unites R. (northwestward) with Sycamore Canyon Rd. at **22.2** *m.*

ARCADY (*not open*), **22.3** *m.* (L), the estate of George Owen Knapp, borders State 150 for more than a mile northwest of the junction with Sycamore Road. The 200-acre property is surrounded by a wall of buff sandstone quarried near Santa Barbara and often used throughout the region. Much of the estate is wooded with native oak, and allowed to remain in its natural beauty; only the water gardens are of formal landscape architecture. A succession of pools connected by stairways lie on successive levels. Three large reproductions of metopes from the frieze of the Parthenon are features of the exterior decoration of the house, in which Italian Renaissance architectural details are suggested by the lines of the red-tiled roof and the arches of the porch and windows. The doors, too, are arched, and the interior is marked by massiveness and simplicity. The breakfast room is finished in Chinese Chippendale. In the music room are an organ loft and pipe organ.

This estate, one of the loveliest in Montecito, is frequently shown to distinguished travelers and groups of garden enthusiasts.

VAL VERDE (*not open*), **22.6** *m.* (R), is the estate of Wright S. Luddington, an artist. The house is an example of the Mediterranean structural designs used early in the development of what is now beginning to be called California architecture (*see Tierra Adorada*). Its architect is Bertram Goodhue. The garden side of the house opens onto a wide terrace, and has an overhanging second story supported by heavy wood beams. The windows are large, and arched. Beyond the entrance is the patio characteristic of Spanish structures.

The exquisitely groomed gardens of the estate are included in the Garden Tours (*see What, Where, When, How*) once or twice each season, but are not open to sightseers under other conditions.

At **23.5** *m.* is the junction with Sycamore Canyon Rd. and Stanwood Dr. State 150 unites R. with Stanwood Dr.; L. (straight ahead) on Sycamore Canyon Rd., the return route to Santa Barbara.

Between the junction of Sycamore Canyon Road with Stanwood Drive and downtown Santa Barbara, the tour covers the first portion of the route followed by Tour 2 to San Marcos Pass and the back country (*see Tour 2*).

At **25.2** *m.,* is the junction of Sycamore Canyon Rd. with the convergence of Montecito and Yanonali Sts. Right from Sycamore Canyon Rd. on Montecito St. to State St. in downtown Santa Barbara, **26.8** *m.*

Tour 2

THE BACK COUNTRY

Santa Barbara — Santa Ynez — Solvang — Buellton — Los Alamos — Santa Maria; 78.2 *m*. De la Guerra St., State St., Montecito St., Sycamore Canyon Rd., State 150, US 101.

Concrete- and asphalt-paved roadbed throughout. Winding road with sharp turns along State 150 in San Marcos Pass.
Accommodations limited except in towns.

After winding up to mountain heights commanding views of exceptional beauty and grandeur, this tour descends and crosses three valleys of pastoral loveliness. Here and there a windmill standing over a solitary clump of shaded ranch houses recalls the farms of the East and Middle West. Purebred beef cattle feed on the vast, rich acres of wealthy gentlemen-ranchers. Little villages that began as stagecoach stations lie along the highway at infrequent intervals. A neat and bustling Danish settlement, where the culture and customs of the mother country are perpetuated, stands in striking contrast to the sad and mellow Spanish-California mission near by, within whose walls time and business seem inconsequential. Near the route's end is a part of the largest commercial flower-farming region in the world.

Southwest from the Santa Barbara CITY HALL, 0 *m.*, E. De la Guerra St. and De la Guerra Plaza, on De la Guerra St. to State St.; L. on State to Montecito St.; L. on Montecito to Sycamore Canyon Rd.; L. on Sycamore Canyon to Stanwood Dr.; L. on Stanwood (State 150).

The SHEFFIELD RESERVOIR (R), 4.1 *m.* (*see Presidio to Channel City*), is a storage unit of the Santa Barbara Water Department. It has two spillways, and a water capacity of 50,000,000 gallons. A low white concrete filtration plant at the northern end has eight filters in which a total of 8,000,000 gallons of water a day can be handled. An 800-foot-long earth dam across a canyon impounds the waters of the reservoir, which was built in 1936 on the site of an earlier one.

At 4.2 *m.* is the junction with Mountain Dr.; the main route continues L. (straight ahead) on State 150.

Right from State 150 on Mountain Dr. This is an alternate route which connects with the main route again after a sharply winding sixteen-mile climb through the mountains on an asphalt-paved highway. The roadstead is sometimes partially obstructed by rock slides after rains (*watch for slide-warning signs*), and the route adds six miles to the total covered on the main tour, but its heights command some of the most remarkable scenic views in southern California. (*Warning: Sun glare excessive after 12 noon.*)

At 0.2 *m.* on Mountain Dr. is the junction with Gibraltar Rd.; L. (*straight ahead*) here to the junction with El Camino Cielo, 7.1 *m.;* L. on Camino Cielo.

At 8.9 *m.* is the junction with a pocked and rutted one-way loop road (L) that climbs 0.2 *m.* to LA CUMBRE LOOKOUT, a national forest observation tower on the crest of La Cumbre Peak (3,985 alt.). Immediately below the lookout station is a very small picnic area with stoves and other facilities (*free*). From the little station's platform, views of coast and ocean extend for a hundred miles on clear days, and even in hazy weather present a grandeur little less than awesome. From this spot the Channel Islands (*see Sierras in the Sea*) are more fully visible than from any other place on the mainland. Below the north platform of the lookout spreads a wide panorama of primitive wilderness in which jumbled folds of mountain pile against one another to the edge of the sky. This rugged country lies in the heart of Los Padres National Forest (*see Sanctuary in the Chaparral*).

On El Camino Cielo is the junction with a paved road, 16.4 *m.* L. here to the PAINTED CAVE (*free; adm. on application*), 1.1 *m.,* a natural grotto decorated with red, white, yellow, and black Indian pictographs of human figures, trees, snakelike creatures, the sun, and circular designs and crosses. Origin of the crudely executed wall designs is undetermined; some authorities attribute them to Zuni or Hopi tribesmen. The cave has been a tourist attraction since its existence was reported to the Smithsonian Institution several years ago. The grotto is about eight feet high, twelve feet wide, and fifteen feet deep. The entrance is protected by an iron grill.

At 18.5 *m.* on El Camino Cielo is a junction with State 150.

The main route is straight ahead (west) from the junction of Mountain Dr. and State 150. At 6.2 *m.* State 150 unites westward with Goleta Foothill Blvd., and turns R. from it at 8 *m.* The main route is R. here with State 150.

Left (straight ahead) from State 150 on Goleta Foothill Blvd. to the junction with Old San Marcos Pass Rd., 2 *m.;* R. here to the LAUREL OF

SAN MARCOS (R), 2.1 *m.,* the largest known California laurel tree (*Umbellularia californica*). It is 91 feet high, has a 100-foot branch spread, and a trunk diameter of 6 feet. At its base, the trunk flares out to a diameter of 12 feet. The tree's age is estimated at 300 years. It is not the true laurel (*Laurus nobilis*) which the ancient Greeks used in making wreaths, but it is a relative. The California laurel is related to the camphor and sassafras, too, and is sometimes called sassafras laurel. The pungent fragrance of its bright, evergreen foliage is rather like that of bay rum, and the leaves when dried are used for flavoring. In this pungence it is very like *Laurus nobilis,* and both sometimes are called the bay tree. Continued smelling of the crushed leaves induces sneezing, and because of this the tree came by another of its names, the pepperwood. Although headache is caused by inhaling the odor of the leaves, the Indians prescribed the use of a leaf in the nostril or several in the hat to *relieve* headache. They had discovered further that a scattering of the foliage about their camps kept fleas away. Tribes in the redwood belt of central and northern California—where the tree is in the middle of its range and grows at its best—roasted and ate the kernel of the olivelike fruit, which succeeds small, greenish-yellow blossoms.

The wood of the tree is hard and heavy, has a figured grain of great beauty, and takes a high polish. It makes good stave timber, and is used in the manufacture of such articles as shoe lasts and bedroom furniture.

The junction of Old San Marcos Pass Rd. and State 150 is at 5.4 *m.*

The main route is R. (north) from the junction of Goleta Foothill Blvd. and State 150, on State 150.

The highway rises from the junction into SAN MARCOS PASS, one of the defiles used by padres and explorers in crossing from the coastal plain to the inland valleys, and by Lieutenant Colonel John C. Frémont when he led his soldiers into Santa Bárbara in 1846 (*see below*). Splendid views of city, harbor, and ocean are revealed in places where the highway curves westward and southward in horseshoe bends as it climbs to the summit. The scenery along the pass is celebrated widely for its beauty, especially in spring when masses of California lilac are in bloom on the slopes. Late in the summer of 1940, much of this scenery was destroyed by a forest fire which raged across the pass, leaving a scene of shocking desolation.

State 150 crosses the boundary of an outthrust arm of Los Padres National Forest (*see Sanctuary in the Chaparral*) at 9.7 *m.*

At 13 *m.* is the junction with a paved road (R) on which is the PAINTED CAVE, 2.1 *m.;* at 13.1 *m.* is the junction with Old San Marcos Pass Rd. (L) on which is the LAUREL OF SAN MARCOS, 3.3 *m.;* at 15.6 *m.* is the junction with El Camino Cielo (R), the road which passes LA CUMBRE LOOKOUT, 9.6 *m.* (*see above*).

At the summit of San Marcos Pass (2,224 alt.), 16 *m.,* is a ten-foot-high slab of native sandstone, the FRÉMONT MEMORIAL (L), which commemorates the crossing of the mountains through the pass by Lieutenant Colonel John C. Frémont and his men, guided by Benjamin Foxen, in the winter of 1846.

On the way downcoast from Monterey to take Santa Bárbara, Frémont and his detachment stopped at the San Luis Obispo County ranch of William G. Dana to rest and replenish their food supply. They had made the march from Monterey in rain and mud, and many horses which had faltered from exhaustion and underfeeding were left behind. Frémont's detachment, the so-called "California Battalion," was made up of about four hundred assorted rangers and frontiersmen armed with various kinds of revolvers, rifles and knives, and dressed in buckskins and Kentucky jeans. About forty Walla Walla Indians were among them. As Frémont prepared to resume the march, Dana gave him the name of an English rancher, Benjamin Foxen, who lived in the Santa Maria Valley country through which their expedition would take them. Foxen, he said, was familiar with the wild region southwest of the valley and could advise them on the last stage of their journey.

Historians do not agree as to whether Frémont was warned by Dana or by Foxen of the rumored ambush set by the Barbareños in Gaviota Pass (see Tour 3), through which it was supposed the battalion would have to come in order to reach Santa Bárbara. However, Foxen made it possible for Frémont to avoid Gaviota Pass by showing him over a difficult and little-known Indian trail through what is now San Marcos Pass.

Rain was falling again as Frémont and his battalion followed Foxen along the steep trail. They had to take the wagons and cannon apart and swing them piece by piece on ropes across intervening chasms. After a day-long struggle they achieved the summit. There they encamped on a spot overlooking the plain of Santa Bárbara and the ocean beyond, and one of Frémont's officers jotted down in his diary, "The descent on the western side is precipitous and appears almost impassable."

There Foxen took leave of Frémont and returned home; his seventeen-year-old son accompanied the troops on the downward march. The officer wrote in his diary, "Dec. 25. Christmas Day and a memorable one to me . . . before we commenced the descent . . . a furious storm began, raging with a violence rarely surpassed. . . . Driving our horses before us we were compelled to slide down the steep . . . rocks, and wade through deep gullies . . . filled with mud and foaming torrents of water that [carried] along the loose rocks and [tore] up the trees. . . . Many of the horses falling into ravines . . . were swept downward. . . . Others, bewildered by the fierceness . . . of the storm, rushed or fell headlong over the steep precipices and were killed. . . . The destruction of horseflesh . . . is . . . frightful. The number of dead animals is estimated at from 75 to 100."

Frémont and his exhausted men marched into Santa Bárbara two days later and took possession of the town while the Barbareños were at morning Mass. Not a shot was fired. A few resident Americans came out to meet the troops, and watched while the Stars and Stripes was raised.

In tribute to Foxen's aid to Frémont, the Church of Sisquoc (see below), at the mouth of Foxen Canyon has been made a memorial. But a somewhat lesser honor came to the rancher while he was living. In 1868, more than a score of years after he had been Frémont's guide,

Foxen again was called upon to show the trail through San Marcos Pass—this time to the county surveyor, who laid out a route for a wagon road which became the San Marcos Toll Road. Foxen was permitted to use it free of charge. The modern road through the pass was incorporated into the State highway system in 1931.

The highway winds down from the summit through areas in which the 1940 forest fire reduced to charred stumps the great old oaks, sycamores and conifers which had graced the landscape throughout several generations of Santa Barbarans and tourists. The full loveliness of these areas will not be reproduced by succeeding growth within the lifetime of those who fought the 1940 conflagration and those who motored from far and near to see what the fire had done to San Marcos Pass.

At 20.3 *m.* State 150 crosses the northern boundary of the arm of Los Padres National Forest and heads across the SANTA YNEZ VALLEY. The SANTA YNEZ RIVER parallels the highway as it descends from the mountains. It flows through the valley region which, in old Spanish days, was the territory of the Santa Inés Mission (*see below*), and therefore was given the mission's name. The discrepancy in spelling between the names arose in the confusion of usage common in those days, there being many illiterates, and the script taught in the mission schools being so ornate that it was difficult to read and write correctly. Inept pupils grew up to spread all sorts of errors about the countryside. The Spanish had a habit of using *I's* and *Y's*, and *S's* and *Z's* interchangeably, especially in proper names. When the Americans came in, the confusion in speech, spelling, and writing knew no bounds. Because the mission was administered by men of higher education, it continued to use in its papers the old correct Spanish form of its name, Santa Inés. But the river, the valley, the mountains, and the town named for them, assumed several spellings as the years went by—Santa Ynes, Santa Inez, and Santa Ynez. How the latter came to be the fixed and accepted form for these place names is undetermined. Many publications use that form for the town, mountains, valley, and river, but follow the Catholic church in its use of the correct Spanish form for the mission's name.

Trees, verdant ravines, and rolling meadows give an idyllic quality to the valley landscape. Hay is grown and cattle are pastured on the broad, rich ranch lands.

Cattle raising had a large part in shaping the history and traditions of Santa Barbara County. The industry here, which claims the longest continuous range-cattle history in the United States, was well established at a time when the wild West beyond the Rockies still was overrun with buffalo. The first Spanish settlers brought their cattle with them, and all during the Spanish and Mexican era of California the chief occupation of the *dons,* the cattle barons who held the great land grants, was cattle raising. There were no fences on the range then, and the lean, long-horned cattle were half wild; it took genuine cowboys to work the herds, "tough *hombres*" such as those who people the cowboy yarns in Western story magazines nowadays. Lack of a market for meat, and limited transportation facilities made hides and tallow the only salable produce of the industry until gold-rush days opened up a market for meat in San Francisco. Cattle were driven up the coast from Santa Barbara and the other "cow counties" adjoining, feeding on ranges along the way.

The first American settlers in the county also took up cattle raising, and many of them became so completely assimilated that they adopted the dress and customs of the native California ranch owners, suffered their given names to be changed to the Spanish form, and even accepted the title *don,* which is equivalent to the English "esquire."

Shortly after 1850, Thomas B. Dibblee and other pioneer American *rancheros* began improving the California cattle by importation and breeding of better stock from the East. The animals were driven across the plains, or shipped around Cape Horn. At the turn of the century, still better stock was introduced, and through years of steady development up to the present day, the county has achieved a national reputation for fine beeves. The stocky, short-horned beef cattle that roam the county's ranges today are considered less hardy than the old stock, of which not a single survivor remains under domestication, although local legend has it that several completely wild descendants still live in the primitive, almost inaccessible Hurricane Deck Country (*see Sanctuary in the Chaparral*).

Many of the cattle ranches of the county are still vast acreages, and some of the original holdings are intact. The roundup remains an annual feature, and the owners of smaller ranches in the Cuyama district behind the Sierra Madre Range to the northeast follow the old Spanish-California custom of pooling all hands to make up a single crew that travels from ranch to ranch, working each one in turn. The custom is not followed on the bigger ranches, where roundup work can be done by a few hands, but hospitalities attending the old Spanish-California roundup visits are perpetuated by the well-to-do ranchers of the Santa Ynez Valley in their annual ranch-to-ranch horseback outing, the ride of the *Rancheros Visitadores* (visiting ranchmen) (*see Fiesta Land*).

Roundup crews on the bigger ranches, such as the Suey Ranch near Santa Maria (48,000 acres), handle an average of 250 to 300 head daily. Branding irons still are used, but the cowboys work on foot in a large circular corral and run each animal through a chute, where it is held by adjustable hurdle bars for branding and dehorning. The county's cattle industry, which is carried on principally in the Santa Ynez, Los Alamos, Santa Maria, and Lompoc districts, brings an annual return of approximately $4,500,000. More than a million of this is accounted for in Los Alamos and Santa Maria valleys, where the ranchers say that more cattle can be ranged to the acre there than in any other part of the State. They specialize in raising white-faced Herefords and Red Durhams.

About five hundred yards off the highway at 24.4 *m.* is the white stucco Spanish-style administration building (R) of RANCHO SAN

FERNANDO REY (*open afternoons; guides*), a seven-thousand-acre domain of grain and pasture lands on which Dwight W. Murphy keeps the stock with which he is working to improve the quality of the Palomino horse, and establish it as a distinct breed.

The Palomino is an ivory-tailed, ivory-maned horse with a solid body color varying in the individual from the preferred shade of pure gold to lighter or darker shades such as copper and cream. The history of the Palomino is exceedingly fragmentary, and facts concerning his origin even more elusive. A few believe the color phenomenon to be the same biological accident which accounts for cinnamon bears among black bears, silver foxes among red foxes, and redheads among human beings. Other theories take into account the horse's early history among the Arab tribes, and the fact that the Palomino is produced only among Arabian horses or those with Arabian blood in their ancestry. One of the theories is that the Palomino is an offshoot of the Arabian strain; another, that he is a throwback to the lost basic color of the Arabian's forerunners.

Whether the Arabs ever were able to control the percentage of foals of this type born among their horse herds is not known definitely. But for fifteen centuries before the Moorish conquest of Spain in the early part of the eighth century the Arabs tried to breed the type out of existence because the metallic brilliance of its golden coat made it conspicuous against the desert landscape, and therefore impractical for warring tribes to use. That they had not rid themselves entirely of the persistently recurring golden horses is known by the fact that when the Moors set up their civilization in Spain, the mares among the Barb and Arabian horses they brought with them still were dropping an occasional golden foal, and even after they crossed with the native Spanish stock, the rare animals continued to appear.

The Spanish people prized them highly, and when Queen Isabella came to power and drove the Moors out of her country in the fifteenth century, she collected a stable of these horses for her coach. Thereafter they came to be known as Isabellas. The queen sent one of the stallions and five matched mares to her viceroy in New Spain (Mexico), and at least one horse of the type was taken on the colonizing expedition led from there across the southwestern deserts and up the Pacific coast to San Francisco by Juan Bautista de Anza. The horse was ridden by a soldier named Juan Palamía, or as some accounts have it, Juan Palomino. Both are old Spanish family names. It is not known exactly how the latter name came to be applied to the horse, but the application is of California origin, and its use dates not earlier than the mission period.

As in Spain, so in the New World colonies settled by the Spaniards, the high civil and military officials and the land-owning *dons* took all the available Palominos for their own exclusive use, and valued them beyond price. Probably there never were quite enough of them to go around, for young *caballeros* (cavaliers), in their burning desire to own a Palomino often would go hunting for them among the bands of wild horses descended from stock which had strayed from *ranchos* and missions, or had been freed when settlements were abandoned. Still no attempt was made to breed Palominos scientifically so that their number might be increased. The entire horse stock of the Southwest finally began to deteriorate in quality through cessation of the intensive and careful breeding that had produced the fine Andalusian horses among which the Isabellas had occurred. The *rancheros* imported heavier horses of European descent from the Americans to draw their plows and wagons, and these were crossed with the native stock, sometimes deliberately and sometimes promiscuously. When the Americans dominated the Southwest and their horse stock freely intermingled with the native, Palominos of any sort became harder to find than ever, and good Palominos nearly disappeared.

As with everything rare and of mysterious origin, conflicting tales grew up about the Palomino during the ensuing "dark ages" of horse breeding in the West. On some parts of the range an unaccountable belief was held that they were inferior types of horses, lacking in stamina and various qualities, but yarns of cowboys in other regions attributed phenomenal powers to them. These tales were kept alive by the persistent occurrence of occasional Palominos of good color and conformation, but the scarcity of such animals by the second decade of the century, at the time Dwight Murphy went in search of a mate for his Palomino, Blondie, was such that nowhere in the State was there a good Palomino for sale at any price.

Murphy decided to breed Palominos to see whether he could increase their number and revive the nearly vanished pure-gold color of those the Spaniards had prized so highly. He extended his search to the other southwestern States, and at last collected several Palomino mares in Texas, which he brought to his Santa Ynez Valley ranch. For several years these mares were bred, but all their offspring either were failures, or if good in themselves, were unable to produce good Palomino colts. The fact that a Palomino's color is not developed fully until he is two years old made the work slow and heartbreaking, for a foal which approached the desired golden color the first season was likely to become too dark when grown to be considered a true Palomino.

At last Murphy decided to breed for Palominos by using Arabian stock. He bought Swedish King, a fine Arab stallion, and bred light Barb mares and Palominos to him. Of the several gold-tinged foals sired by King, one developed into a perfect pure-gold Palomino, the first real reward Murphy had. He was *Del Rey* (Sp., of the king), and sired *El Rey de los Reyes* (the king of the kings), which not only was a superb Palomino, but also the first to produce a majority of good Palomino foals among his offspring. He was the answer to Murphy's prayers. When it was discovered that sons and grandsons of this horse produced a good percentage of fine Palominos among their get, Murphy felt that he had at last succeeded in setting the strain. He is recognized as the first to do so among the breeders in the Southwest who have been experimenting with Palominos. Murphy and other breeders realize, however, that their work still is in the early stages and that the breed is not established fully. Murphy still crosses chestnut Arabs with Palominos, and gets about 70 per cent Palomino foals.

Following Murphy's successes, other Palomino breeders began solving their problems, and within the last score of years, movements arose among them toward organization for the betterment of their work. In Santa Barbara the Palomino Horse Association and Studbook Registry was formed, with Murphy's *El Rey de los Reyes* the first entry in the book. As Palomino classes rose to popularity and importance at horse shows throughout the West, the Palomino Exhibitors' Association was organized. It prepared a concise set of horse-show judging rules, setting forth in detail what qualities a Palomino should have to be best fitted for improving the breed through his offspring, and what faults should disqualify a horse from the show ring or lower his score. This statement is one of the most advanced of the recent efforts judges and breeders have been making to reconcile the controversial opinions as to what constitutes a true Palomino. Because of these often unsound opinions, and the judges' general unfamiliarity with the breeders' aims and problems, many unwise decisions were rendered in the show ring which not only failed to help but also actually hindered the breeders in their task. Competent judging of Palominos at shows is a valuable guide for selective breeding and sets a standard for improvement of the strain.

The elusive color ideal was the judges' principal stumbling block and center of the greater controversies. It is the most important single consideration of the breeder. To many, the most exciting aspect of the color phenomenon is the brilliant metallic sheen present only in the coat of the pure-gold Palomino, and absent in those of lighter or darker shades. Variations from the ideal shade of gold are acceptable in the show ring, according to specifications of the Palomino Exhibitors' Association, but because in the breeding classes color counts as much as all other features combined, a horse of excellent conformation and performance might score very poorly if his color varies too far from the ideal.

Entries in breeding classes are shown "in hand" (led on a halter), but in all other Palomino classes entries are judged under "Western" equipment. Their conformation is judged on Western stock and saddle-horse standards. In the Palomino parade-horse class, the costume of the rider and trappings of the horse are judged as well as the horse's color, conformation and performance. The rider usually is dressed in the early-California costume of braid-trimmed black velvet jacket, bright silk sash, and bell-bottomed trousers. The horse's equipment is commonly of silver-mounted, black-tooled leather; the heavy stock saddle is high-pommeled and wide-skirted, and the rider's feet rest in stirrups ornamented by *tapaderas* (Sp., stirrup covers) that reach to the horse's knees. The ideal parade Palomino, the spectacular brilliance of his coat set off by such glamorous trappings, his heavy mane falling the full width of his neck, and his tail flowing almost to the ground, makes a picture of barbaric splendor familiar not only to Western horse-show spectators but also to every follower of California fiesta parades.

Today it is estimated a thousand Palominos are in the country— three hundred in California, about as many in Texas, and enough more in Arizona, New Mexico, Colorado, Oklahoma, Nebraska, and Oregon to complete the total. A good Palomino saddle mare or gelding sells at $200 and up, but a stallion will bring $1,500 to $5,000. An important sire whose name is well known among breeders will cost several times that amount, if he can be purchased at any price. Many breeders do not like to think of Palominos in terms of buying and selling. Murphy, who named his ranch after an early favorite—a dappled gray Arab stud—considers nothing too good for the most important breeders of his herd. Each stallion has a separate box stall which is equipped with light and running water, and the stable is a model of cleanliness and efficiency. Incoming flies are given an elaborate reception by an electrically charged, honey-baited wire grill. One of these contraptions is placed near the floor at each entrance to the building. The stable is finished inside with knotty pine. Walks of pale brick border the two rows of stalls, and between the walks is an alley of saw-dust, put down fresh and raked perfectly level every day. The stallions are groomed thoroughly every morning for the afternoon exhibition on the ranch.

SANTA YNEZ, 38.1 m. (450 alt., 550 pop.), slumbers beneath spreading oaks and sycamores in the center of the Santa Ynez Valley, dreaming of a railroad that never came. Its red-brick buildings, its general store, the curve of the road through the town, an occasional windmill jutting above the trees, suggest a Midwestern rural scene. The town subsists exclusively on agriculture and cattle ranching. Dairying in the surrounding area is becoming increasingly important. Some fifteen dairies operate through a milk producers' association.

Santa Ynez was founded in 1882 as a trade center for the 35,000-acre College Ranch, part of which had been subdivided and sold to settlers. In 1887, rumors of a pending extension of the Pacific Coast Railroad's narrow-gauge line from Los Alamos caused an active movement in real estate. A hotel and dozens of homes were built. But the railroad never came as far south as Santa Ynez, so the little town remained merely a station on the stagecoach line between Santa Barbara and the railroad's terminus in Los Olivos (*see below*).

The ZANJA COTA INDIAN RESERVATION, spreading from the southern boundary of Santa Ynez along Zanja Cota (Sp., Cota's ditch) Creek, is one of the smallest in the United States. On its eighty-seven acres are a handful of Indians, thought to be the last survivors of those attached to the Santa Inés Mission (*see below*). The reservation, apparently an old Catholic church lease, was turned over to the Indians with the provision that it was theirs as long as five or more of them lived on it. Within the last two years, the Federal Government has been investigating the title to the property to determine whether the Indians have legal right to it.

The low, white adobe buildings of LA MISÍON DE SANTA INÉS (Sp., the mission of St. Agnes), 42 *m*. (L), nineteenth in the chain established by the Franciscan padres, stand on the slightly elevated plateau at the outskirts of Solvang (*see below*). The restored monastery, adjoining chapel, and a bell tower that projects in falsefront style from the north side of the church, face eastward across the fertile Santa Ynez Valley. South of the main buildings are ruins of an aqueduct and a mill.

No two of the rounded Roman arches at Santa Inés have the same measurements. Indian-made bricks compose the floor of the nave, sanctuary and sacristy. The butterfly hinges and old locks on sacristy and choir doors are considered among the best of mission specimens. Over the altar is a statue of St. Agnes, carved by an Indian neophyte. Wooden candlesticks and carved wooden statues of John the Baptist are among church relics. In the museum are Indian-made saddles inlaid with silver, a collection of old music bound in leather with rawhide thongs, a harmonium with rosewood cover, portions of an organ, two old cellos, a heart-shaped bullet mold, and a cannon used in the Indian revolt of 1824.

Santa Inés Mission was founded by Fr. Tapis, successor to Fr. Lasuén as president of the California mission chain, on September 17, 1804, on a site about halfway between missions Santa Bárbara and La Purísima Concepción. The fathers hoped that the new mission would bring to conversion some of the region's fierce Tulare Indians.

Because of the expected hostility of the tribe, a large guard was assigned to protect the fathers, but the natives readily came into the mission community. Neophytes from older missions came to teach the Santa Inés converts to make adobe bricks and tiling for additional buildings. Rafter and beam timbers of pine, oak, and sycamore were bound together with rawhide strips. Lime was made of ground sea shells. Walls and roof were coated with a gluey preparation of prickly cactus plant which resembled whitewash when soaked in water. The first church, monastery, convent for girls and unmarried women, granaries, and workshops were tile-roofed adobes built in a rough quadrangle about a patio and garden. The Indian village was built about two hundred feet from the patio, and as the neophyte population grew, the village expanded. Portions of the cement pipe by which water was conducted underground from the mountains to the community are still used by ranchers. A tannery built of huge river boulders covered with cement was erected in front of the mission at the end of the orchard.

Earthquakes of 1812 damaged many Santa Inés buildings. The church partly collapsed, and religious services were held in the granary until 1817, when the padres finished the second and permanent church of brick and adobe.

Meanwhile neophytes were trained in agriculture, carpentry, shoemaking, masonry, weaving, and other crafts. Study of Christian doctrine and regulated periods of diversion made up the rest of the Indians' life. Many learned to speak Castilian Spanish and to sing the Christion music of their teachers. By 1816 they numbered 750.

The Indian revolt of 1824, which involved several missions, originated at Santa Inés. The *Tulare,* stronger and more aggressive than the other tribes of the region, rebelled against the burden of supporting the territorial soldiers and their families, a duty enforced upon them since the revolution in Mexico had cut off the troops' pay in 1811. The resentment might never have reached the boiling point except for the flogging of a Santa Inés neophyte by a petty officer. The neophytes attacked the mission on February 21, 1824. No one was killed, but much damage was done. Next day, troops arrived from the Santa Bárbara Presidio, and the neophytes barricaded themselves in one of the largest buildings. The soldiers fired it. In retaliation, the Indians burned many other Santa Inés buildings, but left the church unharmed.

About 1829, the Santa Inés community somewhat resembled Santa Bárbara Mission, with gardens and choice fruit trees on one side and the Indian village on the other. The buildings at Santa Inés were of more severe architecture than those of any of the other missions; the most relieving feature was the campanile.

Santa Inés feast day was January 21, *Día de Santa Inés* (day of St. Agnes), and everyone celebrated. Horse races and bullfights were organized. On Holy Saturday, an image of Judas made of wild hollyhock was tied to the saddle of a bronco, and took an exceedingly rough and hazardous ride as the beast plunged and reared in fright. The effigy was ceremoniously burned in the evening. Music for the feast was supplied by Indian musicians with flutes, tambours, horns, and triangles.

Santa Inés was one of the last of the missions to be secularized, and might have escaped entirely, except for an unfortunate incident. In 1835, Governor Chico protested that he was insulted as a result of an inhospitable reception from a Santa Inés padre. The priest explained that, as he had received no notice of the governor's visit, he was unprepared to greet him with the formality due his rank. The mission president informed the governor that he had no claim upon the hospitality of unsecularized missions. Governor Chico thereupon issued an order, which his assembly confirmed, for the immediate secularization of Santa Inés. In 1843, Governor Micheltorena issued a decree returning the missions to the Franciscans, and an ecclesiastical seminary—California's first—was established at Santa Inés. It was erected on a 35,-000-acre tract adjoining the mission land, and was promised an annual contribution of $500 from the government. Then Pío Pico ousted Micheltorena in 1845; the seminary contributions ceased, and in 1846 the mission was leased and afterwards sold to José Covarrúbias and Joaquín Carrillo for $7,000. The college grounds also were sold, and the building fell to ruin. Three weeks after the mission's sale, the American flag was raised over Monterey, and Pico fled to Mexico.

In 1862, a fraction of the original mission lands were restored to the Catholic church, which still holds them. The buildings deteriorated rapidly, for the fathers were more concerned for the welfare of the mission Indians than for that of the buildings. The pulpit fell and was not replaced; arches and walls crumbled; roofs caved in; owls flew in and out of the windows and rested on the images of saints. The south end of the monastery gaped open and become a haunt of snakes.

In 1882, the Donahue family moved in to keep house for the resident priest; they repaired the roofs and made many minor restorations, but lack of funds hindered their work. In 1904 Reverend Alexander Buckler was appointed pastor of Santa Inés, Lompoc, Sisquoc, and the mission Indians, and was authorized to begin restoration of the devastated mission. For more than a quarter of a century he and his niece labored to restore Santa Inés. They found an old oil painting of St. Francis lying under one of the water tanks, partly destroyed; altar stones were dug up from the cemetery; hand-loomed brocaded vestments were found and repaired. They employed transient labor, which could be secured for food and shelter, but they were severely handicapped by lack of money. Nearly $7,000 was raised by contributions, and the bell tower and buttresses were replaced, the monastery roof retiled, a concrete foundation built, and the south end of the building completely reconstructed. The reservoir was repaired, and a cistern built. The mission virtually was restored by the time of Fr. Buckler's retirement in 1924.

SOLVANG (Dan., sunny vale), 42.1 m. (495 alt., 400 pop.), is the largest Danish settlement in California; 75 per cent of the population is of Danish birth or descent. The square-towered white stone DANISH LUTHERAN CHURCH (R), an edifice of fourteenth-century Danish architectural pattern, looks down from its location over the lower-lying business district (L). Covered arcades shade sidewalks before stores and shops, on which signs are lettered in Danish. In this tree-shaded town, surrounded by the farming and dairying lands that suggest its name, traditional customs of the Danish homeland are preserved. A factor in keeping alive native ways and culture is the College of Atterdag, a Danish folk school founded in 1911 as a private enterprise, but operated since 1921 by the local Danish church. Surviving are many of the pioneers who, as members of the Danish-American Corporation, helped to found Solvang in 1911. They and their first- and second-generation descendants annually participate in various folk feats and dances—the *Fastelavn* in spring, the Danish Days Midsummer Festival in June, and others.

Gayest is the *Fastelavn,* celebrated under the sponsorship of all Danish organizations on the evening preceding the first day of Lent. Danish children usually arrive early to spank each other and everybody else with gaily trimmed switches called *Fastelavnris,* in perpetuation of an ancient homeland custom (according to which the parents remained in bed the morning of the holiday until the children arose and switched them with the *Fastelavnris,* when they too arose and bestowed gifts upon the children). Those who have the hardihood—and a horse—participate in such strenuous events as "ring riding" and "knocking the barrelhead," while the more sedate drink coffee and eat *Fastelavn-boller,* a bun. Ring riding is a contest between horsemen who try to take rings from a pole with a spear while riding past; the first successful participant is declared King of *Fastelavn.* Three barrels are used in "knocking the barrelhead"—a strong one for adults, a medium-strength one for older children, and a small one for little children. The winner is the contestant who, with a club, breaks the barrelhead, and originally this accomplishment released a cat from the barrel, but in Solvang it releases a flood of oranges, apples, and candy.

Midsummer Festival, the Danish Days celebration, is usually held the second or third week in June. Church services on Sunday are followed by a noonday dinner. The afternoon is devoted to community singing and speaking. In the evening, the celebration reaches a carnival pitch with a torchlight procession. A Danish language play is produced. A mass meeting is held in the outdoor bowl of Atterdag College. Dramatic presentations of Hans Christian Andersen's tales and folk dances in costume complete the program. Many who attend the festivals dress in native Danish costume—the men wear tasseled caps, short-waisted coats and knee breeches; the women wear rimless bonnets, shoulder shawls and full-pleated skirts; the children wear costumes patterned after their elders.

In 1909, the Reverend J. M. Gregersen, pastor of a Danish church in Iowa, and the Reverend B. Nordentoft and Professor P. P. Hornsyld of Grand View College in Des Moines, urged the establishment of a Danish folk high school on the west coast and the founding of a Danish settlement to support it. In 1911, the Danish-American Corporation was formed with thirty-four stockholders to acquire ten thousand acres of the Jonata Ranch, adjoining the lands of Santa Inés Mission. A private house and a hotel built early that year were the first structures in the town. Later in the year, Atterdag College was founded by Gregersen, Nordentoft, and Hornsyld. The Danish Lutheran Church was organized in 1913, and for fifteen years its services were held in the college lecture hall. The white stone church was built in 1928. Adjoining it was a small country school which was replaced early in 1940 with a long, steep-roofed schoolhouse of old Danish architecture. The stork weather vane on its steeple is a concession to the Scandinavian belief that storks on the roof bring a house good luck.

Crown Prince Frederik and Princess Ingrid of Denmark, on a visit to Santa Barbara County in 1939, attended Good Friday services in the Danish church at Solvang, on April 7.

BUELLTON (490 alt., 107 pop.), 45.7 *m.,* is a small hamlet which has grown up about the junction of State 150 and US 101, somewhat as other towns in the valley started as stage-line stops (*see below*). Buellton styles itself "the Mission Crossroads," because it lies on the old route between the missions Santa Inés and La Purísima (*see Tour 3*). A little more than a dozen years ago, a tavern keeper in

Buellton began making a specialty of split-pea soup prepared after a recipe his French wife had from her mother. As the fame of the dish grew, the tavern's restaurant trade grew with it to such proportions that the entire pea crop of an Idaho farmer—a carload—was sent every year to Buellton to be turned into soup, and the little town became known as "The Home of Split Pea Soup." Competition presently came, and until recent years, three tavern keepers in Buellton disputed each other's claims to the fame of the dish. Two on one side of the main street displayed signs reading, "The Home of Pea Soup," and "The Best Split Pea Soup in the World." From the opposite side of the street a larger sign took issue, "We are the originators of the split-pea soup advertised across the street."

Buellton was named for the R. T. Buell family, pioneers who owned the surrounding ranch lands.

Early in January, steelhead trout begin their annual spawning run up the Santa Ynez River, which flows past Buellton under the bridge on US 101, about three quarters of a mile south of town. From this bridge to the river's mouth, near the little seashore village of Surf (*see Tour 3*), fishing is permitted. The trout run lasts until early summer. The paved county road which branches westward from US 101, a quarter mile south of the bridge, parallels the river for seventeen and a half miles to a junction with State 1 near Lompoc (*see Tour 3*).

In Buellton is the junction of State 150 and US 101; R. on US 101, now the main route.

North of Buellton the highway curves along the western rim of the Santa Ynez Valley, with the green-forested slopes of the La Purísima Hills (L) dropping to the highway's edge.

At 51.3 *m.* is the junction with Los Olivos Rd. Right here.

MATTEI'S TAVERN (R), 2.7 *m.*, a hostelry familiar for many years to travelers through this part of the country, was founded as a wayside inn and stagecoach station by Felix Mattei in 1888, the year after the Pacific Coast Railroad was laid into Los Olivos (*see below*). The inn provided for travelers making the connection between stagecoach and railroad train. Although trains, rails, coaches, and stage lines have vanished from Santa Ynez Valley long since, and the main line of travel is now several miles to the west, Mattei's Tavern still serves its old-fashioned meals with vegetables, fruit, and fowl from its own acres, and trout from streams in the region. Its staid but gracious atmosphere wisely remains as it was and the old Chinese cook still presides over the kitchen.

LOS OLIVOS (Sp., the olive trees), 2.9 *m.* (836 alt., 193 pop.), a trading center for the farmers and turkey ranchers of northern Santa Ynez Valley, began in 1887 as the terminus of the Pacific Coast Railroad, which had been gradually pushing its narrow-gauge tracks south from San Luis Obispo County with Santa Barbara as its ultimate goal. When the line reached the little stagecoach station about which Los Olivos grew up, it stopped because of the anticipated competition of the powerful Southern Pacific Railroad Company, which planned to run its San Francisco-Los Angeles line through the coastal counties. The little stagecoach station at Los Olivos had stood on the spot since 1876, a stop on the stage line between Santa Barbara and San Luis Obispo. The narrow-gauge railway displaced that part of the stage line between San Luis Obispo and Los Olivos station, but the remainder of the line continued in operation until about 1901. That forty-mile stretch between

Los Olivos and Santa Barbara was the last remaining link in the great stage-coach system that had borne passengers, mails, and goods between Los Angeles and San Francisco before the coming of the Southern Pacific Railroad. With the development of motor travel and haulage and the improvement of high-ways, operation of the little railroad from San Luis Obispo County became less and less profitable, and service between Los Alamos and Los Olivos—the southernmost ten or twelve miles of the line—was discontinued. In the middle of the 1930's, regular service between Los Alamos and Santa Maria also was discontinued, and nowadays the line carries only occasional freight and no passengers. The rails between Los Alamos and Los Olivos have been taken up.

Northwest of the junction with Los Olivos Road, US 101 cuts through the Solomon Hills (R) and La Purísima Hills (L). As the pass widens, Herefords and Red Durhams grazing on the slopes herald the proximity of the cattle country in Los Alamos Valley.

At 57.6 *m.* is the junction with the paved *Cañada de los Alisos* (Sp., canyon of the alder trees) road. The main route continues straight ahead.

Right on the paved canyon road. This is an alternate route which con-nects with the main route again after twenty-four and a half miles of hill-and-dale meandering. The little old-fashioned country chapel dedicated to Benjamin Foxen, who helped Frémont across San Marcos Pass, stands in the peace and quiet of Foxen Canyon, through which the tour passes; the tiny town of Sisquoc stands near the convergence of Cat Canyon with the Sisquoc River bed; and up Cat Canyon, through which the tour proceeds, is Blochman City, a town built and operated by elementary-school children.

At 6.5 *m.* on the Cañada de los Alisos road is the junction with another paved road running through Foxen Canyon. Left here to the little gray frame SISQUOC CHAPEL (L), 11.5 *m.,* standing beside a solitary cypress upon a mesa near the head of Foxen Canyon. Adjoining the church is a three-acre cemetery in which many of the graves are marked by simple little wooden crosses with inscriptions obliterated by time and the elements. Among them, marked by a marble shaft carved in the form of a ship's broken mast, is the GRAVE OF BENJAMIN (DON JULIÁN) FOXEN, who in 1846 guided Lieutenant Colonel John C. Frémont and the "California Battalion" along a little-known Indian trail through what is now San Marcos Pass (*see above*).

Foxen, an Englishman, had been a ship captain. He quit the sea in 1827 to settle in Santa Bárbara County, and was christened at Santa Bárbara Mis-sion in order to be eligible to marry the daughter of a local Spanish family. Indians at the christening dubbed him Don Julián, a name he bore throughout the region in which he was known for the rest of his life. With his Spanish wife he went to live on the property he acquired in the Sisquoc River Valley—the Rancho Tinaquaic. He took up cattle raising, and because he never quite forgot the sea, his cattle brand was an anchor.

When Frémont and his motley battalion camped in the wood on Foxen's land in 1846, they were on their way from Monterey to take Santa Bárbara. Frémont had learned of Foxen's familiarity with the country to the southwest from a rancher in San Luis Obispo County with whom he had stayed to rest and provision his men. It is not certain whether the San Luis Obispo rancher or Foxen himself warned Frémont of the rumored ambush set for him by the Barbareños in Gaviota Pass (*see Tour 3*), but doubtless Foxen knew of the rumor from his Barbareño wife before Frémont arrived. Foxen was one of the few who knew the Indian trail through San Marcos Pass, but he was at first hesitant to help Frémont avoid the suspected ambush by revealing the existence of the alternative route to Santa Bárbara. Like many of the old

American settlers in the country, he took no side in the struggle for possession of California. But he became much attracted to the dynamic and courageous Frémont, and when he reflected that the annihilation of the man and his troops would be no deciding factor in the conquest, it was possible for him to make up his mind to help them.

For what the Californianos considered betrayal, Foxen reaped a bitter harvest. Three times his home on the Rancho Tinaquaic was burned and his herds stampeded, until at last he was obliged to live elsewhere. After about seven years, however, it was possible for him to re-establish himself in peace on the ranch.

For years after he first took to the land, Foxen had entertained plans for building a church on it, but in 1874 he died with his plan still unfulfilled. Two or three years later, Foxen's daughter, Mrs. Ramona Wickenden, gave the mesa land for the church, and it was built by the Reverend J. B. McNally, pastor of the district that included Guadalupe and Lompoc (see Tour 3), where he built two other little churches exactly like the one at Sisquoc (these others, however, have been altered). Actual labor of building the Sisquoc Church was performed by friends and neighbors. Lumber was imported at $40 a thousand for haulage. Foxen's remains were taken from the unmarked hillside grave near his ranch house and transferred to the church's cemetery.

Services were held in the church once a month, on the regular visit of the pastor to the district, and perhaps many were content enough that they could not be held oftener, for the building stood on stilts above an open foundation, and the wind blew in from underneath, raising the dust and the skirts of ladies, and chilling feet in winter. Rattlesnakes basked in the cemetery. Automobiles, which began to appear in 1908, were the church's final undoing. It stood in a prominent position near the highway where those who motored on Sundays passed its hitching racks; so, as auto traffic increased, more and more frequently the congregation would diminish suddenly as the men stole out of the pews and ran loudly shouting down the hill to hold their horses while some Sunday auto party went chugging past.

In time, the chapel fell into disuse. Somehow, by a mishap untraceable through the course of years, the deed to the church land had never been recorded, and it stood privately owned and publicly forgotten through a quarter of a century. In 1932, the Santa Maria branch of the Security-First National Bank, which had taken the property, gave both chapel and cemetery to the Santa Maria Cemetery Association as a memorial to Foxen. The next year, descendants of Foxen made a pilgrimage to the church, and dedication services were conducted by representatives of the Santa Barbara Mission. Two years later, the memorial was given to the county to be preserved as a historical landmark. Memorial services are held once a year, not regularly, but usually in June before the grasses turn brown.

At the north end of the paved Foxen Canyon road is the little village of SISQUOC (Ind., quail), 17.9 m. (495 alt., 200 pop.), lying at the terminus of a branch line of the now inactive, but once quite busy Pacific Coast Railroad (see Los Olivos above). Idle cattle-shipping corrals at the junction of the motor road and railroad are surrounded by sprawling frame buildings, perhaps a score of them, whose occupants trade at the tiny town's single general store. The store ministers also to the wants of poultry and cattle raisers in the surrounding region.

In Sisquoc is the junction with the oiled-gravel Palmer road. Left here.

On a hillside (L) among oil derricks, on property adjoining the Blochman Union School, 21.5 m., stand the ten eight-foot-high frame buildings of BLOCHMAN "CITY," the "village that Jack and Jill built," a model town run entirely by children under the mayor-and-city-council plan. The community has its own currency, its government is supported by the revenue obtained in a smooth-working taxation system set up by its first citizens at the founding of the town in 1931, and its police department regulates behavior by imposing fines upon lawbreakers. At the beginning of each school year, the mayor, city councilmen, and chief officers of the Chamber of Commerce are chosen in a general election. Eligible to vote is the entire population of this village of fifty souls, about evenly divided as to sexes, ranging in age from six to nearly sixteen years, and varying in class enrollment from the primary to the ninth grade. The small citizens are required to attend school regularly, so life in Blochman City must perforce be limited to holidays, summer vacations, and the hours before and after the daily school session.

A year's program of public works and civic improvement projects is outlined by the Chamber of Commerce at the beginning of every new term. The mayor and city council oversee all city activities. Everybody in town receives a yearly salary, paid monthly; the amount is determined by the responsibility of the position and the value of the services rendered. The mayor receives the highest salary, $500 a year. Although commerce is regulated by the government, individual enterprise flourishes—a citizen here and there buys a lot, puts up his own building, and starts business. There are many partnerships. The two lads who bought the Bureau of Information one year for $2,000, each putting up half, borrowed from the little city's bank and improved the building so that they sold it the following year for enough to pay off the loan and interest, and made a handsome profit besides. Meanwhile, in operating the Bureau of Information, they had studied everything from tours of their home State to the itinerary of the *Yankee Clipper*. Likewise, youngsters who take over the general store for a term get a practical education in merchandising practice; those who administer the health center study hospital methods and first aid; publishing of the city's little mimeographed daily, *The Static,* starts many an apt youngster on the road to professional journalism; management of the city bank presents the complexities of economics in a manner that, because thoroughly understandable, is never forgotten; and he who is fortunate enough to be chosen mayor or elected to the city council is privileged to study such absorbing subjects as municipal government, zoning, sanitation, public health, and recreation.

Blochman City occupies an area of 2,000 square feet, which is divided into twenty-four small lots and criss-crossed by six gravel-surfaced streets wide enough for two cars to pass each other. The townsite was surveyed and the streets graded by the founding citizens, with borrowed transit, tractor, and grader. A contractor spent a day with the boys, laying mudsills and showing how to erect building frames. The girls helped saw and nail up siding. Dealers in the towns of the region donated wallboard, hardware, nails, paint, and cement for street curbings. In many instances, there were enough of certain materials to create a surplus that was exchanged for other things. After the general store was built, the children received dozens of glass jars of preserved meats, cases of canned milk, and various notions and dry goods. Throughout the nine years of the city's existence, it has had assistance from all manner of business establishments in and out of the State. Mineral samples from a Utah mine are on display in its little museum. Among the city's archives are blueprints for a miniature oil derrick and pumping unit, drawn up by the engineers of a Los Angeles oil company—from these the boys built working models on an inch-to-the-foot scale. Plans for a miniature sawmill sent up by a lumber company in Los Angeles were followed with such skill by the boys that the model they made was exhibited at the San Diego Exposition. When the old post office at Sisquoc was abandoned, the equipment was hauled over and set up in Blochman City, so that the little village now has a post office with lockbox and special combination for every citizen. Blochman City mail is received and dispatched on schedule.

Mrs. Bina L. Fuller, principal of the Blochman School, put one of her long-dreamed-of ideas into effect when she started the Blochman City project in 1931. The land was donated by John Williamson, president of the Palmer-Stendel Oil Corporation, which owns the property on which the little country school stands. Mrs. Fuller says, "One project directed by the children and embracing mathematics, history, English, civics, and sociology is worth more than a thousand recitations."

The junction with US 101 is at 24.5 *m.*

From the junction with the Cañada de los Alisos road, the main route is straight ahead (west) on US 101.

LOS ALAMOS (Sp., the cottonwoods), 60.3 *m.* (560 alt., 500 pop.), is the trading center for Los Alamos Valley cattle ranchers and vegetable, fruit, and hay farmers. The small business center of one-story buildings—some stucco, and some frame with frontier-style false fronts—radiates from a memorial flagpole that marks the dividing line between two old Mexican land grants, the Rancho Los Alamos and the Rancho La Laguna (the lake). Each was 40,000 acres in area. In the 1860's two American settlers, John S. Bell and Dr. J. B. Shaw, each acquired a substantial acreage of these neighboring properties and started raising grain. At the time, the headquarters buildings on these two ranches were the only structures in Los Alamos Valley, but grain production required so many workers that in 1876 the two ranch owners pooled adjoining portions of their lands and laid out a townsite with the principal street running down the dividing line between the properties. This was—and still is—Centennial Street, so named to commemorate the 100th anniversary of the nation's birth, the year the town was founded.

In 1882, the narrow-gauge line of the Pacific Coast Railroad (*see above*) was brought in from San Luis Obispo County, and until the middle 1930's, when that part of the line to Los Alamos was discontinued, the little town became a shipping point to tidewater ports for cattle and farm products from Los Alamos and Santa Ynez valleys.

Although most of the large land holdings about Los Alamos are still used for raising cattle and grain, the sandy loam of the central part of the valley has been converted to vegetable crops. The earliest strawberries in the San Francisco market come from Los Alamos, and the tomatoes, lettuce, cucumbers, and musk melons go to Los Angeles.

At 64.5 *m.* is the junction with the oiled-gravel Palmer road leading to BLOCHMAN "CITY," 3 *m.;* SISQUOC, 6.6 *m.;* and, on the Foxen Canyon road from Sisquoc, the SISQUOC CHAPEL and the GRAVE OF BENJAMIN FOXEN, 13 *m.* (*see above*).

As the highway proceeds through Solomon Canyon, MOUNT SOLOMON (1,336 alt.), which crowns the Solomon Hills, is visible to L. of the highway at 68 *m.* These topographical features bear the name of the outlaw Solomón Pico, who used the mountain as a base for raids on stagecoaches operating between Santa Barbara and San Luis Obispo in the 1850's. Solomón was a cousin of Pío and Andrés Pico, whose names stand in better fragrance in early-California history—the former was one of the State's governors under Mexican rule, and the latter was a chief of vigilantes in Los Angeles. Solomón took to outlawry as a protest against the invasion and settling of California by the United States, and his victims were invariably gringo strangers. The old American population, which had settled into the land before the invasion and lived in harmony with the Californianos, were inclined to tolerate Solomón's activities; they had been generally indifferent as to which country won in the struggle for California, and were not unaware of instances of rather sharp dealings with the Californianos on the part of unscrupulous Americans who had poured in after the conquest to grab land and get rich quickly. Through racial loyalty, and because of the outlaw's ties with the reputable Pico family, the Californianos also tolerated him.

In all stage stations in and between Santa Barbara and San Luis Obispo, notices were posted warning of the stretch of road along which Solomón and his gang operated, and giving advice to ride over it fully armed and only by day, and to drive as fast as possible. By 1853, conditions on the road were more hazardous than in any other spot in southern California. When Solomón went to Baja California, his followers were taken over by one of their number, Jack Powers, whose manners, flare for finery, and superb horsemanship made him the most spectacular bandit in all the bandit-ridden Southwest. His hold-ups became so flagrantly daring that a band of fifty vigilantes from San Luis Obispo drove him out of Santa Barbara County, and the gang— the last of its kind in the State—ceased its plunders and disintegrated.

At 70 *m.* the derricks of the SANTA MARIA OIL FIELD stud the lower elevations of the Solomon Hills in a clump about a mile and a half to the left of the highway. This field is one of several in the region, known generally as the Santa Maria Oil District (*see Tour 3*), which includes the Bicknell, Casmalia, and Lompoc fields, and has the town of Orcutt (*see Tour 3*) as its trading and supply center.

As the last of the Solomon Hills is passed, Santa Maria Valley lies spread out to the north.

SANTA MARIA (Sp., Saint Mary), 78.2 *m.* (204 alt., 8,522 pop.), second largest city in Santa Barbara County, is the trading and shipping center of the surrounding agricultural area and the petroleum-producing region to southward. Trees and shrubbery grow along most of the town's streets, which are of greater-than-average width because the farmers who founded the town in 1875 (as Central City) wanted plenty of space in which to turn the 6-mule teams they used in hauling produce over the hills to Point Sal Landing. Main Street is 120 feet wide.

The Californianos first settled Santa María Valley in 1840. They raised cattle, but there was little farming until the Americans began to come in after the Civil War. The Americans grew beans, grains, a little corn, and a few potatoes. In 1897, irrigation was introduced into the valley by a company of sugar-beet producers, who in that year established beet growing and built a sugar refinery about which the village of Betteravia (*see Tour 3*) has grown. The artesian wells drilled for irrigation of the beet crop opened the way for general ex-ploitation of the valley's water resources (Santa Maria has one of the finest supplies of almost perfectly pure water in the State; it comes from deep wells seven miles south of the city). With water came the gradual expansion of agriculture in the valley to include, and finally to specialize in, diversified vegetable crops.

Oil production became a considerable factor in the economy of the valley a few years after the Santa Maria oil district was opened in 1902. After the initial boom, production settled down to its present steadiness.

About the time of the outbreak of the first World War, commercial growing of flowers for seed was begun in the valley, and is now the most important of its agricultural crops. The combined Santa Maria and Lompoc (*see Tour 3*) districts, which have approximately five thousand acres in flowers, constitute the largest commercial flower-seed-growing region, and produce 90 per cent of the world's flower-seed supply. Before the destruction of great seed fields in Poland, Czechoslovakia, Austria, Holland, and other countries, after the outbreak of the European war in 1939, these districts produced 60 per cent of the world's flower seeds. Best foreign customers, before the war put a crimp in flower-seed demand abroad, were France, Germany, and England. England was particularly fond of improved California wild flowers, known in the trade as "California natives."

The success of the flower-seed industry in Lompoc and Santa Maria valleys is due to a combination of fertile soil and mild, equable climate. Various kinds of soils are found in the valleys—adobe, gravel, sand, etc. Ocean mists and steady west breezes keep the district cool in summer, and winter temperatures hover closely about the all-year average of 60 degrees.

More than a thousand acres of flowers of some two thousand varieties are grown in Santa Maria Valley alone. Sweet peas predominate, but marigolds, nasturtiums, delphinium, larkspur, poppies, cosmos, snapdragons, calendula, petunias, and others are grown in scores and hundreds of acres, each variety in its own separate plot of land. During the blooming season—June to September—visitors come, many from distant places, to see the sight.

Flower farming is an interesting combination of painstaking hand methods and modern machine processes. Much of the work done by hand is performed by women workers. All flower plots are carefully watched for "rogues"—abnormal or off-type specimens. When one appears, it is removed as soon as color shows in the bud, to prevent cross-pollenization of standard types. A weak plant also is removed, and plants of unusual beauty and vigor are marked and studied for possible hybridizing. The harvesting of seeds is done by hand by skilled workers. Small seeds are threshed with flails, and larger seeds with mechanical rollers. They are spread out on large canvases to be given a preliminary drying, then taken to the cleaning rooms for finishing by electric machinery which blows, whirls, brushes, polishes, and grades them mechanically. Undersize seeds are discarded. Orders for seeds are booked at the farm's offices, filled in the stockrooms, and shipped as through a post-office system. Wholesale prices for the seeds range from a few cents an ounce for some common varieties to as much as $200 an ounce for seed of the giant ruffled petunia, which is thus worth six times its weight in gold (1940).

Some farms confine their business to the production of seed of standard flower varieties by the ton; others specialize in a few varieties; but some also develop new strains, or more specialized variations of established strains, by hybridizing (*see Tour 3*). Staffs of trained women hybridists are kept for this work. Occasionally nature takes a hand in it—even on the farms of growers who do no hybridizing—and presents the grower with a small fortune in one plant. This happened in the case of the dwarf sweet pea, a chance development which brought its nonexperimenting owner several thousand dollars. One firm has several collectors scouring Mexico for wild flowers suitable for development for the seed industry. Among other flower improvements brought about by the growers of the district are the odorless marigold, the winter-blooming and the giant ruffled sweet peas, the giant ruffled petunia, the giant cosmos, the rust-proof snapdragon, and the double golden nasturtium.

Tour 3

COAST AND MOUNTAINS

Santa Barbara—Goleta—Gaviota—Las Cruces—Lompoc—Orcutt—Betteravia—Guadalupe; 83.5 *m.* De la Guerra St., US 101, State 1, County Roads.

Concrete- and asphalt-paved roadbed throughout.
Southern Pacific R.R. parallels route between Santa Barbara and Gaviota.
Accommodations limited except in towns.

After following the narrow shelf along the southern coast line of Santa Barbara County for about thirty miles, this route abruptly turns and climbs into the mountains, where it winds through semiwild cattle country of notable beauty, passes a mine in which Miocene fossil deposits are dug for use in various manufacturing processes, and descends into Lompoc Valley, where mustard fields and commercial flower-seed farms cover hundreds of acres. After a visit to an old mission, one of the most important State landmark restorations in California, another mountain climb takes the route through more agricultural regions to its end in a peculiarly cosmopolitan village of prosperous Swiss and Portuguese dairy farmers and agricultural laborers of mixed Oriental and Latin races.

Southwest from Santa Barbara CITY HALL, 0 *m.,* De la Guerra St. and De la Guerra Plaza, on De la Guerra St.; R. on Rancheria St. (US 101).

At 3.6 *m.* is the junction with La Cumbre Rd. The main tour continues straight ahead on US 101.

Left on La Cumbre Rd. to the junction at 0.1 *m.* with Modoc Rd.; R. here to the junction at 0.3 *m.* with Las Palmas (Sp., the palms) Drive. Left on this drive, which winds through HOPE RANCH, 0.3 *m.,* a two-thousand-acre residential park with more than a hundred and fifty fine homes fronting on thirty miles of shaded drives which curve among fragrant lemon groves to elevated spots overlooking the ocean and Santa Cruz Island. The homes are predominantly of California architecture and the drives have mellifluent Spanish names. Hope Ranch is part of a territory once included in the Santa Bárbara Mission holdings, and which later became the land grant called *Las Positas y La Calera* (the little springs and the lime kiln). The ranch is named for its original owner, Thomas Hope, who in 1863 bought land in the region for seventy-five cents an acre. At Vieja (old) and Nogal (walnut tree) Drives in the north end of the ranch, Hope's two-story house still stands, serving as ranch headquarters. It is pointed out as an interesting example of ranch-house architecture of the period 1870-85.

More than fifty thousand lemon trees are planted in the groves of Hope Ranch, which has been found to be suited particularly for growing the fruit. Proximity of the ocean eliminates destroying summer temperatures which make lemon culture hazardous in many other southern California areas. The inward bend of the coast, the position of the mountainous Channel Islands, and the bulwark of the Santa Ynez Range combine to eliminate harsh winds and frosts.

Almost all the lemon trees of Hope Ranch are grafted to sweet orange rootstock—a practice found to be better than the former custom of grafting them to sour orange root. All citrus trees are prepared for the orchard by grafting: bud-bearing twigs, cut from trees especially propagated for fruit-producing qualities, are grafted to the trunk of a rootstock seedling of a citrus variety especially propagated for root strength; the top of the seedling then is cut off, and the grafted twigs are trained to form the new top.

The Hope Ranch engineering department keeps a map of the entire tract which shows location, age, and pedigree of every lemon tree. Irrigation lines and outlets also are indicated. The practice of irrigating an entire grove at one time by sending water down the rows in ditches is not followed at Hope Ranch. Instead, the trees, during their first and seconds years, are irrigated individually by hoses attached to faucets in convenient locations. Thereafter the faucets serve the water for sprinklers placed either on the ground near the trees or overhead. The ranch management owns a complete

FLOWER SEED HARVEST IN LOMPOC FIELDS

EL REY DE LOS REYES,
DWIGHT MURPHY'S GOLDEN BROWN PALOMINO

NATIONAL GUARD ARMORY, SANTA BARBARA

RANCHEROS VISITADORES—SANTA
BARBARANS RE-LIVING THE PAST

THE HOUSES THAT JACK AND JILL BUILT, BLOCHMAN CITY

A CREAKING CARRETA IN THE
FIESTA PARADE, SANTA BARBARA

HOME, SWEET HOME,
IN THE SANTA YNEZ MOUNTAINS

A HOME IN MONTECITO,
WEALTHY SUBURB OF SANTA BARBARA

stock of orchard equipment, from tractors and spraying machines to hoses and hand tools, which it rents to growers in the tract. Many of the growers, some because they are inexperienced in lemon culture and others because they do not live on their property, arrange with the ranch management for care of their groves. Few citrus growers anywhere harvest their own crops; it is done for them by experienced crews sent out from the packing house of the citrus association to which the orchard owner belongs. Most of the product of the Hope Ranch groves is harvested, packed and marketed by the big packing house at Goleta (*see below*). Lemons are picked about ten times a year, for the crop continuously matures. The fruit is picked while still green in color, and ripens while in storage at the packing house.

On Hope Ranch are a lake, a golf course and country club, children's playground, beach pavilion and cabins, and many other recreational facilities. More than twenty-five miles of bridle paths wind through the ranch. The Santa Barbara Riding and Hunt Club maintains stables, a training ring, and a steeplechase track there, and a polo field lies south of the lake.

At 5.3 *m.* on US 101 is the junction with San Antonio Rd.

Right on this road, which passes through the middle of GOLETA CEMETERY, 0.2 *m.*, to the grounds of the County Hospital. Robert Ripley was delighted when it was called to his attention that in Santa Barbara County "you have to go through the cemetery to get to the hospital," and made mention of the fact in his newspaper feature, "Believe It or Not."

As if going through the cemetery to get to it were not enough to indicate that here no expected order of things prevails, the cream-white buildings of the SANTA BARBARA COUNTY GENERAL HOSPITAL, 0.3 *m.*, stand informally among lawns and gardens, looking less like a public institution than a private estate. The buildings are of one- and two-story height, of hollow-tile construction, and California architecture. Together they afford quarters for 300 patients. A staff of 60 prominent Santa Barbara physicians is in attendance at the hospital, which has a first-class institutional rating with the American College of Surgeons.

The first Santa Barbara County Hospital was established early in the 1860's on the eastern outskirts of the city, and was little more than an old people's home. In 1915, the patients were transferred to a group of buildings on the County Farm, which is still on its old acreage at the east side of the hospital grounds. The present hospital buildings evolved little by little over the following twenty-five years at a total cost of about $500,000, more than half of which went into additions and new structures within the last ten years. Gradual expansion of the hospital continues.

With walnut orchards and small vegetable farms bordering the route, pepper-tree-lined US 101 proceeds to GOLETA (Sp., schooner), 8.2 *m.*, (50 alt., 1,200 pop.), packing and shipping center of the surrounding agricultural region. The Santa Barbara airport is in the southwestern part of this town. One of Goleta's steadiest industries is packing hampers of green peas shipped in refrigerator cars to Middle Western and Eastern markets. About seventy-five thousand sacks of beans and forty thousand bags of walnuts a year are produced in the region. The Goleta Lemon Packing House, one of five such plants in the county, handles the produce of growers in Goleta and Hope Ranch districts. On La Patera (Sp., the duck pond) Ranch, west of town, lemon trees more than sixty years old still bear. The thirty-five acres of lemons planted there by W. W. Stow about 1874 are reputed to be the first commercial planting of the fruit in California. On country estates and ranches about Goleta many crops besides lemons, walnuts, peas, and beans are grown. Avocados, oranges, grain, hay, and alfalfa are among the others, and many acres are used in diversified vegetable farming. Blooded horses and Hereford cattle are bred on some of the ranches.

Goleta received its name from the bleached timbers and rotting hulk of an American schooner which had anchored in the estuary there and been left high and dry when the tide went out. The ruins lay for many years, but have vanished long since.

In Goleta is the junction with Beach Road.

Left here to GOLETA BEACH PARK, 1.2 *m.,* a county recreation ground on the Goleta sandspit. Where the estuary (upon which the American schooner was stranded) extends a half mile inland, a bathing beach lies on the ocean side of the spit, and a children's wading beach on the landward side. The waters at high tide are excellent for aquaplaning. The park has a pier for stillwater fishing, a picnic pergola with barbecue pits, and dressing rooms and rest rooms.

Wells of the ELWOOD OIL FIELD (L) 12.9 *m.,* tap oil sands underlying the flat land between the highway and the sea, and subocean pools. Steel derricks mounted on piers extending over the surf mark the wells which pierce the ocean floor. Subocean drilling was introduced at Summerland (*see Tour 1*) in the 1890's, but it has been developed better at the Elwood field, where there are a dozen derrick piers. The field became one of the largest producers in the county after its opening in 1928, when the discovery well was brought in by the Barnsdall and Rio Grande companies. Drilling history of the well, the Luton-Bell No. 1, is an oil man's classic. When the bit had bored 3,170 feet into the ground and still there were no favorable showings, the company ordered drilling stopped. The field superintendent worked a while longer anyway, and within a few hours Luton-Bell No. 1 came in. It flowed 2,500 barrels of high-gravity oil before being put on the pump.

The highway continues westward, passing the fields of the Elwood Ranch (L), which are surrounded and bisected by columns of tall old eucalyptus trees. Elwood Cooper, owner and developer of the ranch, was a pioneer whose experiments with the eucalyptus as a windbreak served to introduce its permanent and widespread use throughout the southern part of the State. The tree, indigenous to Australia, is so prolific here and grows so readily that it commonly is regarded as native.

Oil from the ORELLA FIELD, 20.8 *m.,* is conducted in a small pipe to an anchorage offshore, where tank ships load from the valve projecting above water. There is no pier at the anchorage.

The green-shingled cabins of a trailer camp at 25 *m.,* strung along a U-shaped inlet at the mouth of Cañada del Refugio (Sp., vale of refuge), occupy the approximate SITE OF THE ORTEGA WHARF built by Don José Francisco de Ortega, one of the Spanish-California land barons of the early 1800's. The Cañada del Refugio, which cuts northward into the Santa Ynez Mountains from the sea, was the eastern boundary of Ortega's land, the Rancho Nuestra Señora del Refugio (ranch of Our Lady of Refuge), which extended along a 25-mile ocean frontage. Ortega received the grant from the Spanish Crown in 1800 for his services in Portolá's 1769 expedition to Monterey. In 1818, the pirate Hippolyte de Bouchard destroyed Ortega's first home, on one of his hacienda-sacking forays. Of Ortega's second home, built three miles up the canyon, only traces of the foundation remain. The road past this house and through the canyon was used by the Franciscan padres as a short cut between the Santa Inéz and Santa Bárbara missions.

GAVIOTA (Sp., sea gull), 31 *m.* (94 alt., 157 pop.), which styles itself "The Gateway to Gaviota Pass," is a town consisting of a general store and a gasoline filling station. The coves notching the shore line west of Gaviota were hideouts for Yankee sailing vessels which smuggled trade goods inland to the *ranchos* and missions at night to avoid paying high Mexican tariffs.

At 31.9 *m.* is the junction with a paved road.

Left here to GAVIOTA BEACH COUNTY PARK, 0.3 *m.*, a county recreation area at the mouth of Gaviota Canyon. The park covers a small crescent-shaped beach, and contains picnic tables under pergolas, and barbecue pits. High above is the steel trestle of the Southern Pacific Railroad, which today transports by land freight once shipped by sea from the old GAVIOTA LANDING on this spot.

As the main route turns inland from the ocean, it begins the ascent into GAVIOTA (sea gull) PASS, so named because one of the soldiers of Gaspar de Portolá's party shot a sea gull as the expedition passed through in 1769. In those days the pass was exceedingly narrow, and wagons could not be drawn through it. The Spanish and Mexican settlers, and even the earlier Americans, let it remain so for nearly a century. All during the mission and land-grant eras, and long after the beginning of the American influx, it was the only outlet to the northern part of the county, yet a boulder fallen from a cliff blocked it so that two animals could not pass through it abreast. If any of the natives thought of making it wide enough for wagons, they always postponed doing anything about it until *mañana*—tomorrow. A series of trails, few of them wide enough for any but horseback travel, served as roads in Santa Barbara County, and until 1855 not one of them was set aside lawfully for public use. There was not a single bridge. In 1855, seven years after California had become a part of the United States, the Santa Barbara *Gazette* began to protest.

"In this county," it indignantly declared, "there had never been a pick and shovel used on a road until some emigrants in 1854 cut their way through Gaviota Pass. In two days they accomplished what the combined strength of Santa Bárbara had not ventured to attempt in almost a century. Carriage after carriage has been conveyed in pieces ʌross the insignificant defile, team after team has suffered shipwreck there, and the united labor that is annually expended by individuals in making their way through the obstacle would suffice not only to remove it, but to build in its place a causeway worthy of the Roman Emperors."

At last, in 1859, officials of Santa Barbara and Los Angeles counties put in operation the governmental machinery necessary to start building a road between the two county seats, and before it was completed, a road was built through Gaviota Pass between Santa Barbara and San Luis Obispo. The routing was essentially the same as that of US 101 today. In 1861, the first Overland Stage went through Gaviota Pass on its way from San Francisco to Santa Barbara.

In the pass (200 alt.), a boulder with a plaque, 32.8 *m.,* set against the cliff face (L), commemorates the GAVIOTA PASS AMBUSH which local legend insists was set by the *Barbareños* in 1846 for Lieutenant Colonel John C. Frémont and his troops, who were marching down from Monterey to take Santa Bárbara. No official account made up in those days relates the incident, but the story has persisted among settlers of the county that the *Barbareños,* warned of Frémont's coming, and supposing he would have to go through Gaviota Pass because it was the only way to Santa Bárbara from the north, hid themselves at the top of the cliffs at the defile's narrowest place and planned to blast rocks down upon the Americans as they marched through. Frémont was told of the ambush as he came through San Luis Obispo County, and on advice of the ranchers there he sought aid from Benjamin Foxen, an English settler in Sisquoc Valley, who took him over an obscure and difficult Indian trail through San Marcos Pass into Santa Bárbara (*see Tour 2*).

LAS CRUCES (Sp., the crosses), 34.1 *m.* (339 alt., 64 pop.), shaded by immense old sycamores, is a cluster of homes about an inn, a wayside store, and a garage. The spot was once a gathering place for early-California cattlemen who took their cattle through the pass and down to the old Gaviota Landing for shipment. In still earlier times, the region was a battleground during the tenacious wars between the coastal tribes and the Tulare Indians from the San Joaquín Valley.

At 34.3 *m.* is the junction with State 1. The main route is L. from US 101 here.

Right on US 101 to the junction at 2.4 *m.* with an oiled road, part of the former routing of US 101. Right on this road, which branches at 3.3 m. Right here to NOJOGUI FALLS COUNTY PARK (*picnic facilities; camping prohibited*), 4 *m.*

Through the park from the oiled highroad runs a graveled road. Right on this road to its end, 4.3 *m.,* from which a footpath continues to NOJOGUI FALLS, 4.8 *m.* Here, between steep canyon walls, the waters of Nojogui Creek slide in a smooth, silver sheet over nearly vertical, moss-covered limestone. A clear pool of purest water receives the fall. The name is sometimes spelled *Nojoqui* and pronounced nó-jo-kee. The local pronunciation is nó-howee, the pronunciation which the Spanish would have given the name in spelling it *Nójogui.* The meaning has been lost.

The main route, following State (L) from its junction with US 101, is through a mountainous region, one of the finest stock-raising areas in California. Virtually all the stock is cattle. El Jaro (Sp., the boar) Creek parallels the highway a part of the distance between Las Cruces and Lompoc (*see below*). Billboards are barred from the countryside between these two towns by mutual agreement of all land owners. It is a region of exceptional natural beauty. The hills are wooded with large sycamores and oaks, many of them hung with be-draggled veils of gray-green air moss. Often the stream beds carry water throughout the year, and the ravines through which they run are overgrown with willow and elder, and various blooming shrubs. Much of the country was a part of the 48,000-acre Rancho San Julian (*see below*).

At the entrance to RANCHO SAN JULIAN (R), 42.9 *m.*, the red roofs of the ranch houses appear through trees about a quarter mile off the highway. Here in April or May gather the score of expert horsemen invited each year to participate in the rounding up and brand-ing of the cattle raised on the 23,000-acre hill-and-meadow property. In the evenings, the men relax in the hospitality of the big ranch house. They work four or five days, handling some 200 head of cattle daily. The animals are marked with Rancho San Julian brand, a cross encircled by the letter D.

The Rancho San Julian, in its original 48,000 acres, was granted to George Rock in 1837, and acquired that same year by Captain José Antonio de la Guerra y Noriega, who perfected the title and put beef stock on the land. Don José Antonio was the fifth *comandante* of the Santa Bárbara *Presidio,* and continued to live in his great *casa* in town (*see Points of Interest*), although he spent much time on the ranch. It was an important meat-supply base, and the soldiers of the *presidio* built an adobe on it.

Occupants of the ranch today are third-generation descendants of Don José Antonio. Fine, registered cattle are the beef stock. Horses are bred for racing and for range work. Hay, grain, beans, mustard, and other crops are grown.

Chalky slides (L) which first appear at 49.4 *m.* and streak the hillsides at intervals for about a mile thereafter are dumps from the workings of the CELITE MINES of the Johns-Manville Corporation. Celite is the trade name of the material mined here—a chalklike fossil substance called diatomaceous earth, composed of the skeletonic cell walls of a microscopic sea plant, the diatom. The Celite bed covers about five thousand acres, and is composed of an estimated hundred million tons of the substance. It is one of the largest uniform deposits of pure diatomaceous earth yet discovered. Some one hundred and fifty men are employed regularly in working the mines, which have been exploited steadily since 1896 but still contain enough diatomite to outlast the lives of the workers mining it.

In the Miocene period, from ten to twenty million years ago, this entire region was underneath the ocean. Masses of diatoms, unicellular algae not visible to the naked eye, lived in the water. As they fulfilled their life span and died, their limestone-like cell walls settled on the ocean floor. The deposits were laid down at the rate of about a half inch a year until the bed was a solid mass of fossils about fourteen hundred feet thick.

The Lompoc deposit was not developed until John and Arthur G. Balaam began full exploitation of the bed in 1896. The property passed through many hands until the Johns-Manville Corporation took over the rights to the deposit in 1929. At first diatomite was used chiefly in tooth powder, silver polish, scouring compounds, and as a filter. German scientists—who call it *Kieselguhr*—discovered its value as a sound-proofing and insulating material in 1912. Now it is used in making heat-proof walls for blast furnaces, water heaters, etc.; in the manufacture of molded plastics, rubber products, paints, concrete and asphaltic compositions; and, because it is an absorbent for nitro-glycerine, in the making of high explosives.

Only part of the diatomite mined here is processed at the company's Lompoc plant; the rest is shipped to other firms and factories in various parts of the world.

Beyond the Celite mines, State 1 begins an easy descent into LOMPOC VALLEY, blanketed to its encircling foothills with the fields of commercial flower-seed farms. During the spring and autumn blooming seasons, the fragrance of the flowers may be detected before the fields themselves come into view. Lompoc and Santa Maria Valleys (*see Tour 2*) form an area which is now the world's largest flower-seed-growing region (about 90 per cent of world supply). In Lompoc Valley approximately 5,000 acres annually for the past five years have been planted to mustard for its seed. Fine saddle and show horses, purebred beef and dairy cattle, and sheep, hogs, and poultry are raised on the ranches about Lompoc. Great fields of grain and alfalfa are grown for fodder and pasturage, and experiments with cultivated range grasses are carried out on hillside ranches. Some of the farmers grow sugar beets, augmenting the large sugar-beet plantings around the Union Sugar Refinery in Betteravia (*see below*). The tops of these beets are used to fatten beef cattle in fall. Cherries, apples, apricots, walnuts, lettuce, and carrots are among the larger crops in the valley's agriculture. About thirty-five tons of honey are produced annually.

At 53.7 *m.* is a junction of State 1 and State 150, which unite westward into Lompoc (*see below*) at this point. The main route is R. here on State 150.

Left from this junction on the combined stretch of State 1 and State 150 to LOMPOC (Ind., shell mounds), 1.3 *m.* (95 alt., 3,379 pop.), trading center for surrounding flower-seed, mustard and truck-crop growers and cattle ranchers. During the June blooming season of the flower-seed farms, a flower show is held in the town, and Independence Day is observed with a general community celebration featuring a typical Western rodeo. This is one of the big events of its kind, and it draws spectators and competing cowboys from Santa Barbara, Ventura, and San Luis Obispo counties.

Lompoc was the first successful American land colonization in California.

In 1874, portions of the Ranchos Lompoc and Misión Vieja (Sp., old mission) were purchased and subdivided by the California Immigrant Union. Small farms and ranches sold for $40 to $75 an acre, and town lots for $500 to $800. During the height of the land-sales boom, one corner lot sold for $1,200. A week's land sales were $700,000, including $70,000 in town lots. Building followed sales at the same boom pace, and eighty families were living in homes of their own within two months after the subdivision was opened. Clauses which forbade the sale of liquor on the land were inserted in the deeds of sale by the former owners of the *ranchos,* and lend documentary support to Lompoc's claim to prohibition pioneering in California. In the 1880's a posse of Lompoc citizens wrecked the drugstore of a violator of the liquor-selling prohibition; the store of another early-day "bootlegger" blew up in an explosion one night, and next day's newspaper reported that an earthquake had singled out the store for destruction, accommodatingly sparing every other building in town. With the passing years, however, Lompoc modified its stand on liquor, and since the repeal of national prohibition in 1933, relief for parched throats has been available in a number of drink emporiums.

As the side tour continues, passing through Lompoc on State 150 (Ocean Ave.), the highway is bordered with the fields of commercial seed farms. More than a thousand varieties of annuals and perennials are under cultivation here. The flower crops are rotated from season to season to insure purity of stock. As part of the hybridizing program, several thousand trials a year are conducted. The trials consist of cross-pollenating selected plants and keeping them under close observation until the second generation, when definite flower characteristics develop. Those individuals which develop the most desirable characteristics with greatest vigor are used in the purity tests. They are "caged"—enclosed in muslin netting—to prevent repollenization by bees. The experiment is not pronounced successful or otherwise until the purity tests have indicated whether the subjects will breed true.

A detailed account of the flower-seed industry and farming methods of the Lompoc-Santa Maria Valley region is given in the discussion of industries in Santa Maria (*see Tour 2*).

State 150 continues in a northwesterly direction to the coast and ends there in the little village of SURF (sea level, 100 pop.), 10 *m.,* where the Southern Pacific spur track to Lompoc joins the main line along the seacoast. At the northern limit of the hamlet, on the south bank of the Santa Ynez River, is OCEAN COUNTY PARK, in which is the ANZA CAMPSITE. Here Juan Bautista de Anza, Spanish explorer, camped in 1775 on his way from San Gabriel to Monterey along the route broken by Gaspar de Portolá, Pedro Fages and Fray Junípero Serra. From here, Anza rode all the fifty miles and more to San Luis Obispo Mission without again stopping to camp. On his way back from Monterey along the coast, he camped on the north bank of the Santa Ynez River. In 1776, leading the band of San Francisco colonists upcoast, Anza camped again where Ocean County Park now lies.

Ocean County Park is the only spot on the coast for many miles in either direction where camping is permissible and swimming advisable. Other beaches in the vicinity are reserved for picnickers only, and treacherous ocean currents make swimming unsafe between Gaviota and Oceano, in San Luis Obispo County. The lagoon and several stretches of the Santa Ynez River, which empties into the sea on the northern edge of the park, are good for swimming. Fishing in the surf at the mouth of the river is a popular sport. Steelhead trout begin their annual run up the river to spawn early in January, and continue at intervals until summer. Fishing is permitted along the thirty miles of spawning grounds between the river's mouth and the point where it is spanned by the bridge at Buellton (*see Tour 2*).

From the junction of State 1 and State 150 east of the town of Lompoc, the main tour route continues R. (northeast) on State 150.

At 54.2 *m*. the highway crosses the Santa Ynez River on a bridge built in 1878, the first to be built over the river.

A little brown shack among willows a few feet off the road is the FORMER HOME OF GIN CHOW (L), 54.4 *m*. Gin Chow was a Chinese farmer whose fame as a weather prophet burst the bounds of Santa Barbara County early in the 1930's and was carried by his own books and the public press throughout southern California. Several years before publication of Gin Chow's *First Annual Almanac,* in 1932, Lompoc had already begun to hear the first of Gin Chow's prophecies. The small, wizened Oriental foretold with uncanny accuracy the earthquakes which devastated Yokohama in 1923 and Santa Barbara in 1925. He warned of rains, floods and heat waves which came to pass as he had said. He predicted that people would go to the city to work, "but not to live there," and that there would be less sickness in time to come because when a man became ill his neighbors would shame him, for "nobody will feel sorry for sick man as much as now because it will be his own fault." In 1931, Harry Carr, columnist of the Los Angeles *Times,* wrote the first of his feature paragraphs on the Lompoc weather wizard. The little Oriental appeared in motion-picture newsreels. He became a featured speaker at southern California business clubs, delivering his addresses in the dialect in which his two almanacs are written.

Gin Chow said that his system of prophecy was based upon a "key" to the weather cycles left to the Chinese people many centuries ago by a sage. Other California Chinese declared that this "key" was doubtless the lunar calendar Chinese farmers have used for centuries to predict weather.

Gin Chow left China in 1873 at the age of sixteen, and came to Santa Barbara to join relatives there. He was one of those Chinese immigrants who became a part of California life as American pioneering stock began to settle in, serving with profound faithfulness and dependability in the early-American California ranch families, washing, cleaning, cooking, tending babies, and sharing the vicissitudes of pioneer life with their masters. Gin Chow worked with families in Santa Barbara, Montecito, and near-by canyon ranches. He saved his small earnings, and bought land near Goleta for vegetable farming. The Southern Pacific Railroad Company wanted to buy the land, but Gin Chow firmly refused to sell it until the company met his price. In 1911, six months prior to enactment of the law prohibiting Chinese from purchasing real property in the United States, he bought land in Lompoc and moved there.

Gin Chow's court actions were many and varied. He was the first to sue the city of Santa Barbara for Santa Ynez Valley water rights, an action in which seventy other farmers joined afterwards.

Gin Chow's second wife (the first died) bore him five children, of whom two daughters and a son are living.

In the summer of 1932, a bull from a neighboring ranch trampled Gin Chow, and was found with the old Chinaman's lantern hanging on one horn. But Gin Chow declared that he would live over his injuries because it was not his time to die. It was then that he predicted his death "within a year." And the next summer, shortly after publication of his second almanac, his career ended as he had foretold. A truck driven by a Japanese (ironically, a son of a friend of Gin Chow), struck and injured him fatally.

At 55.6 *m.* is the junction with a paved county road. Left from State 150 on this road, now the main route.

LA PURÍSIMA STATE PARK, 56.2 *m.,* is a 507-acre preserve in which stands the MISIÓN LA PURÍSIMA CONCEPCIÓN DE MARÍA SANTÍSIMA (Sp., mission of the Immaculate Conception of the Most Holy Mary), founded in 1787 by Presidente Fermin Francisco de Lasuén as the eleventh of the California missions and now being restored (1940). The three buildings undergoing restoration— the monastery, workshops, and the church building—form a long row facing eastward upon the road; northernmost is the monastery, in the middle is the reproduction of a building which housed workshops and soldiers' quarters, and southernmost is the church with its tall *campanario* (bell tower). The monastery is an excellent example of mission architecture, and the square, fluted columns of the east-cloister colonnade are considered the finest in any of the missions, but the restoration of La Purísima is still more interesting because the lands about it are being brought back to their early mission-days appearance—a project made possible because the region has remained almost unchanged throughout the years.

When the State began its restoration upon receiving the acreage in 1935, nothing remained of La Purísima's buildings except some of the walls, the tile flooring of the church, and the crumbled wall bases of the monastery. In the latter building not enough was left to indicate what the window positions or roof angle had been, but these were determined by careful measuring on old photographs taken before the walls had crumbled away. The height of the roof was determined from a single intact pillar. An approximation of interiors was made from foundation alignments. When actual labor—by a company of 170 Civilian Conservation Corps boys—was begun, the ruins were found unsafe as a basis for the restoration, so the mission was rebuilt entirely with adobe identical in composition with that of the old structures, brought from pits dug on the grounds. Concealed pillars of reinforced concrete were built into the walls to conform to modern safety requirements, but visible parts of the buildings have been restored with elaborate care to reproduce the originals, with primitive tools as used by the Indians. CCC boys moulded 110,000 adobe bricks, 24x21x4 inches each, and made by hand 32,000 tiles. It was found that professional plasterers did not produce a finish crude enough to resemble the original, even with the special trowels, so the trowels were given to the CCC boys, and having had no more experience at plastering than the Indian neophytes who built the old structures, they turned out a quite satisfactory reproduction of the first mission plaster work. Scrapings of plaster from fragments of the old walls were analyzed to determine the exact nature of the dyes used on the wall surfaces.

Redwood timbers were hand hewn by CCC boys who also made and "aged" the mission doors and many pieces of furniture. The great iron locks of the mission doors were designed in early nineteenth-century patterns. A few rooms of the restored mission are partly furnished with original mission furniture returned by museums, collectors, and individuals into whose hands they had passed.

After extensive research by the Index of American Design, WPA Art Project of Southern California, Henry Helmle, an artist loaned by the Project, supervised the decoration of the church building. Sketches were made, using mission motifs only. These were ornamental designs from various missions, as recorded by the Index of American Design, such as Santa Inez, Santa Barbara, San Juan Capistrano, San Fernando, San Miguel, San Luis Rey, etc. The records showed that the nave of the original church had little decoration, most of it being in the Sanctuary and the choir loft, upper and lower. In the difficult task of redecoration, the motifs for the ornamentations were transferred onto the walls by means of a pounce, with a suitable dry color, and when the design was lightly visible it was scratched in with a sharp tool. The woodwork—pulpit, altar rail, etc.—was done in oil. Some of the dry colors used can be found in the near-by hills surrounding the valley.

Already planted about the grounds, or under cultivation in the mission nursery, are 15,000 shrubs and trees which will complete the restoration. The pear orchard is being rep.. 'ed with young trees from the missions nearest La Purísima, and with c. 'tings from one lone, gnarled survivor of the old orchard. Grapevines i.. m the original Purísima vineyards have been retransferred from the Jalama district on the coast about fourteen miles south. In the garden are old-fashioned hollyhocks, which commonly were planted at all the missions, Castilian roses from San Antonio de Padua Mission in Monterey County, and medicinal herbs used by the padres. The stone garden fountains, the cistern, and the aqueduct of tile pipe and tile-lined *zanjas* (ditches), which brought soft spring water to the mission from a mile or more upcanyon, are being restored.

Vaulted in concrete within the restored mission church is the body of Fray Mariano Payeras, head of La Purísima during her fullest years and most difficult crises. As anticipated by technicians in charge of the restoration, his remains were discovered during excavations of the church site when workers shoveled into his decomposed redwood coffin.

Fray Payeras was appointed to La Purísima in 1804, when the mission was seventeen years old and flourishing in an era of productiveness. At that time it stood four miles south of the present site, across the Río Santa Rosa (now the Santa Ynez River). Its population of a thousand or more consisted of Indian neophytes, Spanish soldiers, and padres. Payeras taught the Indians how to deal constructively with the white people, for whom they often worked. He compiled a religious doctrine for them in their own tongue. He also practiced the Franciscan custom of teaching them to speak Castilian Spanish, although both the fathers and the Indians conversed with the soldiers in a jargon of Mexican and Indian dialects.

Daily the Indians worked four or five hours at the mission, the women making shoes and weaving cotton into coarse mission cloth from which they were taught to make suits for the men and gowns for themselves. They wove wool into blankets worn by both sexes. The men worked at construction and maintenance of buildings and grounds, tended mission livestock, and cultivated mission crops, and gathered wild grains in season to supplement the domestic supply.

Morning and evening meals at the mission settlement consisted of *atole,* a gruel of corn meal. For the midday meal there was *pozole,* a thick porridge of barley and beans. On feast days the Indians received rations of wheat, and every year there was a slaughtering of mission cattle for meat and hides.

There was little cash in the country at the time. The mission fathers bought dry goods, groceries, shoes, church goods, candles, tools, and furniture from Mexico and paid for them with tallow and hides produced from their thousands of sheep and cattle. The people of the mission settlement applied to the mission store for these goods and for agricultural products, paying for them as they could with horses and with their own labor. (At this time the mission store's account books carried such well-known California family names as Carrillo, Ortega, Alvarado, Reyes.) The horses and other necessities were sold to soldiers from the Santa Bárbara *Presidio,* who paid for them with soap and cigars.

At the peak of a quarter century of steady development, the mission was producing an abundance of grains, vegetables, and fruits. Some of California's finest sheep, cattle, and horses grazed on the pastured hills. Housing was adequate. Good wine came from neighboring vineyards while La Purísima's own late-planted vines were maturing. The birthrate rose among the Indian neophytes and they progressed rapidly in weaving, silver- and wood-working, building of pillared adobes, and other crafts. More than fifteen hundred of them had been baptized, and they apparently were advancing in their study of Christian doctrine to the deep satisfaction of Fray Payeras and his associate missionary. In their daily leisure hours they sang, played musical instruments, and enjoyed various other diversions popular among them.

On December 21, 1812, an earthquake split the mission site. The buildings were shattered and their walls, together with images, paintings, and furniture, fell into the chasm and were buried. Many persons were injured. The open earth belched water and black sand, and heavy rains added to the disaster. Only a few of the most urgent necessities were rescued from the devastation, and most of the Indians deserted the ruined mission. Those who remained took refuge with the two fathers in shelters of poles and grass.

Father Payeras realized the inadvisability of rebuilding the demolished structures and continuing the mission on the original location, so he petitioned Church and State for a new site. In the spring of the following year they settled in the present spot, a dale they called Cañada de Los Berros (Sp., canyon of the watercress). It was on the Camino Real between Santa Inés and San Luis Obispo Missions.

In re-establishing the mission settlement, Father Payeras faced his most trying obstacles. Because of the three-year-old Hidalgo Revolt still raging in Mexico, the previously available goods and money from the Pious Fund no longer were forthcoming. The soldiers likewise were deprived of salaries from Mexico and therefore looked to the missions for support for themselves and their families. Slow as the labor of mission building was, these hardships made the labor even slower—but the fathers staunchly gathered their frightened neophytes at the new site, and reassuring them as well as they could, set them to work at building temporary quarters of thatched-roofed palisade-houses and a church of adobe-veneered poles. A garden and crops were planted, and the aqueduct that ran from the river to the Old Mission was extended to the new site. Reservoirs for spring water were built. By the end of the first year in the new location, more than a thousand Indian families were living again under dominion of the mission. A year or two following, Fray Payeras was appointed head of the Catholic church in California, and as he chose to remain at La Purísima, the mission accordingly became the ecclesiastical headquarters of the country. All the major structures which stood on the new site until the beginning of the present restoration were built during the next eight years (1813-21).

Although hardships were many during those years—loss of crops and livestock in droughts, destruction of neophyte houses by fire, and an outbreak of stillborn cases among the Indians, all of which resulted in desertion by many of them from the mission—yet La Purísima produced grains, livestock by-products, and handicraft goods in abundance, and was able to extend the usual hospitality to travelers, including the customary gift of a horse and supplies to last during the journey to the next mission post. Gradually the new buildings at La Purísima were furnished, and equipped with statues of saints, Mexican framed mirrors, oil paintings, and fine altar linens embroidered by the mission women.

After Fray Payeras was made head of the mission, he was obliged to journey continually among the nineteen others in the chain, and the hardships of these travels, after six years of exhausting labor in re-establishing La Purísima, hastened his death, which came in the spring of 1823. The disintegration of the mission progressed with increasing rapidity after his death. An uprising of the Purísima Indian neophytes, instigated by revolting Indians of Santa Inés Mission who chafed under the confining life and unending demands for supplies to feed, clothe, and equip the soldiers and their families, resulted in intervention of troops from Santa Bárbara and San Luis Obispo Missions, and the execution of seven young Purísima Indians charged with responsibility for the uprising. Scores of Indians deserted the mission because of the affair, and in 1832 there were only about three hundred left.

Secularization further hastened La Purísima's disintegration. The Purísima estate at the time was valued at about $60,000. Administrators shifted the property from person to person, and each change of ownership entailed a loss of furnishings and scattering of cattle. The neglected buildings deteriorated rapidly. No missionary was stationed there after 1836, and the Indian population dwindled. Many of them became ill, and in 1839 the inspector of the missions permitted slaughter of about three hundred cattle to purchase clothing for them.

Governor Micheltorena's decree of 1843, restoring management of mission temporalities to the Franciscan fathers, meant little to La Purísima. After nine years of secularization, few of its properties were left to be worked, and the population was estimated generously at two hundred. Under Pío Pico's governorship in 1845, mission properties were distributed ruthlessly among favorites or auctioned away to the highest bidders. Thus the remains of La Purísima—the neglected buildings and two vineyards—went to John (Don Juan) Temple of Los Angeles for $1,100 in 1845. During the following thirty years of abandonment, highwaymen made their lairs in the crumbling structures and stolen loot filled the vestment cases. After them, respectable *rancheros* and their families used the church as a home. For a time it became a store, the only one in the county outside of Santa Bárbara. During this time the mission served as a religious house only for services held on Easter Sundays. Under United States President Ulysses S. Grant, the mission and its properties were restored to the Catholic church (1874), but over the following years it was necessary to sell tracts of the land to seculars. Meanwhile the mission buildings aged and were ill used—sometimes as stables or sheepfolds—and with the turn of the century the roofs fell, the corridor arches crumbled, the painted pulpit on the chapel wall hung with its sounding board awry, the canvas ceiling drooped in tattered strips, the heavy beams and handmade roof tiles collapsed and were carried away by trespassers, stone and rubbish collected behind the broken altar rail, and wild mustard choked the gardens and doorways and sprang up through chinks in the tile floors.

First move toward restoration was made by the Union Oil Company in 1903, when it bought the property and offered it to the county or State on condition that it be reclaimed. But general interest in restoration was not aroused until Father John Raley of Lompoc, after two or three years of effort, brought about in 1910 a celebration of the 125th anniversary of La Purísima's founding. This was followed by press and public-speaking campaigns which further stimulated interest in the project. At length the land bearing Purísima ruins was deeded to Santa Barbara County, which passed it on to the State in 1935; the Catholic church donated part of the old cemetery grounds, additional lands were purchased which brought the area to its present size, and actual restoration was begun.

At 60 *m.* is the junction with State 1. Right on State 1, now the main route.

After ascending a short, steep pass through the Purisima Hills, the highway achieves a vantage point at 61.5 *m.* from which much of the countryside is visible; the view of Lompoc Valley to the rear is spectacular. The highway winds in hairpin curves over the crest of the Purisima Hills and down the northern slopes, so that careful driving is necessary to avoid accident.

Shortly after achieving the crest of the pass, the highway passes a stand of Bishop Pine (R) covering several hundred acres. This tree, native to the coastal regions of the State and Lower California, bears an abundant crop of cones which remain closed on the trees for many years. When these trees are victims of fire in the forest, the cones open prematurely in the excessive heat and release their seeds, thus sowing a new forest crop. This stand of Bishop Pine is an example of such reproduction, the result of a forest fire among the preceding stand about ten years ago.

Descending from the pass and touching the edge of the little village of Harris at 65.2 *m.,* State 1 proceeds through pastoral hillscapes marred occasionally by an oil derrick or a storage tank, and graced at intervals by a stand of eucalyptus or sycamore trees lining the roadside.

ORCUTT (314 alt., 470 pop.), 72.4 *m.,* is an oil town dominated industrially by properties of the Union Oil Company, which has tool plants and tank farms there. It is the shipping center for petroleum produced in the heart of the SANTA MARIA OIL DISTRICT, to which the Orcutt, Bicknell, Casmalia, and Lompoc fields belong.

Oil prospectors began to investigate the district in 1896, but it was not until 1902 that the first well to tap the vast resources of the field was brought in. Several oil companies entered the scene at once, and before the year was out another heavy-producing well came in. Among the oil seekers who thereupon flocked to the Santa Maria District was the Union Oil Company. Its geologist, W. W. Orcutt, mapped a surface geology of the entire district and wrote an appraisal of the territory. The company began buying land and leases, and by 1904 brought its holdings to 70,000 acres, thereby controlling most of the oil pool. Within its land was what had been the 10,722-acre Todos Santos (Sp., all saints) Ranch, granted by the Mexican government in 1841 to William Hartnell. The town of Orcutt, named after the company geologist, was established on the tract in 1903, while it was still under lease to the company.

The Pacific Coast Railway, which ran from old Port Harford (now Port San Luis) through the Santa Barbara County back country (*see Tour 2*), built a spur track to the new oil field and took crude oil out in tank cars. The Union Oil Company put down 32 miles of 6-inch oil pipe along the railroad right-of-way. The year-old town of Orcutt became a thriving little oil center with a continual stream of 6-horse trucks moving through its streets carrying supplies for the wells.

At this time (1904), one of California's earliest and most remarkable gushers came in, Union Oil's Hartnell No. 1 (named after the Hartnell property, on which it stood). Terrific gas pressure forced oil up the 8-inch casing and 150 feet into the air. It flowed 12,000 barrels a day for three months, and continued to flow vigorously for two years before being put on the pump. Hartnell No. 1 continued to be one of the wonders of California until the big Midway Field gushers of Kern County came in, about six years later.

At the western edge of Orcutt, State 1 jogs L. from its junction with the Orcutt road, turning right at 72.5 m. to resume its northerly direction.

At 73.1 m. is the junction with a paved county road. State 1 branches L. at this point. The main route is straight ahead on the county road.

The route is through a rural district lying south of Santa Maria (see Tour 2).

At 76.5 m. is the junction with another paved county road. L. on this road, now the main route.

BETTERAVIA (Fr., betterave, beet), 80 m. (185 alt., 250 pop.), is surrounded by fields of sugar beets that supply the raw material used by the Union Sugar Refinery (L). The refinery, more than seven acres of sprawling, red brick buildings massed along a spur of the Southern Pacific Railroad, is the economic focus of this little settlement of beet field and factory workers, with its service station, garage, and scattering of homes. For eight months of the year Betteravia slumbers quietly among the beet fields, its refinery idle, its road little used except by an occasional motorist taking a short cut between Guadalupe and southern Santa Maria Valley. Then early in August the smoke again belches from the tall stacks of the sugar plant, and caravans of trucks bring in beets from the 16,000 acres of surrounding fields.

The sugar beet, although it belongs to the same family as the red garden beet, is not used as a garden vegetable. It is larger than the red beet, and white in color. The sugar beet and sugar cane produce almost all the sugar sold commercially. The product of the two plants is identical when completely refined, but the raw beet sugar has a very disagreeable flavor and never is offered on the market. Beet sugar is extracted by the diffusion method, as contrasted to the expression method of obtaining sugar from cane. First the beets are washed, then sliced mechanically, and put into a battery of twelve or more diffusing vessels, into which hot water is forced under pressure. The water, charged with sugar diffused into it from the plant cells, is forced from vessel to vessel until it is so heavily saturated with plant sugar that it cannot take up any more. At this stage it is called "diffusion juice." Then it is purified with hydrate of lime, bleached with sulphur dioxide, and heated to a temperature of 140 degrees Fahrenheit. The heat removes emulsified air, lowers the density of the liquid, and kills living organisms which would cause fermentation and acidity. Then hot mother-liquor (molasses) is passed through a filter to remove the non-sugars which have been made separable by the heat and chemical agents.

Slow cooling brings about a condition of supersaturation, in which sugar crystals are formed. These crystals are removed from the liquor in a perforated rotating drum with a gauze lining through which the fluid passes by centrifugal force, leaving the sugar crystals free.

In refining, the crystals are washed to remove adhering molasses, and melted to form a liquor, which is filtered under pressure through cloth to purify, and filtered through bone char to render it colorless. The clear liquor is then boiled in the vacuum pan, and again crystals form. The liquor is removed from these in centrifugal machines, and they are purged with water, syrup, or steam. The finished crystals are dried, and are ready at last for the package.

A hundred tons of beets will yield between fifty and sixty-five tons of by-products, mostly beet pulp, some wet filter-press cake, and a little molasses. The beet pulp is made into cattle fodder, and is sometimes sweetened by adding molasses. The filter-press cake is used for fertilizer. The molasses is used principally in making alcohol, and some is used in fertilizers. Nothing of the beet is wasted. Even the tops are used in fattening cattle.

The Union Sugar Refinery distributes more than a million dollars a year among the farmers and laborers of the district in wages and beet purchases. During the refinery's four-month seasonal run—August through November—from 1,500 to 2,000 workers are employed in the fields and factory. During the rest of the year they turn to the dairies and truck gardens of neighboring districts for work.

The sugar-beet industry was introduced to the region in 1897 by the Union Sugar Refining Company. Until the beet growers drilled artesian wells for irrigation, water resources of Santa Maria Valley were unexploited. Thereafter, however, the practice of irrigation spread, bringing about a gradual transition of the valley's agriculture from dry farming of grains, beans, and pasturage to diversified fruit and vegetable farming.

At 83.9 *m.* is the junction with State 166; L. here to the junction with State 1 at 84.8 *m.*; R. on State 1, now the main route.

GUADALUPE (80 alt., 2,000 pop.), 85.8 *m.*, is the center of a prosperous dairying industry carried on by thrifty Swiss and Portuguese. In the town, English is rarely spoken without an accent. In addition to the Swiss and the Portuguese there are Mexicans, Filipinos, Chinese, and Japanese. Most of the Japanese own farms, as do most of the nondairying Portuguese. The Mexicans, Filipinos, and Chinese are field hands or dairy workers, and some of them find seasonal employment in the Betteravia sugar factory and beet fields (*see above*).

Rancho Guadalupe was a 30,000-acre land grant given in 1840 to Teodoro Arrellanes and Diego Olivera. The Arrellanes home was the first in Santa María Valley, and when Americans began to settle in the district after the Civil War, they built their homes about it. The straggling settlement which thus grew up was not given its name until 1874, but it was a trading center for an agricultural and stock-raising region of 125,000 acres, and became the first town of any importance in the northern part of the county. The year after it had been graced officially with the name Guadalupe, the town which was to outgrow and supplant it in importance was founded—Santa Maria (*see Tour 2*), then called Central City.

The main line of the Southern Pacific Railroad runs through Guadalupe. The Santa Maria River skirts the northern edge of town, marking the boundary between Santa Barbara and San Luis Obispo counties. The river has no source under its own name, for it is formed by convergence of the Cuyama and Sisquoc Rivers at the eastern end of Santa Maria Valley.

Part 4

Appendices

Chronology

1542   Oct.—Juan Rodríguez Cabrillo discovers Channel Islands. Drops anchor off Santa Bárbara coast.

1543   Jan.—Juan Rodríguez Cabrillo, deceased, buried on one of the Channel Islands (San Miguel or Santa Cruz).

1579   Sir Francis Drake sails by Santa Bárbara.

1602   Dec. 4—Sebastián Vizcaino, on exploration trip for Spanish Crown, visits Santa Bárbara Channel. Santa Bárbara region named by Father Antonio de la Ascención, a Carmelite friar and member of Vizcaino party.

1769   April—Galleon *San Antonio,* commanded by Juan Pérez, lands at a channel island; Santa Cruz (Sp., holy cross) Island named.

Aug. 18–20—Captain Gaspar de Portolá with expedition visits Santa Bárbara.

1772   Sept. 6—Father Junípero Serra, with Comandante Pedro Fages, arrives at site of present city of Santa Bárbara for first time.

1774   April 15—Captain Juan Bautista de Anza passes present site of Santa Bárbara, on his trail-blazing expedition from Mexico to Monterey.

1782   Jan. 1—Father Crespi, early historian of Santa Bárbara Indian life, dies at Monterey.

April 2—Presidio Real of Santa Bárbara founded by Governor Felipe de Neve, Padre-Presidente Junípero Serra and Captain José Francisco de Ortega, first comandante.

1784   Captain José Francisco de Ortega relieved as Comandante of Santa Bárbara Presidio, transferred to Monterey.

1786   Dec. 4—Father Fermín Francisco Lasuén, third Padre-Presidente of the Alta California missions, presides over ceremonies dedicating Santa Bárbara Mission.
Dec. 31—First Mission baptism at Santa Bárbara Presidio.

1787   First buildings at Santa Bárbara Mission erected.
Dec. 8—La Purísima Concepción Mission founded by Father Fermín Francisco Lasuén.

1788   Original chapel of Santa Bárbara Mission enlarged to provide for increasing number of Indian converts.

1789   A second church built at Santa Bárbara Mission.

1793   A third mission church is begun, of adobe construction.
Nov.—Captain George Vancouver, noted British navigator, visits Santa Bárbara.

1797   Presidio chapel finished and consecrated.

1802   Five great vats built at Santa Bárbara Mission for tanning of hides.   Thirty-one new adobe houses built.

1804   Sept. 17—Santa Inés Mission founded by Father Estevan Tapis.

1806   First reservoir to supply water to city of Santa Barbara built under direction of Father Ripoll.

1807   Stone prison constructed near Santa Bárbara Mission.
Mission dam built by Indians under direction of Franciscan fathers of Santa Bárbara Mission.

1810   Sept. 16—Revolution in Mexico against Spanish domination breaks out.   Santa Bárbara cut off from Old Mexico.

1811   Dec. 8—Earthquake at Santa Bárbara.

1812   Sept.—Earthquakes at Carpintería and Santa Inés.

1812   Dec. 21—Earthquakes destroy Missions Santa Bárbara and La Purísima Concepción.

1815   José de la Guerra becomes Comandante of Santa Bárbara Presidio.

1818   Joseph Chapman, said to be first Yankee settler, arrives at Santa Bárbara as unwilling member of privateer crew.

1820   Sept. 10—Old mission church completed and ceremoniously dedicated with Governor Sola and staff, prelates, neophytes, Comandante José de la Guerra, officers, and troops of presidio present.

1822   April—Santa Bárbara takes oath of allegiance to Mexico and lowers Spanish flag.

1824   Feb. 22—Santa Bárbara Mission Indians revolt against Mexican soldiers; several lives lost on both sides.

1826   Dec.—First Ayuntamiento by order of Governor Echeandia changing Santa Bárbara Presidio from military to civil government.

1828   Don Daniel Hill builds adobe house with first wooden floor in Santa Bárbara (now known as Carrillo Adobe, named after one of California's most distinguished families).

1829   First Mexican school established in Santa Bárbara.

1833   Aug. 17—Mexican congress decrees secularization of Alta California missions.

1835   Jan. 14—Richard Henry Dana, of the crew of brig *Pilgrim* and later author of *Two Years Before the Mast,* first visits Santa Bárbara.

      Oct. 29—Governor Figueroa buried at Santa Bárbara Mission.

1840   Santa Bárbara's estimated population, 900.

      Apr. 27—Appointment of Father Francisco García Diego y Moreno as California's first bishop signed by Pope.

1842   Jan. 11—Bishop Diego y Moreno establishes residence at Santa Bárbara Mission.

      Jan. 24—Sir George Simpson, celebrated English traveler, visits Santa Bárbara.

1845   Dec. 4—La Purísima Concepción Mission sold to John Temple for $1,110.

1846   Bishop Diego y Moreno dies; buried at Santa Bárbara Mission.

      Feb.—Governor Pío Pico sends Don José María Covarrúbias of Santa Bárbara to Mexico for aid in impending war with United States.

      Aug. 4–5—Commodore Robert Field Stockton, in command of American forces, anchors at harbor of Santa Bárbara. Captures city, leaving small garrison in charge. Stars and Stripes fly for first time over Santa Bárbara.

      Oct. 1–2—Stockton's garrison captured; Lieutenant Talbot and men escape to Monterey.

      Dec. 27—Major John C. Frémont leads reinforcements to Santa Barbara. Retakes town.

1847   American brig *Elizabeth* wrecked near Santa Barbara; salvaged cannon becomes object of local intrigue.

      July 4—One hundred and eighty men of Stevenson's regiment leave Santa Barbara for Los Angeles.

1849   First Santa Barbara school established under American flag.

1850   Apr. 9—Santa Barbara begins legal existence as American city. First post office established.

      Aug. 26—First Common Council of Santa Barbara convenes under presidency of Luis T. Burton, with Don Francisco de la Guerra as Mayor.

      Sept. 9—State of California admitted to Union.

1851   Santa Barbara surveyed and streets laid out by Capt. Salisbury Haley.

1853   July—George Nidever rescues the "lost woman of San Nicolás" Island and brings her to Santa Barbara.

1855   May 24—B. W. Keep and R. Hubbard locate in Santa Barbara to publish the *Gazette,* a weekly newspaper.
July 5—First shipment of twenty-eight flasks quicksilver from Santa Barbara County mines.

1856   July 3—Lighthouse erected two and one-half miles west of Santa Barbara.

1860   Santa Barbara population, 2,351.

1861   Apr. 1—First overland stagecoach from San Francisco to Santa Barbara arrives.

1863   Great drought sears county land, continues through 1864, closing era of vast ranches.

1864   Santa Barbara reverts to Spanish for language of public records.

1868   May—E. B. Boust launches Santa Barbara *Post,* newspaper.

1869   Santa Barbara College founded.
First charting of rainfall made.
Trinity Episcopal Church, first Protestant church in Santa Barbara, erected.
Erection of first wharf in Santa Barbara at foot of Chapala Street.

1870   Santa Barbara population, 2,970.
English finally supersedes Spanish as language of Santa Barbara public records.
Sept. 26—First telegraph line brought to Santa Barbara from San Francisco.

1871   July 1—Santa Barbara *Press* (formerly *Post*) comes out as daily paper.

1872   Stearns Wharf erected at foot of State Street, Santa Barbara.
Charles Nordhoff visits Santa Barbara. Charmed by beauty of community, he writes best-seller book of travels, thus encouraging immigration of hundreds.
Pioneer fire company organized.
Feb. 21—Lamps of Santa Barbara lit with gas for first time.
Feb. 22—Ventura County created from Santa Barbara County.
José Lobero dedicates Lobero Theater, first community playhouse in California.
May 31—Four leagues of pueblo land confirmed to city of Santa Barbara by President Ulysses S. Grant.
Oct. 7—Cornerstone of a new courthouse laid.

1873   Mar. 3—National Gold Bank organized.

1875   Apr. 10—The Lompoc *Record,* newspaper, established by H. H. Broughton.
July—Santa Barbara County Bank organized.

July 10—Arlington, first tourist hotel in Santa Barbara completed.

1876   First National Bank building completed.

June—Santa Barbara County Jail erected.

1878   First bridge across Santa Ynez River at Lompoc.

Jan.—Santa Barbara *Democrat,* newspaper, launched by E. B. Boust, B. W. Keep and F. A. Moore. Name changed to *Independent* later in year.

1880   Santa Barbara population, 3,460.

1882   Feb. 16—City Council establishes free library and reading room.

1884   Santa Barbara *Independent* first issued as daily newspaper.

1886   Natural gas and crude oil discovered in Summerland.

1887   Peak of land boom reached.

March 19—City streets first illuminated with electricity.

Aug. 17-20—Southern Pacific runs branch from main line at Saugus to Santa Barbara. First train occasions great jubilee, with 5,000 visitors. Transportation Pageant.

1890   Santa Barbara population, 5,864.

1891   Apr. 25—President Benjamin Harrison visits Santa Barbara. "Battle of Flowers" arranged.

1895   Petroleum strike at Summerland. Scramble for water frontage for drilling purposes.

Santa Barbara *News* launched as daily paper.

1897   Cold Springs tunnel supplies water to Santa Barbara.

1900   Santa Barbara population, 6,587.

Jan. 1—Thomas M. Storke purchases Santa Barbara *Independent*.

1901   Santa Barbara Mission dedicates St. Anthony's College to prepare young men for the priesthood.

Mar. 31—Completion of Southern Pacific Railroad to link Santa Barbara with Los Angeles and San Francisco.

May 10—President William McKinley visits Santa Barbara.

1902   Jan. 19—Potter Hotel opened. Gala affair, with many wealthy visitors attracted to Santa Barbara.

1903   May 9—President Theodore Roosevelt visits Santa Barbara.

1905   Southern Pacific Railroad lays double track through city and erects $20,000 depot.

Two new schools costing $40,000 constructed.

Powerhouse constructed at cost of $50,000. City flooded with electric light.

1908   Anna S. C. Blake Normal School established.

1909   Santa Barbara State Normal School of Manual Arts and Home Economics (now Santa Barbara State College) founded on co-educational basis.

1910   Santa Barbara population, 11,659.

American Film Manufacturing Company locates in Santa Barbara to make motion pictures under "Flying A" trade-mark.

1911   City purchases complete control of water system for $150,000.

1913   Base of Gibraltar Dam laid.

Thomas M. Storke acquires *News,* effects merger with *Independent* under name of Santa Barbara *Daily News.*

1918   Sheffield Reservoir constructed to store water for Santa Barbara.

1919   King Albert and Queen Elizabeth of the Belgians visit Santa Barbara for three days.

1920   Santa Barbara population, 19,441.

Jan.—Community Arts Association formed, composed of artists, musicians, writers, and friends of the arts.

Gibraltar Dam completed, impounding Santa Barbara's water supply.

1921   Apr. 13—Potter Hotel (now Ambassador) burns. Site (Burton Mound) released for archeological investigation.

1922   Plans and Planting Branch of Community Arts Association organized to concentrate on task of beautifying the city.

Carnegie Foundation grants $25,000 yearly for cultural activities of Community Arts Association.

First building in Museum of Natural History erected on land donated by Miss Caroline Hazard.

1923   Excavations revealing existence of Indian cultures found in Burton Mound by Museum of the American Indian, Heye Foundation, New York.

Sept.—Seven United States Navy destroyers wrecked near Honda, above Point Concepción; twenty-three lives lost.

1924   De la Guerra Studios created by Plans and Planting Branch of Community Arts Association, demonstrating possibilities for creation of distinctive Spanish-California architecture for the city.

Aug.—New Lobero Theater opened by Community Arts Association.

"Old Spanish Days" fiesta initiated, thereafter an annual event.

1925   KDB Radio Station established.

June 29—Earthquake hits Santa Barbara at 6:23 a.m. Estimated total loss between ten and twenty million dollars. Twelve lives lost. Sheffield Reservoir shattered.

1926   Santa Barbara Mission restored after damage caused by 1925 earthquake.

Blaksley Botanic Garden (now Santa Barbara Botanic Garden)

established under auspices of Museum of Natural History by Mrs. Anna Blaksley Bliss.

1927 Elwood oil field discovered. Produces 86,000 barrels this year.

1928 Aug. 17—Presidential candidate Herbert Hoover makes campaign visit.

1929 Aug. 14—New Courthouse dedicated at Santa Barbara.

1930 Santa Barbara population, 33,613.
Elwood becomes fifth oil field in volume of production in State.
June 30—Breakwater, 2,364 feet long, formally presented to city.
Oct. 15—Faulkner Memorial Art Gallery opened as wing of Public Library.

1932 Santa Barbara *News* and Santa Barbara *Press* combine to make Santa Barbara *News-Press,* sole daily and Sunday newspaper in city. Thomas M. Storke, president.

1936 Goleta Airport dedicated.
City rebuilds Sheffield Reservoir, increasing capacity to 50,000,-000 gallons.

1937 May 8—Half-million-dollar Federal building completed on site where presidio was founded in 1782.
Oct. 31—KTMS Radio Station sends initial broadcast.

1939 Old Post Office building purchased by county to be used as Art Gallery, augmenting facilities of Faulkner Art Gallery.
Thomas M. Storke appointed United States Senator to succeed William Gibbs McAdoo, resigned.
Apr.—Crown Prince Frederik and Princess Ingrid of Denmark visit Santa Barbara and the Danish settlement of Solvang.

1940 Santa Barbara population, 34,438.

Bibliography

This bibliography is of necessity a selective list. In addition to the sources listed below, interviews with persons and organizations of Santa Barbara have been of inestimable value in the preparation of this volume. For a complete bibliography of Santa Barbara consult the Division of Bibliography, Library of Congress, for *A List of References Relating to California*.

Alliot, Hector. *Art in California*. R. L. Bernier, San Francisco, 1916.

Bancroft, Herbert Howe. *History of California* (7 Vols.). The History Co., San Francisco, 1886.

Bell, Katherine M. *Swinging the Censer*. Finlay Press, Santa Barbara, 1931.

Bent, Arthur Cleveland. *Life and History of American Birds of Prey*. Smithsonian Institute, Washington, 1920.

Berger, John A. *Fernand Lundgren*. Schauer Press, Santa Barbara, 1936.

Bolton, Herbert Eugene. *Crespi's Diary: Explorer, 1769-1774*. University of California Press, Berkeley, 1927.

Brooks, Charles S. *A Western Wind*. Harcourt, Brace & Co., New York, 1935.

Cleland, H. G. Fitzgerald. *Our Prehistoric Ancestors*. Coward-McCann, Inc., New York, 1928.

Dana, Jr., Richard Henry. *Two Years Before the Mast*. Houghton Mifflin Co., New York and Boston, 1911.

Davis, Emily C. *Ancient Americans*. Holt, New York, 1931.

Division of Fish and Game, State of California. *Fish Bulletin No. 28*, 1939.

Drury, Aubrey. *California, An Intimate Guide*. Harper & Bros., New York, 1935.

Ellison, W. H. *Life and Adventures of George Nidever*. University of California Press, Berkeley, 1937.

Engelhardt, Father Zephyrin. *Franciscans in California*. Holy Childhood Indian School, Harbor Springs, Michigan, 1897.

Foster, J. W. *Prehistoric Races of the United States*. University of California Press, Berkeley, 1929.

Garrison, Myrtle. *Romance and History of California Ranchos*. Harr Wagner Publishing Co., San Francisco, 1935.

Gidney, C. M. *Santa Barbara, San Luis Obispo and Ventura Counties in California*. (Written in collaboration with Benjamin Brooks and Edwin M. Sheridan.) Lewis Publishing Co., Chicago, 1917.

Graves, Jackson A. *My Seventy Years in California*. Times-Mirror Press, Los Angeles, 1927.

Grinnell, Dixon & Linsdale. *Fur-Bearing Mammals of California.* University of California Press, Berkeley, 1937.

Guinn, J. M. *A Historical and Biographical Record of Southern California.* Chapman Publishing Co., Chicago, 1902.

———. *A History of California and an Extended History of Its Southern Coast,* etc., Historical Record Co., Los Angeles, 1907.

Harrington, John P. *44th Annual Report of Bureau of American Ethnology: Exploration of the Burton Mound at Santa Barbara.* Government Printing Office, Washington, 1928.

Hawley, Walter A. *Early Days of Santa Barbara.* Privately printed. Santa Barbara, 1920.

Hill, Laurence L. & Parks, Marion. *Santa Barbara, Tierra Adorada.* Security First National Bank, Los Angeles, 1930.

Hoffman, Ralph. *Birds of the Pacific States.* Houghton Mifflin Co., New York and Boston, 1927.

Holder, Charles Frederick. *The Channel Islands of California.* A. C. McClurg, Chicago, 1910.

Kroeber, Alfred L. *Handbook of Indians of California.* Smithsonian Institute Bulletin No. 78 of the Bureau of American Ethnology, 1925.

Mason, Jesse D. *History of Santa Barbara and Ventura Counties of California.* Thompson & West, Oakland, 1883.

McGroarty, John Steven. *California: Its History and Romance.* Grafton Publishing Co., of Los Angeles, 1911.

Newmark, Harris. *Sixty Years in Southern California.* Houghton Mifflin Co., New York and Boston, 1930.

Nunn, Herbert. *Municipal Problems.* Bulletin of the Seismological Society of America, Stanford University Press, Palo Alto, December, 1925.

Ogden, Adele. *Hides and Tallow.* California Historical Society Quarterly, Vol. 6, San Francisco, 1927.

Older, Mrs. Fremont. *California Missions and Their Romances.* Coward-McCann, Inc., New York, 1938.

O'Neill, O. H. *History of Santa Barbara County.* Harold McLean Meir, Publisher, Printed by Union Printing Co., Santa Barbara, 1939.

Phillips, Michael J. *History of Santa Barbara County.* S. J. Clarke Publishing Co., San Francisco and Los Angeles, 1937.

Reed, Ralph D. *Geology of California.* American Association of Petroleum Geologists, Tulsa, Oklahoma, 1933.

Rensch, H. E. & E. G. *Historic Spots in California.* Stanford University Press, Palo Alto, 1932.

Rider, Fremont & Cooper, Frederick T. *Rider's California: A Guide for Travelers.* Macmillan Co., New York, 1925. (Rev. Ed.—1927.)

Robinson, Alfred. *Life in California.* (A revised edition, published privately in 1925 by T. C. Russell, bears the title: *Life in California Before the Conquest.*) W. Doxey, San Francisco, 1891.

Rogers, David B. *Prehistoric Man of the Santa Barbara Coast.* Santa Barbara Museum of Natural History, 1929.

Sanchez, Nellie Van de Grift. *Spanish Arcadia.* A. M. Robertson, San Francisco, 1922, and Powell Publishing Co., San Francisco, 1929.

Sansum, W. D. *A Manual for Diabetic Patients.* Macmillan Co., New York, 1939.

Santa Barbara Chamber of Commerce, Bulletins issued at intervals on recreations and resources.

Sheldon, Harry H. *The Deer of California.* Santa Barbara Museum of Natural History, 1929.

Shuck, Oscar T. *Representative Men of the Pacific.* Bacon & Co., San Francisco, 1870.

The Society of California Pioneers. *San Francisco Quarterly,* Vol. VII, No. 1, March, 1924.

Southern Pacific Railway. *Historic Outline.* San Francisco, 1931.

Southworth, John R. *Santa Barbara and Montecito, Past and Present.* Schauer Press, Santa Barbara. (Orena Studios) 1920.

————. *Historic Adobes of Santa Barbara.* Schauer Press, Santa Barbara, (Orena Studios) 1920.

Spicer, Dorothy G. *The Book of Festivals.* New York Women's Press, New York, 1937.

Staats, H. Philip. *California Architecture in Santa Barbara.* New York Architectural Book Publishing Co., New York, 1929.

Storke, Mrs. Yda Addis. *A Memorial and Biographical History of the Counties of Santa Barbara, San Luis Obispo and Ventura, California.* Lewis Publishing Co., Chicago, 1891.

Thomas, George C. & George C., III. *Game Fish of the Pacific, Southern California and Mexican Coasts.* Lippincott, New York, 1930.

U. S. Forest Service, Department of Agriculture. *Los Padres National Forest.* Bulletin No. M.F. 23-R.5., 1939.

Wickson, Edward J. *Rural California.* Macmillan, New York, 1923.

Willis, Bailey. *The Santa Barbara Earthquake.* Bulletin of the Seismological Society of America, Stanford University Press, Palo Alto, December, 1925.

MAGAZINES

Architectural Review. "Santa Barbara: The Case for Unified Architecture." July, 1933.

Brown, Rexwald. "A New Santa Barbara." *American Review of Reviews,* August 25, 1925.

Chase, Pearl. "Better Small Homes in Santa Barbara." *The Architect and Engineer Magazine,* July, 1926.

Fuller, Bina L. "The Village that Jack and Jill Built." *Woman's Home Companion,* November, 1936.

Morrow, Irving F. "New Santa Barbara." *The Architect and Engineer Magazine,* July, 1926.

National Geographic Magazine, February, 1939.

Simpson, R. V. "The Government of the City of Santa Barbara." *Western City Magazine,* August, 1938.

Survey Graphic Magazine, March, 1940.

Overland Monthly, Out West, Land of Sunshine.

NEWSPAPERS

The files of the following newspapers, covering the last fifty years, were consulted frequently:

Santa Barbara *Gazette*
Santa Barbara *Morning Press*
Santa Barbara *Daily News*
Santa Barbara *Independent*
Santa Barbara *Labor News*
Los Angeles *Times*
Los Angeles *Evening Herald and Express*
Christian Science Monitor.

Index

(Where more than one page number is given, the first number is the principal reference.)

Abbas, Philip, 92
Adam, Ronald M., 98
Agriculture, 50-51, 163, 167, 181-182
Aguirre, Don José Antonio de, 114
Airports, 167
Aleut fishermen, 68
Alhecama Theater, 93
All-Breed Dog Show, 101
Alvarado, Governor Juan Bautista, 73
Ambassador Hotel, 121
American rule, 37-39
Ancient Ones, 25-28
Andrea, Italo de, 96
André Clark Bird Refuge, 119, 64, 103
Anthropology (Channel Islands), 76-77, 66, 73, 74
Anza, Juan Bautista de, 173, 150
Arcady, 143
Architecture, 56-58, 91
Architectural Advisory Committee, 47, 91
Arrellanes, Don Teodore, 118, 182
Art, 95-97
Ascención, Father Antonio de la, 29
Ayuntamiento, 38

Backus, Standish, Jr., 97
Bagdatopolus, William S., 96
Balaam, Arthur G., 172
Balaam, John, 172
Barbareños, 170, 112, 120, 147, 159
Bayes, Gilbert, 140
Bell, John S., 162
Bennett Point, 75
Betteravia, 181-182, 163
Better Homes Committee, 91
Big Grapevine, 137
Biltmore Hotel, Santa Barbara, 133
Birthday of Buddha (féte), 90
Bishop Pine, 180
Blaksley, Henry, 129
Bliss, Mrs. Anna Blaksley, 129
Bliss, Arthur, 92
Blochman City, 160-61
Board of Architectural Review, 47
Boderero, James, 97
Borein, Edward, 105, 95

Borg, Carl Oscar, 96
Botanic Gardens, Santa Barbara, 129, 103, 125
Bottome, Phyllis, 94
Bouchard, Hippolyte de, 121, 169
Boust, E. B., 97
Breakwater, 120, 47, 58, 60, 101, 102
Britz, John R., 92
Brooks, Robert L., 74
Broughton, H. H., 98
Buckler, Reverend Alexander, 156
Buchanan, Walter, 92
Buell, R. T., 158
Buellton, 157-58
Burke, James, 121
Burton Mound, 121-22, 38, 45, 130

Cabrillo, John Rodriguez, 25, 27, 28, 29, 65, 66, 70, 73, 74, 112, 119, 120
Cabrillo Pavilion, 132
Cachuma District, 82
Caire, Justinian, 72, 71
California Battalion, 147
California Immigrant Union, 173
California-Hawaii Race, 101
Californianos, 162-63, 34, 36
Californios, 34-35
Cameron, Margaret, 94
Cañada de Los Alisos, 159
Cañada de Los Berros, 178
Cañada del Refugio, 168-69
Canaliños (see Indians)
Carnegie Foundation, 91
Carpenter, Dudley, 96
Carpinteria, 135-37, 61, 38
Carrillo, Antonio, 73
Carrillo, Carlos, 73
Carrillo, Concepción Pico de, 118
Carrillo, Don Dominguez, 118
Carrillo, Guillermo, 114
Carrillo, Joaquín, 114, 155
Carrillo, Luis, 38
Casa de Aguirre, Site of, 114
Casa De la Guerra, 116-17, 90, 103
Casa del Herrero, 141
Cascarone, 100
Casmalia, 52

Castillero, Andrés, 71
Castle Rock Bluff, 120, 121
Cattle Industry, 148-49
Cat Canyon, 159
Celite Mines, 171
Cemetery, Santa Barbara, 138
Central City, 163, 183
Chambers, H. C., 95
Channel Islands: 65-78, 27, 36, 40, 53, 60, 62, 63, 103, 145; Aleut fishermen, 68; Anacapa, 68-70, 60, 63, 65, 66, 68; Anthropology, 76-77, 66, 73, 74; Bennett Point, 75; Cuyler's Harbor, 74; Fauna, 68, 65, 69, 70, 73, 76; Flora, 68, 76, 77; Geology, 66, 69, 70, 72, 74, 76, 77; Indians, 66-67; La Posesión, 74; Los Islas de San Lucas, 73; National Monument, 66, 68, 76; Princess, 73; San Clemente, 76-77, 65, 66, 72, 75; San Clemente Fleet Training Base, 76; San Clemente Island Naval Defense Sea Areas, 76; San Miguel, 73-75, 60, 61, 63, 65, 66; San Nicolás, 77-78, 65, 66, 75; Santa Barbara, 76, 65, 66, 68, 75; Santa Catalina, 75-76, 65, 66, 72; Santa Cruz, 70-72, 30, 61, 63, 64, 65, 66, 68, 73; Santa Rosa, 72-73, 61, 62, 63, 65, 66, 68, 135; San Salvador, 70
Channel, Santa Barbara, 25, 64
Chapman, Joseph, 36, 121
Cheever, Walter, 96
Chico, Governor, 155
Child, Mrs. John H., 119
Chinese Benevolent Association, 90
Churches (see Religion)
Cineguitas, village, 54
Cities, Towns, and Villages: Betteravia, 181-182, 163; Blochman City, 160-61; Buellton, 157-58; Carpinteria, 135-37, 38, 61; Casmalia, 52; Elwood, 44; Gaviota, 169-70, 37, 147, 159; Goleta, 167-68, 47; Guadalupe, 182-83, 58; Harris, 180; Las Cruces, 170; Lompoc, 172-73, 52, 58; Los Alamos, 162; Los Olivos, 158; Montecito, 140-41, 38, 45, 58, 61, 80, 133, 137, 139; Orcutt, 180-81, 163; Santa Maria, 163-64, 58, 80, 183; Santa Ynez, 153; Sisquoc, 160, 159; Solvang, 156-57, 154; Summerland, 134, 52, 168; Surf, 173, 158
City Hall, Santa Barbara, 117-18
City Recreation Commission, 102
Civic affairs, 50
Civilian Conservation Corps, 24-25, 81, 82, 175-76
Clark, Arthur M., 98
Clark, Mrs. Anna E., estate of, 119, 133

Clements, Colin C., 93
Clements, Edith S., 94
Clendenning, Dr. Logan, 95
Climate, 62
Club activities, 90-91
Coats, John, 141
Coats, Newton M., 141
Cold Springs Tunnel (see Water Supply)
Coleman, George, 95
Colleges (see Schools and Colleges)
Colman, Ronald, 93
Community Arts Association, 45-47, 90, 91, 93, 103, 115, 139
Community Drafting Room, 91
Compañía del Muelle de Santa Bárbara, 120
Condor, Sanctuary, Sisquoc, 83-85, 64, 79, 80
Constantia, 140
Cooper, Colin Campbell, 96
Cooper, Elwood, 168
Cottage Hospital, 122
Coulter, Mary, 97
County (see Santa Barbara)
Couper, Mildred, 92
Covarrúbias, Don José María, 118, 106, 155
Craig, James Osborne, 116
Cram, Allan, 96
Crespi, Father Juan, 27, 28, 30, 91, 94
Cueva Pintada, 70
Curtiss, Wilbur, 141
Cuyama District, 149
Cuyler's Harbor, 74

Dana, Richard Henry, 94, 117
Dana, William G., 146-47
Daniels, Charles Cabot, 96
Danish Days Midsummer Festival, 156-57
Daughters of the American Revolution, 78
Davis, Cecil Clark, 95
Dawson, William, 95
Den, Don Nicholás A., 35
Department of Agriculture, 78
Devighne, Dr. Harry, 95
Día de Santa Inés, 155
Dibblee, Thomas B., 149
Dibblee, T. Wilson, 121
Doll festival, annual, 90
Domínguez, Doña Marcelina Feliz de, 142
Diego y Moreno, Father Francisco García, 35, 123, 126
Dominguez, Don Nemicio, 141
Donahue Family, 156
Drama, 92-93

Drought (1863-64), 41, 48
Du Pont, Miss Amy, estate of, 140

Earthquake (1812), 177, 125, 154
Earthquake (1925), 45-46, 62, 90-91, 113, 117, 118, 127, 174
East Beach, 132
Eaton, Captain Ira, 72
Economics, 49-53
Edwards & Plunkett, 119
Edwards, Stanley, 97
Eicheim, Henry, 92
El Camino Cielo, 80
El Cañón Perdido, 112-13
El Cuartel, 115
Eldred, Raymond, 92
El Fureides, 142
Elizabeth, ship, 112
El Jaro Creek, 171
Ellison, William, 94
El Paseo, 116-17
Elwood, 44
Englehardt, Father Zephyrin, 94

Fages, Governor Pedro, 32, 173
Fair and Horse Show, annual, 101
Fastelavn (féte), 156-57
Faulkner Memorial Art Gallery, 114, 95, 96
Fauna, 63-64, 65, 68, 69, 70, 73, 76, 83
Federal Building, 114-15, 47
Fenton, 134
Ferrelo, Bartholomew, 28, 66
Field, Isobel, 93
Field, Salisbury, 93
Figueroa, Governor José, 34, 123
First National Bank, Santa Barbara, 42
Fishing, fresh water and deep-sea, 102, 158, 173
Fishing Industry, 53
Fleischmann, Major Max C., estate of, 114, 120, 134
Fleischmann Polo Field, 134, 138
Fletcher, Frank Morley, 96
Flora, 62-63, 68, 76, 77
Flower and Seed growing, 164-65, 57, 58, 172, 173
Forbes property, 141
Ford, Henry Chapman, 95
Forest Service, 80-82, 83, 84
Fossils, 62, 66, 75, 138, 171-72
Founding of Santa Barbara, 37-39
Fox Arlington Theater, 96
Foxen, Benjamin, 159-60, 37, 121, 146-48, 170
Frémont, John C., 146-48, 37, 116, 121, 159-60, 170
Fuller, Mrs. Bina L., 161

Gálvez, José de, 27, 29
Gamble, John Marshall, 96
Garden Tours, Santa Barbara, 103, 139, 140, 141, 143
Gaviota, 169-70, 37, 147, 159
Geology: 60-62; Channel Islands, 66, 69, 70, 72, 74, 76, 77; Earthquake (1925), 45-46, 62, 90-91, 113, 117, 118, 127, 174; Marine formations, 60-62; Mesa Fault, 62; Miocene Period, 171; Old Asphalt Pit, 137-38; Pleistocene age, 66, 69; Pleistocene forest, 139; Tertiary age, 61; Santa Ynez thrust fault, 62
Gherini, Ambrose, 70
Giant Eugenia Tree, 135-36
Gibraltar Dam (see Water Supply)
Gibraltar reservoir area, 82
Gillespie, J. M., estate of, 142
Gin Chow, 174-75
Goleta, 167-68, 47
Goodhue, Bertram, 143
Gould, Mrs. William P., 114
Graham, Martha, 93
Grant, Campbell, 96
Gray, David, 96
Great Carpinteria Grapevine, 137, 142
Groesbeck, Dan Sayre, 96, 111
Guadalupe, 182-83, 58
Guerman, Marcel, 92
Guerra, Comandante Don José de la, 33
Guerra, Miss Delfina de la, 117
Guerra, Don Pablo de la, 112
Guerra, Don Franciso de la, 38
Guerra Plaza, de la, 117, 118
Guerra Studios, de la, 90
Guerra y Noriega, Captain Don José Antonia, 116-17, 126, 171

Hamilton, John B., 97
Hancock, R. K., 98
Hancock, S. C., 98
Hanson, Mella, 98
Hanson, Walter L., 98
Harbor, Santa Barbara, 120, 101-02
Harcoff, Lyla M., 97
Harmer, Alexander F., 95
Harris, village, 180
Hartnell, William, 180
Hawley, W. A., 94
Haynes, Colonel, W. A., 141
Hazard, Caroline, 94, 129
Headley, Klyne, 92
Hebert, Marian, 97
Helmle, Henry, 176
Herter, Mr. and Mrs. Albert, 96
Hervey, Harry, 94
Hill, Daniel, 35, 114

Hilton, Frank, 94
Hinkle, Clarence, 96
Historic Buildings: Burton Adobe,
121; Carrillo Adobe, 114; Casa de
la Guerra, 116-17, 90, 103; Casa
Del Herrero, 141; Covarrúbias
Adobe, 118, 106, 155; "Historic"
Adobe, 118, 106; Lobero Theater,
115-16, 92-93, 103; Massini Adobe,
94; Oreña Adobe, 117
Historical Society Museum, Santa
Barbara, 112
Hobo jungles, 119
Hoffman, Bernard, 90, 116
Hoffman, Eleanor, 94
Hoffman, Ralph, 95
Holder, Charles Frederick, 77
Hollister, Colonel William, 92
Honda, 45
Hope Ranch, 166-67, 54, 58
Hot springs, 141
Hubbard, R., 97
Hueneme Light, 68
Hunter, Robert W., 94
Hunting People, 26-28, 138
Hunt, Myron, 95
Hurricane Deck Country, 83, 149

Indians: Ancient, 25-28; Canaliños,
25-28, 29, 31, 53, 54, 55, 86, 91, 120,
125, 129, 135; Channel Islands, 28,
66-67; Chief Yanonalit, 31; Cieneguitas, village, 54, Hunting People,
26-28, 138; Juan Justo, 54-55; Neophytes, 125-26, 27, 34, 35, 68, 154-55,
176-79; Oak Grove Men, 26-28;
Revolt of 1824, 126, 155; Santa
Bárbara, 126; Santa Inés, 126; Sho-
shone, 27; Swetete, Canaliño village, 133; Tulare, 154, 155, 170;
Walla Walla, 147; Zanja Cota
Reservation, 153
Indian pictographs, 145
Indian Pitch Spring, 138
Islands belonging to U. S. Government, 66

Jackson, Charles H., Jr., 139
Japanese Association (Nissei), Santa
Barbara, 90
Japanese Citizens' League (Issei),
Santa Barbara, 90
Jefferson, John Percival, estate of, 133
Johns-Manville, 171-72
Johnson, J. A., 97
Johnson, Reginald D., 115, 133
Jones, Robert E., 93
Jones, Mr. and Mrs. Robert Edmond,
140
Juana Maria, 77-78

Julian, Paul, 96
Juncal watershed (see Water Supply)
Justo, Juan, 54-55

Kaplun, Grace, 92
Keep, B. W., 97
Kelsey, Richmond, 97
Kerry Blue Kennels, 139
Kimberley, Martin, 71-72
Knapp, George Owen, estate of, 143
Knowles, Joseph, 96
Kraft, Klyde, 93

La Cumbre Lookout, 145
Ladd, Anna Coleman, 96
La Purisima Hills, 158, 159
La Purisima State Park, 175
Larkin, Isabelle, 114
Las Cruces, 170
Las Posadas, 100
Las Positas y La Calera, 166
Lasuén, Father Fermin Francisco de,
32, 31, 154, 175
Laurel of San Marcos, 145-46, 63
La Victoria, ship, 25
Lawhoren, Roy, 97
Lebrun, Rico, 96
Lehmann, Lotte, 92
Lemon Industry, 136-37, 166-67
Lester, Herbert S., 75
Lester, Mrs. Herbert S., 75
Lighthouse Service, 66, 68, 69, 76
Lippet, Captain, 112
Literature, 94-95
Little Town Club, 114
Lobero Theater, 115-16, 92-93, 103
Lompoc, 172-73, 52, 58, 149, 164
Los Alamos, 162
Los Olivos, 158
Los Padres National Forest, 79-85, 64,
102, 145
Los Rancheros Visitadores, 105-6, 100,
103, 118, 149
Luddington, Wright S., 96-97, 143
Lundgren, Fernand, 96

Maas, Charles, 142
Maas, Sebastian, 142
MacManus, Joseph, 92
Martinez, Alfredo Ramos, 133
Marine formations (see Geology)
Mason, Colonel Richard B., 112
Massini Adobe, 94
Matilija Canyon, 42
Mattei, Clarence, 96
Mattei, Felix, 158
McAdoo, Eleanor Wilson, 94
McCoole, Paul, 92
McDougall, George B., 127
McLennan, Eunice C., 96

McNally, Reverend J. B., 160
Meeker, Arthur, 140
Mellinger, Eleanor, 92
Mesa Fault (see Geology)
Mexican Rule, 33-34
Micheltorena, Governor Manuel, 126, 155, 179
Mihran Studio Building, 114
Mills Brothers, 75
Miocene Period (see Geology)
Miraflores, 133
Mission Choristers, 98
Mission Creek, 112, 113, 125, 129
Missions: Misión La Purísima Concepción de Maria Santísima, 175-79, 103; Neophytes, 125-26, 27, 34, 35, 68, 154-55, 176-79; Santa Barbara, 123-27, 32-33, 34, 35, 44, 46, 48, 89, 98, 103, 104, 105, 112, 166; Santa Inés, 154-56, 96, 103, 106, 126, 148, 178; Secularization, 34-35, 126
Mitchell, Lieutenant Commander John J., 106
Moley, Raymond, 94
Montecito, 140-41, 38, 45, 58, 61, 80, 133, 137, 139
Monterey Cypress, 138-39
Montgomery, Ross, 141
Moore, F. A., 97
Mooser, William, 112
Moreton Bay Fig Tree, 122
Motion Pictures, 93
Mountains: Frazier, 80; La Cumbre, 46, 60, 145; Pinos, 80; Solomon, 162; Picacho Diablo, 70; Santa Monica, 66; Santa Ynez, 48, 56, 60, 61, 62, 63, 105, 141; Sierra Madre, 149; Soledad, 72
Murphy, Dwight W., 150-53
Museum of Natural History, Santa Barbara, 129, 26, 94, 96, 103, 138
Music, 91-92
Mutual Citrus Association, 136

National Guard Armory, 118-19, 106
National Monument, Channel Islands, 66, 68, 76
Native Daughters of the Golden West, 106
Native Sons of the Golden West, 115
Natural History Society, 42
Naval disaster, 45
Navy, U. S., 106, 76, 77
Negro population, 89
Neighborhood House, 118
Neophytes, 125-26, 27, 34, 35, 68, 154-55, 176-79
Neve, Governor Felipe de, 31
Newspapers; Carpinteria Chronicle, 98; Carpinteria Herald, 98; Goleta

Valley Leader, 98; Headlines of 1856, 39; Lompoc Record, 98; Santa Barbara Advertiser, 97; Santa Barbaran, 97; Santa Barbara Daily News, 97; Santa Barbara Daily Republican, 97; Santa Barbara Democrat, 97; Santa Barbara Gazette, 39, 97, 169-70; Santa Barbara Independent, 97; Santa Barbara Index, 97; Santa Barbara Morning Press, 43; Santa Barbara News, 97; Santa Barbara News-Press, 97-98; Santa Barbara Post, 97; Santa Barbara Press, 97; Santa Barbara Times, 97, 141; Santa Barbara Weekly Independent, 43; Santa Maria Courier, 98; Santa Maria Times, 98; Santa Maria Valley Vidette, 98; Santa Ynez Valley News, 98; Static (Blochman City), 161; Union Labor News, 53, 98
Nidever, George, 74-75, 77, 78
Nojogui Falls County Park, 170
Nordhoff, Charles, 42

Oak Grove Men, 26-28
Oak Park District, 45
Ocean County Park, 173
Oil Industry (see Petroleum)
Oland, Warner, 93
Old Asphalt Pit (see Geology)
Old Mission Dam, 129-30
Old Spanish Days Fiesta, 104-05, 87, 100, 103
Old Spanish Settlement, 142
Olivera, Diego, 182
Orcutt, 180-81, 163
Orena, Don Gaspar, 117
Oriental population, 89-90
Ortega, Captain Don José Francisco de, 30-31, 97, 115, 168
Ortega, Guadalupe, 36
Ortega Hill, 41, 52, 133
Ortega Settlement, 134
Ortega Wharf, Site of, 168
Otte, William L., 97
Ousdal, Dr. Asbjorn P., 54, 95
Overland stage, first, 170
Owen, Blossom, 96

Pacheco, Romualdo, 114
Painted Cave, 145
Painted Indian Caves, 83
Palm Park, 119, 132
Palominos, Royal Golden, 150-53, 57, 101
Parra Grande Lane, 142
Parshall, DeWitt, 96
Parshall, Douglas, 96
Payeras, Father Mariano, 176-78

Peake, Channing, 97
Peattie, Donald Culross, 94
Peattie, Louise Redfield, 94
Pedregosa Creek, 31
Pelican Bay, 72
Penal Colony, 71
Peor es Nada, ship, 77
Perkins, Charles, 94
Pershing Park, 101
Petroleum: 51-52; Barnsdall, 168;
    Bicknell, 163, 180; Casmalia, 52,
    163, 180; Elwood, 168, 52, 57;
    Goleta, 52; Lompoc, 163, 180;
    Luton-Bell No. 1, 168; Oil wells in
    the sea, 133, 134; Orcutt, 180;
    Orella, 168; Palmer-Stendel, 161;
    Rio Grande, 168; Santa Maria, 180-
    81, 57, 163; Summerland, 52; Union,
    179, 180
Phillips, Michael, 94
Phelps, Edith Catlin, 96
Pichel, Irving, 93
Pickford, Lottie, 93
Pickford, Mary, 93
Pico, Andrés, 162
Pico, Governor Pío, 118, 126, 155, 162,
    179
Pico, Solomon, 162-63
Playbox Theater, 93
Pleistocene age (*see* Geology)
Pleistocene forest (*see* Geology)
Point Concepción, 73
Point Sal Landing, 163
Polo Association, Santa Barbara, 101
Portuguese Society of America, 74
Porter, Rebecca N., 94
Portolá, J. Caspar de, 27, 29-30, 91,
    135, 169, 173
Post, Frank, 97
Potter Hotel, 45, 121
Potter Theater, 93
Powers, Jack, 163
Presidio Real, Santa Bárbara, 31, 121,
    155, 171
Press and Radio, 97-98
Prisoners' Harbor, 71
Public Library, Santa Barbara, 113
Puerto de Santa Bárbara, 121
Punta Gorda, 41
Purisima Hills, 180
P. W. A., 49

Quail Canyon, 92

Racial groups, 89-90
Radio beacons, 69
Radio Stations: Columbia Broadcast-
    ing Company, 98; Don Lee System,
    98; KDB, 98; KTMS, 98; Mutual

Broadcasting System, 98; National
    Broadcasting Company, 98
Railroads: Pacific Coast Railway, 153,
    158, 160, 162, 180; Southern Pacific
    Railroad, 43-44, 57, 158-59, 174, 183
Raley, Father John, 179
Ranches: College, 153; Elwood, 168;
    Jonata, 157; Higgins, 138; Hope,
    166-67, 54, 58; La Patera, 167; San
    Ysidro, 93; Suey, 149; Todos San-
    tos, 180
Ranchos: Dana, William G., 146;
    Guadalupe, 182; Juan y Lolita, 106;
    Laguna, 162; Lompoc, 173; Los
    Alamos, 162; Los Fuentes, 140;
    Misión Vieja, 173, Nuestra Señora
    del Refugio, 169; San Carlos, 139;
    San Fernando Rey, 149-50; San
    Julian, 171; Tinaquaic, 159, 160
Rare birds, 63-64, 70
Religion: African Methodist-Episco-
    pal, 89; Buddhist Temple, 90;
    Chinese Presbyterian Mission, 90;
    Church of Our Lady of Mount
    Carmel, 141-42; Colored Baptist,
    89; Congregational, 89; Danish Lu-
    theran, 156, 157; Japanese Congre-
    gational, 90; Sisquoc Church, 160,
    147, 159; Trinity Episcopal, 89
Religion, history, 89
Revolt of 1824, 126, 155
Riding and Hunt Club, Santa Barbara,
    101, 167
Riley, Mrs. Ann W., 98
Rincón Point, 41
Ripley, Thomas E., 94, 97
Ripoll, Padre, 123
Rivers: Cuyama, 80, 183; Río Santa
    Rosa (Santa Ynez), 176; Santa
    Maria, 183; Santa Ynez, 148, 48,
    61, 63, 64, 102, 158, 173, 174, 176;
    Manzana, 102; Sisquoc, 83, 102, 159,
    183
Robinson, Alfred, 94
Rock, George, 171
Rogers, David B., 26, 94
Rogers, Robert Cameron, 94
Russell, Charles, 95
Russian otter hunters, 40

Sailors' Sycamore, 119
Saint Barbara, 29
San Antonio, ship, 30
San Carlos, ship, 30
Sánchez, Father, tomb of, 124
San Clemente Fleet Training Base, 76
San Clemente Island Naval Defense
    Sea Areas, 76
San Marcos Pass, 146, 37, 63, 80, 147,
    159, 170

San Rafael Wild Area, 82-83
San Salvador, ship, 25
Sansum Clinic, 122-23, 95
Santa Barbara: Botanic Gardens, 129, 103, 125; Cemetery, 133; Channel, 25, 64; City Hall, 117-18; Community Arts Association, 45-47, 90, 91, 93, 103, 115, 139; County Bank, 42; County Bowl, 91, 104; County Courthouse, 111, 57, 96, 104; County Farm, 167; County General Hospital, 167; Founding, 37-39; Garden Tours, 103, 139, 140, 141, 143; Harbor, 120, 101-02; Historical Society Museum, 112; Japanese Association (Nissei), 90; Japanese Citizens' League (Issei), 90; Museum of Natural History, 129, 26, 94, 96, 103, 138; Polo Association, 101; Presidio Real, 31, 121, 155, 171; Public Library, 113; Riding and Hunt Club, 101, 167; Santa Barbara Foundation, 114; Streets and Avenues, 57
Santa Maria, 163-64, 58, 80, 183
Santa Maria Cemetery Association, 160
Santa Ynez, 153
Santa Ynez Trust Fault (*see* Geology)
Schools and Colleges: Ana S. C. Blake Normal School, 88, 128; Blochman Union School, 160-61; College of Atterdag, 156, 157; Moore Dental Foundation, 88; Saint Anthony's College, 44, 124; Santa Barbara College, 42, 88; Santa Barbara Nature School, 103; Santa Barbara School System, 88; Santa Barbara State College, 127-29, 88, 121; School of the Arts, 90, 91; State Teachers' College, Santa Barbara, 128; St. Vincent's School, 88
Schott, Mrs. Max, 93
Secularization, 34-35, 126
Security-First National Bank, Santa Barbara, 160
Sedgwick, Francis, 97
Seed and Flower growing, 164-65, 57, 58, 172, 173
Seegart, Helen M., 96
Selover, Marshall, 98
Semana Nautica, 106-07, 69, 100, 103
Serra, Father Junipero, 29-32, 34, 173
Shaw, Dr. J. B., 162
Sheffield Reservoir (*see* Water Supply)
Sheldon, H. H., 94
Shepherd, S. F., 136
Simpson, Sir George, 53

Sisquoc, 160, 159
Smith, George Washington, 115, 133
Snider, Ann Louise, 96, 97
Solomon Hills, 162, 159, 163
Solvang, 156-57, 154
Southern California Championship Regatta, 101
Southern California Music Project, 91
Southworth, John S., 94
Spanish Fortress, Site of, 121
Spanish Parent Teachers' Association, 89
Spaulding, Seldon, 95
Spiritualist colony, 134
Stanton, Edward L., 70
Stark, Jack Gage, 96
State Relief, 50
St. Charles Hotel, 116
Stearns, John P., 120
Stearns Wharf, 120
Steedman, Mrs. George, 141
Stevenson, Colonel J. D., 112
Stockton, Commodore Robert Field, 37
Stokowski, Leopold, 92
Storke, Thomas M., 97, 98
Stow, W. W., 167
Streets and Avenues, Santa Barbara, 57
Sugar Beet Industry, 181-82, 172
Summerland, 134, 52, 168
Sunkist, 136
Sun Wah Association (Chinese), 90
Surf, 173, 158
Swanson, David, 96
Swetete, Canaliño village, 133
Sycamore Canyon, 46

Talbot, Lieutenant, 37
Tapis, Fray, 154
Taylor, Hobart C. Chatfield, 94
Taylor, William Desmond, 93
Telegraph, first, 41
Temple, John (Don Juan), 179
Tequetis Dam (*see* Water Supply)
Tertiary Age (*see* Geology)
Thayer, Ernest L., 94
Thompson, Captain Alpheus B., 115
Thompson, Doña Francisca (Mrs. Alpheus B.), 115
Thompson House, Site of, 116
Torrey Pine, 63, 68, 73, 135, 138, 139
Tourists, 51
Trebon, E. R., 98
Troccoli, G. B., 96
Tuckerman, Lilia, 96

Union Sugar Refinery, 181-82
U. S. Government: 49; Channel Islands National Monument, 66, 68, 76; Civilian Conservation Corps,

24-25, 81, 82, 175-76; Department of Agriculture, 79; Federal Building, 114-15, 47; Forest Service, 80-82, 83, 84; Islands belonging to, 66; Lighthouse Service, 66, 68, 69, 76; Naval disaster, 45; P. W. A., 49; Radio beacons, 69; U. S. Navy, 76, 77, 106; W. P. A., 92, 119, 176

Vail-Vickers, 72
Valk, Ella Snowden, 97
Valleys: Arroyo Principal, 70; Carpinteria, 49, 134; Goleta, 49, 61; Lompoc, 172, 58, 164; Los Alamos, 162, 149, 159; Santa Maria, 163-64, 149, 170, 172, 182; Santa Ynez, 148, 49, 63, 149, 153
Val Verde, estate of, 143
Van der Voort, Antoni, 92
Vaughn, S. E., 96
Veterans' Memorial Building, 96
Vigilantes, 163
Vila, Jayme, 54
Villa Reposa, estate of, 140
Vizcaino, Sebastián, 29
Vultures, Extinct: Neogypo errans, 138; Teratornis, 62, 138; Vagabond, 138

Wack, Ethel B., 97
Wagner, Rob, 94-95

Ward, Thomas W., 135
Waters, Captain, 75
Water Supply: 47-49, 125, 130; Cold Springs Tunnel, 48; Gibraltar Dam, 48-49; Juncal watershed, 80; Mission Tunnel, 48; Santa Ynez River, 48; Sheffield Reservoir, 145, 46, 47, 48, 49; Tequetis Dam, 49; watershed protection, 80
Watson D. West, ship, 75
Webb, Margaret Ely, 96
Welch, Thaddeus, 95
Wentworth, Marion C., 93
West Beach, 120
White, Roderick, 92
White, Stewart Edward, 94
Wickenden, Mrs. Ramona, 160
Wiggin, Kate Douglas, 94
Wilkinson, Marguerite, 94
Williams, H. L., 52, 134
Williamson, John, 161
Wilson, Captain John D., 114
Wilson, Ramona (Mrs. John D.), 114
Winfield Scott, ship, 69
Winslow, Carleton M., 113
W. P. A., 92, 119, 176
Wrigley, Wm. Jr., estate of, 75

Yanonalit, Chief, 31

Zanja Cota Indian Reservation, 153